'One of the funniest navigations of the mid-life crisis – and half of Europe – I've ever read. I loved it.'

JOHN NIVEN, author, screenwriter and music writer

'There's a fine line between midlife crisis and sacrificial offering to the memory of your pop hero. And if you're James Briggs, it's the cycle route from Ibiza to the Norfolk Broads – or, depending on which way you look at it, from one end of his perineum to the other. I wholly enjoyed following the former, but maybe I'll give the latter a miss.'

PETE PAPHIDES, music journalist, broadcaster, author of *Broken Greek*

'A curiously engaging (space) oddity of a book: part rock biography, part memoir, part sociological study, part endearingly off-kilter conceit.'

MARK RADCLIFFE, BBC 6 Music presenter, journalist and author

'Sweet, touching and funny – a proper fan's odyssey.'

JUDE ROGERS, music journalist, author of *The Sound of Being Human* and BBC broadcaster

'When two of the greatest things collide (Bowie and Bikes), there's only one possible outcome. I love this story. I'm rather jealous that I didn't think of it first.'

NED BOULTING, sports broadcaster, author and podcaster

'Hugely readable, charming and poignant.'

LEAH KARDOS, author of *Blackstar Theory: The Last Works of David Bowie*

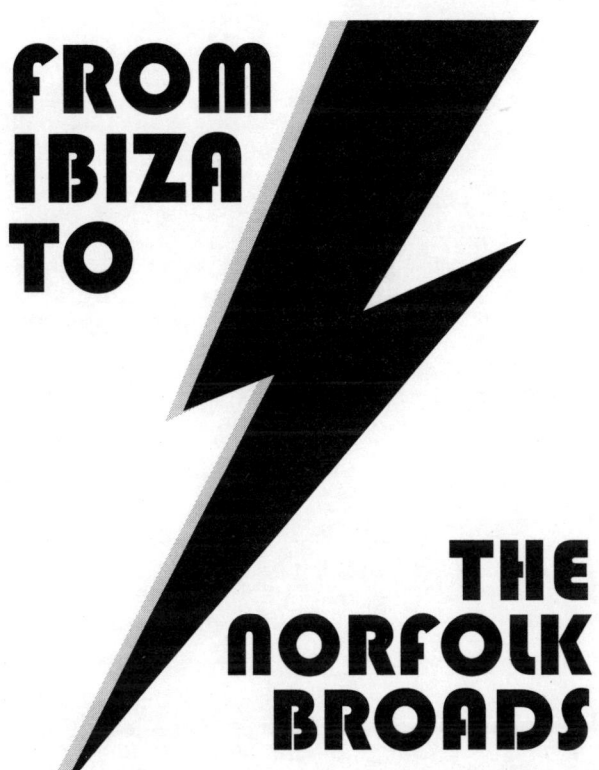

FROM IBIZA TO

THE NORFOLK BROADS

FROM IBIZA TO

A Bowie Bike Odyssey

James Briggs

THE NORFOLK BROADS

ICON

Published in the UK and USA in 2025 by
Icon Books Ltd, Omnibus Business Centre,
39–41 North Road, London N7 9DP
email: info@iconbooks.com
www.iconbooks.com

ISBN: 978-183773-311-8
ebook: 978-183773-312-5

Typesetting by SJmagic DESIGN SERVICES, India

Printed and bound in the UK

Appointed GPSR EU Representative: Easy Access System Europe Oü, 16879218
Address: Mustamäe tee 50, 10621, Tallinn, Estonia
Contact Details: gpsr.requests@easproject.com, +358 40 500 3575

For Mum and Dad

CONTENTS

CONTENTS

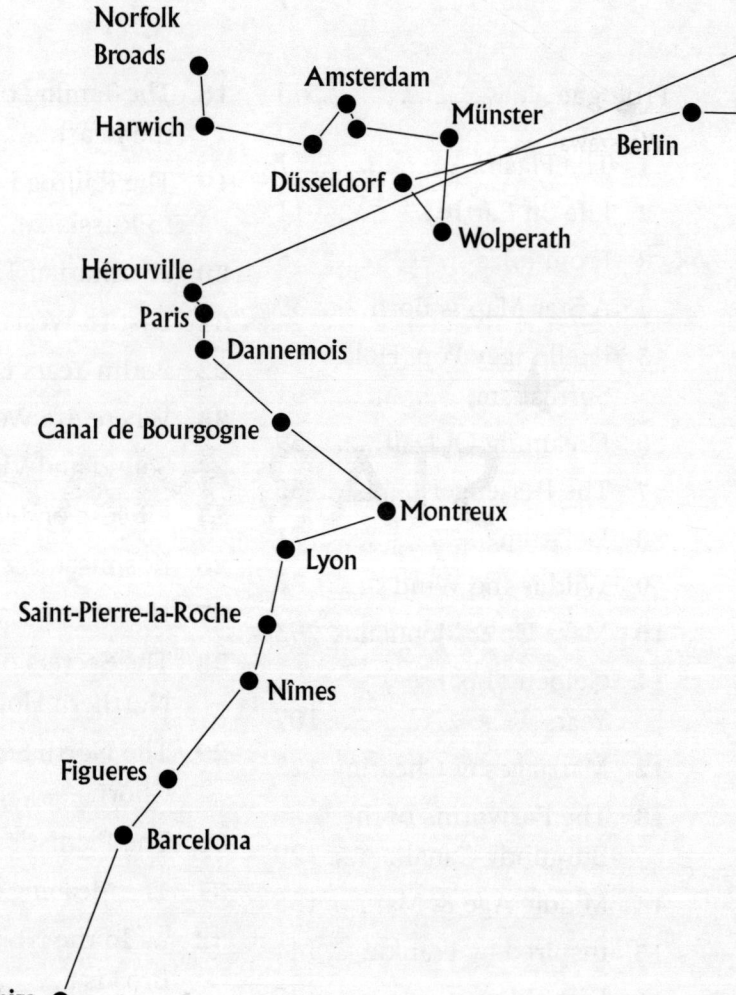

Norfolk
Broads

Amsterdam

Münster

Harwich

Berlin

Düsseldorf

Wolperath

Hérouville

Paris

Dannemois

Canal de Bourgogne

Montreux

Lyon

Saint-Pierre-la-Roche

Nîmes

Figueres

Barcelona

Ibiza

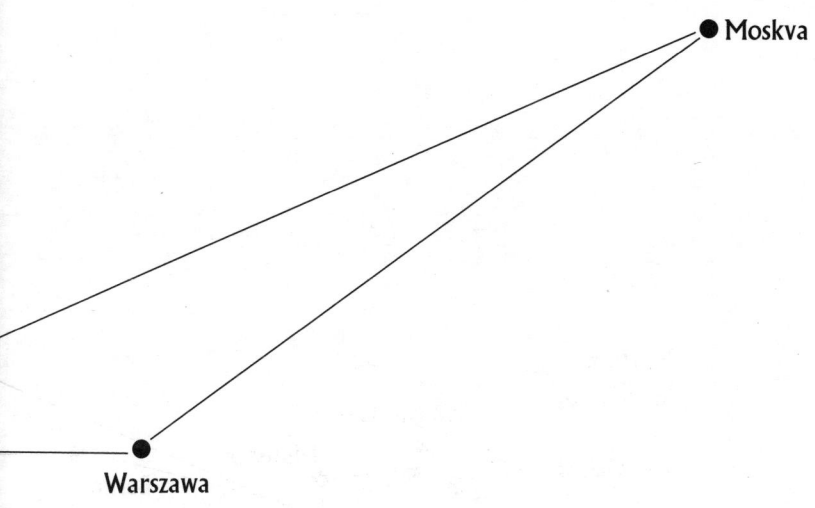

Moskva

Warszawa

STAR MAP

PROLOGUE

They say lightning never strikes twice, but it happened to me. In 1994, the first bolt sent me hurtling to the stars, which was a good thing, because I was fourteen and awkwardly shuffling around a school disco having a terrible time trying to kiss girls. Marooned on the edge of the dance floor, I felt cut adrift, abandoned to another planet. The white-washed assembly hall pulsed with the sound of novelty records, the air brimming with the sickly scent of gobstoppers as a hundred and forty hormonal teenagers desperately tried to get off with one another.

The DJ played a collection of frenetic beats that encouraged hyperactivity. A slick mix of beeps and bops that had prepubescent geeks bobbing around like barrels in an ocean. My head lolloped from the neck of an extra-large Global Hypercolor T-shirt, my train-ers wanting to move but held prisoner by a slick of Panda Pops. It didn't matter. I had gangly arms to wave. I desperately tried to keep time with the music but looked more like an octopus trying to high-five a swarm of electric eels. This wasn't the mating dance the girls of year 9 had been waiting for.

I smiled at Amy Fraser but her fingers were deep in a bag of cheese and onion crisps. I scanned the room for help. The DJ, Steve Baker's dad, thumbed a wallet of counterfeit CDs – then fumbled the lot, sending them skidding across the laminate floor.

The music went dead.

Boys and girls stared gormlessly at one another. The only sound, the slop of bubble gum rattling around teeth and tonsils. Then, from nowhere, a piano note dropped from the heavens. Boys with wispy beards fell from plastic chairs, girls' bubble-gum bubbles popped in an apocalyptic frenzy and Amy Fraser's jaw dropped open to reveal a row of shimmering braces that sparkled like Elizabeth Duke diamonds.

That note, that piano chord, couldn't have been more electric if it was thrown by Zeus himself. Impudent bass followed, pouring from speakers, bristling between centre-parting haircuts; piano notes chased, tap dancing around fluorescent hair bobbles, while serene orchestral strings pirouetted under billowing jeans and chequered culottes, searching for the stars. The seventies had transported themselves to nineties Somerset. As the poetic lyrics transformed young ladies with hairspray-stiffened fringes into girls with mousy hair, a dizzying finale erupted, and we were hastened to look to the skies and question if there really was life on other planets.

Oh man! What a ride.

Off my tits on Dolly Mixture, my head swirling with galaxies and supernovas, I couldn't begin to comprehend the bounty of surreal images that waltzed before my eyes, blazing like stardust as they went. I had no idea what it meant, but David Bowie's 'Life on Mars?' was the greatest thing I'd ever heard.

1. THE FLASH

It was winter when lightning struck again. Two decades had passed and it was a normal day. But every day had been normal since we lost him. Barely a month had gone by since Bowie blasted off to another planet for good and anyone with a musical soul was still in mourning. I was in no better frame of mind myself; I passed my bicycle, propped among the clutter of my hallway, which was also my front room, and shuffled towards the shower. The pre-dawn parade: wash away the morning blues, awaken the senses and gather your thoughts for the day; perhaps remember that it's your mum's birthday, you need to pay the electricity bill, or, as a 36-year-old man, consider buying a leather jacket.

I stared down at the swaddle of stomach blubber – too many post-work beers – as clumps of thinning hair washed down the drain for ever. This wasn't how it was meant to be. Not yet. I'd travelled a bit in my twenties but got stuck in my thirties. I had a career that was grinding every ounce of life from me and a relationship in which I was happy but hadn't said the 'L' word. Even without the cloud of steam and shower gel suds gathering in my love handles, I'd worked myself into a right middle-aged lather. I looked down at the blocked water pooling around my ankles. I was in a rut, an expensive one-bedroom London rut – with dreadful plumbing. I'd lost my way, as well as my hair.

Fortunately, my record was cued. I was softly and sadly singing the lyrics to David Bowie's 'Life on Mars?' – slowly murdering the first verse and chorus. But among the foam, dead hair follicles and monotone murmurings, a storm was brewing. The rumblings of my mind fired off neutrons, a maelstrom of errant thoughts criss-crossing one another like intergalactic rockets – the bike in the hallway, the regrettable decision to grow a moustache, the impending misery of another working week. The pressure built, the humidity fizzing to an unsustainable crescendo, and at the sixth line of the fourth verse, it collapsed – a flash of fury, a bolt of lightning: I should cycle that; I should cycle from Ibiza to the Norfolk Broads.

Ordinarily, lightning bolts in showers are a no-no if you want to continue padding around this earth, but this one had a certain spark. I could follow Bowie's lyrical path, make a pilgrimage to the Starman, chat to Bowie fans from around the world and find the meaning of life or, at the very least, the meaning of 'Life on Mars?'

As I wrestled damp socks onto damp feet, the implications of such mid-life heroics began to dawn on me. I had a career. I had a girlfriend. And this wasn't ideal holiday territory with either. Why had it been that song stuck in my head, why not 'Kokomo' by the Beach Boys? As those lyrics tease, I could be swanning from the Caribbean to the Florida Keys. Instead, I was going to be awful and spend time pedalling the unglamorous hard shoulders of European motorways. I broke it to Lucy, said this was the holiday Bowie would have wanted: get off the beaten track, lead don't follow, find our own path. I suggested we do it together, maybe on a tandem.

Lucy fancied Greece.

'Greece would still be there next year,' I offered obviously and ignorantly.

She politely said, 'No, thanks.' But, seeing the words 'blistering mid-life crisis' emblazoned across my forehead, encouraged me. Next, I had to convince my boss that this was an important pilgrimage, a creative sabbatical that deserved a light ripple of applause rather than a P45. After a short period of wrangling, it was tenuously but suspiciously approved, letting the idea consume my thoughts.

Had anyone cycled a song lyric before? More importantly, had anyone died cycling a song lyric before? Anyway, the path was set. Or at least I thought it was. In truth, I didn't really have one. A common theme over the next few weeks was pub conversations going around in circles a lot like this:

'I'm going on a cycling trip!' I'd announce like the screaming mid-life crisis cliché I clearly was.

'Oh, right. Whereabouts?'

This was the kicker. I'd take another sip of beer and casually say, 'From Ibiza to the Norfolk Broads,' somehow restraining myself from clambering on the table and performing an elaborate jazz hands routine. After explaining to the less enlightened that this was a major Bowie lyric and not a minor breakdown, the snippets of wisdom came pouring forth.

'I don't know why anyone would do that,' said someone I thought of as a friend.

'The Spanish are drunk drivers,' said an English drunk drinker.

'That's weird,' offered a colleague who had exactly the same sandwiches at exactly the same time each day.

Then the drama was ratcheted up even further.

'That's a long way, aren't you worried about bears?' proffered someone with a fear of distance and furry man killers.

It's true, I hadn't thought about the size of Europe or razor-toothed forest assassins. But there was one particular query that was infinitely more bothering.

'Yeah, but where are you going to go?'

'I've told you, from Ibiza to the Norfolk Broads,' I replied, performing jazz hands under the table.

'Yeah, but where?'

Jeez.

'From Ibiza to the Norfolk Broads,' I said, whistling the melody and pointing from floor to sky like it was some kind of star map known only to those dumbstruck by lightning.

'Yes. But where, specifically?'

I was getting tired of waiting for the applause and handshakes to roll in. I sighed wearily and sang the lyric for the fourth time.

'We know that, you blathering testicle, but what do France, motorways and mountains have to do with Bowie?'

Ah.

I'm sure Bowie probably was massively fond of France and motorways, plus I remembered reading somewhere he liked to ski, so that'd be no problem. And we all know DB is everywhere. Look around you, gaze lustily at the star-strewn skies, he's embedded in the very fabric of the universe. Isn't he? So that would include Norfolk, obscure French B-roads and Ibiza, definitely Ibiza.

The black hole in my plan had been exposed. This probably merited further investigation. I know, I'd ask the fans: the David Bowie Wonderland message forum – a fantastic source of Bowie trivia and nuggets populated by Starman fans left, right and centre of the galaxy – they would have the answer. I applied my fawning index fingers and tapped out a long, meaningful message:

Did Bowie visit Ibiza?
July 26 2016 at 9:54 PM

I'd let that percolate for a day or two before announcing to my friends that my plan was sound because Bowie loved Ibiza, French motorways and long aimless bike rides. Either that or, like all internet forums, it would spiral out of control and end up with people talking about their cat, a dead grandparent, or their cat who killed their grandparent. But always trust a Bowie fan; they have more substance, if not clarity on the matter. Fans were playful, saying the Ibizans were keeping quiet to keep the tourists away, suggesting Cyprus was his island – a nod to another Bowie lyric from his *Lodger* album. That or delivering small socio-geographic essays outlining the extremities of them as holiday destinations, arguing that the Norfolk Broads was a traditional spot, whereas Ibiza was more for the middle classes on the lookout for a leisurely getaway.

The evidence was thinner than my hairline. A sudden fright took hold, the possibility of a slow descent into madness while cycling nearly three thousand miles, occasionally bumping into people eating packets of Mini Cheddars in service stations and asking pathetically if they liked David Bowie. As I hunched over my laptop in my miniscule flat, far away from the jazz hands of the pub, I began to realise there's nothing more reckless than a man on the brink of a mid-life meltdown with access to a bike and Google Maps.

Poking around on the internet, I began to see that Bowie was kind of everywhere. As I typed 'Bowie France' into Google, a not too shabby 11.3 million search results cascaded down the screen. 'Bowie Space' turned up a whopping 18.3 million titbits, and even 'Bowie Motorway Service Stations' a teasing 323,000 leads.

As I cast my net wider, I began to see the cosmos – a shining path of everything Starman, places he'd played, studios he'd recorded, houses he'd lived. I frantically jotted them down, plotting a loose constellation across Europe. A 'Star Map' – a route that would free my soul and, using Bowie as a compass, start to unravel the mysteries of 'Life on Mars?'. I hoped the answers I found would propel me in the direction I sought from my ageing life on earth.

Unfathomably, Bowie had written the song at 24. Twenty-four. Let's put that in perspective: in my early twenties I was failing anatomy and getting fat at university. So tubby, in fact, that when I came home for the summer my mum ignored the laws of mothering and spent two months actively feeding me down, rather than up. But why had it been *that* song that dribbled from my mouth in the shower?

Everyone comes to Bowie in a different way. We're familiar with the stories of how he made it OK to be different, to dress how you wanted, to be yourself, embrace your identity and sexuality, and to be downright weird. But these people were from the Bowie generation, they'd grown up with his music. This would be another problem for me. I'd spent much of my formative musical years exposed to my dad's taste: Barry Manilow, Genesis – crap like that. I'm not sure what happened, he had a good record collection – Motown, Hendrix, The Stones – but sometime in the eighties he slipped down a side road of musical bilge inhabited by the likes of Richard Marx, Wham! and Michael Bolton. My sister and I used to sit with our ears pressed to a Celestion speaker as 'Uptown Girl' by Billy Joel *wo-oh-oh*-ed from the coils with Dad air-drumming furiously behind. Like the Bowie fans, I was different alright, just in a pop and soft rock kind of way.

I had to furrow my own path. Take things into my own hands. Which meant an act of juvenile delinquency – nicking my sister's CDs. The Stone Roses and Nirvana, the gateway discs to an indie rabbit hole where the likes of Pulp, Blur and Oasis were waiting to steal my ears. A Somerset childhood meant that, by 2000, I was jumping the fence at Glastonbury where Bowie delivered an 'Oi, don't forget about me' elbow to the ribs. In a field of black and orange, cider and substance highs, he sashayed through a career-spanning set, playing to the biggest festival crowd ever assembled. With his flowing bleached-blond hair and Alexander McQueen suit he introduced 'Life on Mars?'

'I'm very fearful tonight,' he teased, 'because I got struck down by laryngitis this week. So, if I give out and any of you know any of the words – for gawd's sake join in. Counting on you!' As the immortal lyrics drifted over the Somerset ley lines, my sticky school disco feet were knocked off balance again. While small fires burned and wellies stuck in gluey mud, we heeded Bowie's call to sing our little hearts out.

I was desperate to claim that, as a child of the eighties, it was Bowie's ball-smothering trouser turn in *Labyrinth* that did the trick, or that, being born in 1979, I'd caught the breeze of the Berlin Trilogy. But really, after having my world shook twice, both at the school disco and Glastonbury, I was still playing hard to get. The following year, 2001, was lost to the restricted blood flow of skinny jeans and shades-wearing bands from New York, but by the following year I was ready. I'd love to say I cycled to Our Price to experience *Low* or dug deep in record racks for an original copy of *Aladdin Sane*. But there was another reason, and it wasn't cool. My official inauguration into one of the wonders of the musical universe was a *Best of Bowie* double CD. A greatest sodding hits. The album cover shows a mosaic of Bowie characters and personas spanning his career – released in 2002 as EMI / 5 39821 2 (for those aroused by catalogue numbers).

So, where do you start with all this? It doesn't take a steamy shower to realise that if you're going to do a Bowie pilgrimage properly, you'll need a sense of David in your direction. I returned to the

Greatest Hits CD and ummed and arred over a route, pressing play as I mulled over the size of his cosmos.

If I was going to do a Bowie bike ride properly, I'd need a proper bike. My rust-bitten racer was unlikely to withstand the weight of my middle-age spread. Another option was required and, sadly, buying a bike meant talking to people in bike shops, and a good few out there are dastardly plonkers intent on belittling you for not knowing your wheelies from your endos.

A few sample conversations to support my case:

'What valve you after, mate?'

'Oh, you know, a good one.'

'Presta or Schrader?'

'Pardon me?'

It was like a secret code for those in the know to humiliate you with.

'Put your hand on the butts.'

Was he the leader of a sexual cult?

'Both of them.'

He was.

I'd later learn the 'butts' he referred to were more commonly known as 'hoods'. The place you rest your hands over the brake levers, but it may as well have been a sub-dialect of Northern Mars.

It made more sense to start this journey where Bowie did, so I made a pilgrimage to 40 Stansfield Road, Brixton, South London, where David Robert Jones landed on this planet on 8 January 1947. On a bright summer's morning, the three-storey Victorian terrace shrouded by an ash tree bore no sign of its famous son – no flowers, letters or records. But there was a bike shop nearby. As well as being a short walk from where Bowie was born, the good folk at Brixton Cycles were not egotistical eggs. As I was talked through the various options, lots of bikes were thrillingly described as 'bulletproof'. Not planning on any form of warfare, my priorities lay rather more prosaically along the lines of something that wouldn't get too many punctures. Choosing one of the lower-end models for a test ride, this wasn't guaranteed. As I edged into Brixton Road, aligning myself with chugging buses, marauding taxis and lunatic cyclists, my feet became tangled in foot braces and my legs whirred like Wile E. Coyote mid-cliff. Before long I was panting like a polar bear in a sauna. At least the bike felt reliable and, more importantly, sturdy enough to withstand the weight of my blossoming moobs.

I returned to the shop, where I breezily picked up items I hoped would prove useful, things with odd names like hex tools, bidons and panniers: not only bulletproof, but waterproof. Finally, with all the gear and one silly idea, I hopped on my steed and cycled back to Bowie's birthplace, gave a hearty salute and placed the first pin in my hastily jotted Star Map.

2. LIFE ON EARTH

So I had the T-shirt – a Ziggy Stardust one – and the bike. Now I just needed to do some training. But anyone who goes near London roads knows they are an aggressive shitstorm of taxi drivers, pedestrians and cyclists all intent on injuring one another or, if that fails, lobbing volleys of abuse at each other. But on last night's cycle home, pedalling between chuntering cabbies, Lycra dingbats and gormless phone-tapping pedestrians, I think I figured out why.

Now, I'm quite partial to a mutter at people's driving habits, just loud enough to vent my frustration, just inaudible enough for them not to hear and get out and smash me in the face with a tin of travel sweets. I remember cycling through London and seeing a car cut up another cyclist by veering left without indicating, provoking a shout of, 'Nice indicating, knobhead!' But then he made the same left turn, again without indicating, and I found myself shouting after him, 'Yeah, nice indicating, knobhead!' I was so incensed at the cyclist's hypocrisy that I then also slung a left without indicating. Faintly, in the distance, I heard someone shout, 'Yeah, nice indicating, knobhead!', before they too peeled left without indicating. Indeed, if you listen very carefully at any time of day in London, you'll hear the words, 'Yeah, nice indicating, knobhead!' echoing like wildfire across every borough.

Things had somehow happened all too quickly. Winter was coming, I'd booked a flight and only had time for one last ride. Judging by the Tour de France hopefuls riding round London getting asphyxiated by their Lycra outfits, I'd probably need some specialist clothing. Bowie wasn't a conservative dresser, but I needn't have worried, most cycling apparel is handily arranged in the colour palette of vomit. It's also made from body-hugging Lycra, so a tube of glitter here and some superglue there and I was bang in showbusiness. I slapped a £20 note on the counter of a budget sport shop and stepped out looking like I'd mugged Mr Motivator.

With the omnipresent dangers of being called a knobhead, it made sense to do my last training ride in a quieter part of London, so I took my garish green shorts and man-tit hugging space fibres to the suburbs. Prime territory for Bowie – and Bowie fans, kooks who, like me, had ordinary, humdrum childhoods spent getting our kicks behind fly-postered bedroom doors from music, fashion and art. In preparation, stuffed into my panniers were four litres of water, two bags of Jelly Babies and half a loaf of sandwiches. All of which did nothing to keep me dry in the torrential downpour emptying itself over South East London. As my energy receded around Blackheath, so did the city, the gallivanting concrete jungle melting into the suburban order of Bromley. Clocking a not so cosmic twelve miles, I fired my burners at a big hill until those same burners fizzled out with a whimper and left me gasping against a garden wall like I'd been thumped in the windpipe by a gorilla.

I'd hit zero – and Bowie's suburbia.

With my cover assured by the garden's pampas grass draped over my limp body, I earwigged on a Sunday conversation. 'Well, we've got a hedgehog, which is what I wanted,' said a middle-aged woman, as if spiked mammals were high on the suburban bucket list after a three-bedroom bungalow with a bird bath and a gnome that looked like a sexual deviant. I lobbed some sweets into my mouth, remounted and slipped along the sleepy streets. As I did, I began to see a strange alchemy of contentment and boredom. People either drove too fast or too slow. For every open car boot with protruding flat-pack furniture, there was a brainlessly smashed alcohol bottle littering the pavement. For every dazzling flower bed, a scattering of discarded nitrous-oxide canisters. You can take your boredom as you please out here, contentment and frustration living side by side.

I was about to provide another outlet for it.

'Faggot!'

My colourful presence hadn't gone unnoticed. As flab stretched against Lycra, three twelve-year-olds stood sniggering like the acne-flecked turds they clearly were. But I wasn't just here to try to run over pimpled youths at speed. No, because in 1953 the Jones family moved from Brixton to Bromley and 106 Canon Road. I ground to a halt outside a two-up, two-down; another bygone Bowie residence which in direct defiance of the young homophobes was painted a fabulous blancmange pink.

Bowie's parents switched between various houses in the area, moving to Plaistow Grove, where David would walk to the local school, Burnt Ash. He became part of the choir, a teacher describing his voice – perhaps in the biggest miscalculation ever – as 'adequate'. Bowie wasn't deterred. While most of us were trying to save up for records, he wanted to make them. He was fascinated by the sounds coming out of America, especially Little Richard with his unusual standing-up piano-playing style, androgynous look and hints of sexuality in his lyrics, confessing to *Vanity Fair* that when he first heard him his 'world was set on fire'.

He took a job at a local butcher's delivering sausages on a heavy iron bike. Like me, he was pedalling to escape order, routine and calm. But his aspirations were loftier; he wanted to save for a saxophone so he could play in Little Richard's band. London was only a short distance from where his legs whirled as his mind travelled ever faster. He wanted to be just like the man who stood at a piano playing rock and roll, he wanted to sing, he wanted to play – he wanted to be famous.

After earning his bacon delivering sausages, he bought that saxophone, took lessons and threw himself into his dad's records. He studied singers and performers like the creative tour-de-force Anthony Newley. He was inspired by his half-brother Terry, diving into beat poetry and devouring Kerouac. A restless mind in too restful a place. As the suburbs slept around him, they became a conduit for his creativity. He searched for identity in a series of bands: The Kon-Rads, The King Bees, The Manish Boys, and The Lower Third. The latter's 'Can't Help Thinking About Me' song expressing themes of leaving home, a sign of the restless direction in which he was heading. He set up a folk night which would become the Beckenham Arts Lab. His foppish hair and liberal tendencies meant he surrounded himself with mime artists, musicians and actors, learning not only how to sing but how to project different personas. His self-titled debut album, released in 1967 on the same day as The Beatles' *Sgt. Pepper's Lonely Hearts Club Band*, was a set of precocious and parochial teenage tales set to vaudeville and music hall stylings, which received little fanfare, although two songs did have lyrics about bicycles.

Regardless, Bowie was moving fast, travelling through suburban space and time as the sixties rocketed into the seventies. He was drawn to the lights, sounds and textures of London; journeying with Terry to Soho where fashion, girls – and boys – became a fixture in his cosmos. He used the capital to pilfer ideas and clothes from dumpsters, toiled with musical genres like mod, folk and music hall, each influence sending his imagination spiralling higher into the stratosphere. On his second album, he finally achieved blast off. Inspired by the moon landings and a mind-expanding cannabis joint, 'Space Oddity' became his breakthrough hit; and from there it was only a short journey to Mars.

I felt like I'd already done a lap of the galaxy, my lungs howling in protest as I swerved into Croydon Road Recreation Ground. Like Bowie,

I'd undertaken some childhood bike training. My schoolboy paper round ran a gauntlet of frothy-mouthed dogs that menaced back and forth behind frosted glass looking for wrists to sever. Sailing through the thick of dawn as the winter sun set light to my imagination, I had dreams, too – I'd be an explorer, a footballer, a tub-thumping drummer. Hunching over the handlebars I'd pick up pace, the cold air burning at my knuckles. Then, unburdened by the weight of newspapers, I'd cycle as hard as I could back to the shop and exchange a dew-drenched bag for a small manila envelope. Payday. This is where Bowie and I took different paths. He bought a saxophone and changed the fabric of the music universe; I bought, and slowly killed, two goldfish.

My childhood dreams faded into the distant London smog as I sugar-crashed between two palm bushes and began tearing at jam sandwiches. Faculties restored, I turned to face a tired green fence surrounding an Edwardian bandstand. On its roof, a crown and mitre postured alongside a sorry-looking weathervane. Wooden roof slats lay hither and thither, blistered and world weary. Blue and white balloons hung lifelessly from once ornate ironwork. And cracks in the paintwork revealed that burning roots of rust had laid siege to its foundations. Its only redemptive feature was a flower bed erupting with a poem of oranges and yellows. It had certainly seen better days. But it had also seen greatness – because this is where David Bowie sat and wrote 'Life on Mars?':

> 'This song was so easy. Being young was easy. A really beautiful day in the park, sitting on the steps of the bandstand. "Sailors bap-bap-bap-bap-baaa-bap." An anomic (not a "gnomic") heroine. Middle-class ecstasy.'[1]

---

[1] David Bowie speaking to the *Mail on Sunday*, 29 June, 2008.

Bowie, rightly so, was rather pleased with his afternoon's work under the shade of the bandstand. I sat and looked out – another beautiful day. I narrowed my eyes and tried to picture it. Did he see what I saw? Two young mums with pushchairs, a big Alsatian walking a small Indian man, and a white feather bustling across the grass at the whim of a shallow breeze. I wondered if it was all circumstance that led to those lyrics. Could it so easily have been, 'Doooooogs weeing on the seesaw'? It could, and it might have. Bowie's original lyrics differed wildly from the ones we all know. There are mentions of stars but also shoulder rock movements and great lords sighing in vain. Then it's a muddle of wordplay about buying and bargains being made before he arrives at the song's title. Either way, the seed was planted:

'I took a walk to Beckenham High Street to catch a bus to Lewisham to buy shoes and shirts but couldn't get the riff out of my head.'

I was hooked. I didn't chase a bus to Lewisham, but I inhaled the belching fumes of one as I skidded into Southend Road. It was here where Bowie set up home with first wife Angie and a rotating cast of squatting musicians. Haddon Hall was a rambling gothic mansion with stained glass windows and ceilings painted with swirls of silver; it was here that he knocked up the music to 'Life on Mars?'.

'Workspace was a big empty room with a chaise lounge; a bargain-price art nouveau screen ("William Morris," so I told anyone who asked); a huge overflowing freestanding ashtray and a grand piano. Little else. I started working it out on the piano and had the whole lyric and melody finished by late afternoon. Nice.'

David Bowie there, making it sound as if writing one of the greatest songs of all time was like knocking up a slice of buttered toast. To him it probably was. I gazed around Southend Road, Haddon

Hall now demolished, renamed Shannon Way, and replaced with retirement homes. The comings and goings of Bowie's 'Beckenham Palace' – the groupies, band members, wild fashions and artists – replaced by delivery drivers juggling towers of cardboard and slinging them in hedges when they thought no one was looking.

All of Bowie's suburban frustration and efforts to break free had manifested into a girl who daydreamed about life on Mars. Who was she? Someone he knew, someone who saw the world the same way as him? In 1971 he went to record the song in Soho's Trident Studios with his band, The Spiders from Mars. Mick Ronson on electric guitar, mellotron and strings; Woody Woodmansey on drums; Trevor Bolder on bass and classically trained collaborator Rick Wakeman on piano. The lyrics he'd written on the Beckenham bandstand, an intergalactic swirl of themes and abstract imagery of other worlds, all tied together by the yearning of a disillusioned girl, now had music. 'Life on Mars?' was ready for the godly universe.

As he hurtled towards Mars our stars aligned, kind of. While Bowie entered the slip road for the intergalactic highway, I took a two-hour jaunt back across London as a stream of taxi drivers, pedestrians and cyclists all turned left without indicating and the word knobhead gathered again and again in the grey sooty skies. But troubled skies were the least of my worries. Mum and Dad had grown suspicious of the recent uptake in middle-aged pursuits. The sudden interest in maps, bike racks and mutual benefits of the E111 health card. They smelled a Mars-shaped rat and, under duress, I told them the plan. They immediately threw a Steve and Pauline shaped spanner in the works, handily transcribed through more 'Life on Mars?' lyrical themes.

Because my mummy is yelling, No!
Because 'dual carriageways are full of terrible drivers and it's dangerous to camp by the side of the road'.

And my daddy has told me to go.
Dad hadn't told me *not* to go, but he did say, 'David Bowie? He's weird!', before counterbalancing his argument with, 'Made some great records, though.'

The spanners came down thicker and faster. In an act of corporate arse-clownery, work had decided not to let me go after all.

Hi James,
Not sure this is going to work. We're just too busy. Let's talk.
Susan.

HR Manager

The demands of the corporate world were too pressing, the need to flog this little minion more urgent. That's that then, I conceded, a little too easily. I'd always been a shit rebel. Never quite going the distance, forever on the edge of minor anarchy: putting extra penny sweets in my bag, mumbling at a teacher, perhaps coming into work ten minutes late – those wild, rebellious sorts of things. I sighed. Cycling around London was fun, and it was a nice dream, but 'Life on Mars?' and its otherworldly meaning would have to stay unresolved.

And yet, I was already in character, like the girl in the song who was also addicted to the silver screen. Although hers is a fantasy world born of boredom – a silver screen her escape, one she longs to be in – my own inertia, my life-sapping ennui, was all wrapped in a similar longing, except I wasn't a teenage girl or a starry-eyed child; I was a middle-aged man. One who had just eaten six chocolate biscuits before 11am.

There were obvious parallels, I could see that. My silver screen was grey, the computer I idly stared into for fifteen hours a day, most weekends and then every other second of my increasingly flabby existence. Indeed, if you focused a camera down, you'd see a harmonious triangle of laptop, sedentary human and biscuits.

I would cycle my jowls home and be too exhausted to do anything: to plan for the future, to give Lucy the time she deserved. I had tried to find myself by throwing myself into a career, but found myself stuck. I'd never known which direction to take. I'd never really known what I wanted to be, whereas Bowie had from the moment he picked up that saxophone.

Was he going to save me?

Or was I going to save myself?

I rolled the dice.

I could do this ...

Hmm, I did like sitting around eating biscuits.

What if I just went for it ...

Excitedly race home on bike.

Exhausted from work, barely talk.

Patchy sleep.

Ruinous thoughts.

Repeat.

For ever?

It came worst at night. My bed a temple devoted to sighing. If I wasn't sleeping, I was huffing, tossing, worrying; a tangle of confusing thoughts raced against themselves to no destination. Panicked introspection chased – shouldn't I know what I was doing with my life by now? Under the cloak of night, it went far beyond the exhausted reasoning of daylight. I scrunched it up and buried it inside. I felt like I was drowning, but I wouldn't talk about it. I'd play it safe, be sensible, sit still in a straitjacket of low-level depression. More late nights. More working for the man. Progress, careerism, conformity. My road mapped out for me. It was OK, I told myself. I could go next year, or the year after. Work comes first, pay the bills, run faster than the rest of the rats. The world would keep turning, Bowie's legacy would keep shining. But one night, in between some particularly frenzied bouts of sheet wrestling, I broke what Lucy must have thought was a sponsored silence and confessed, 'I've got to do it, or I'll never do it.'

Feeling my desperate muggy night breath she said, 'Then go, do it.'

As it turned out, Bowie's legacy was besmirched by my filling the office with deep dramatic sighs and passive-aggressive stationery behaviour. Staplers were noisily dumped onto tables, crocodile clips weren't returned to rightful owners and Pritt Stick lids were carelessly left off. The 'A' in James A. Briggs *finally* stood for Anarchy rather than the more passive Andrew. In the dying embers of summer, my dream of a reckless cycle odyssey only burned brighter, a raging flame that refused be extinguished.

What was I going to do? What would Bowie do?

'If you feel safe in the area you're working in, you're not working in the right area. Always go a little further into the water than you feel you're capable of being in. Go a little bit out of your depth. And when you don't feel that your feet are quite touching the bottom, you're just about in the right place to do something exciting.'[2]

As big thoughts gathered in my small brain, Bowie's words stirred my soul and begged me to stick two fingers up at sensible and give the bird to pragmatism. My stationery dissent hadn't gone unnoticed, and I was hauled in front of HR Susan. My voice cracked as I laid it on the line.

'I have to go.'

'I see,' said HR Susan with a sympathetic nod.

'I've got to do it.'

---

[2] David Bowie in the 1997 Michael Apted documentary *Inspirations*

'I see.' Second sympathetic nod.

'I'm sorry, but it means a lot to me.'

'I see.' No third nod.

HR Susan was good at seeing, like a blouse-wearing Cyclops; I literally could have said anything right now.

'I've eaten all the Post-it notes.'

'I see.'

'Been stealing toilet roll for years.'

'I see.'

'Been dealing the office milk to cats.'

Seeing was all very well, but I had to start doing. I took a deep breath, doggy paddled to the deep end, and as the floor fell away beneath me let go of the corporate towline.

'If I can't go, I'm leaving.' Inside I was moonwalking and shitting my pants.

'I see.'

HR Susan could see the bright burning cosmos. Unfortunately, my boss couldn't. The news filtered through to her unsympathetic ear on a Sunday night, resulting in a testy phone call where my threat was called out in a bluster of corporate aggression.

'Is it true what you said?'

'Afraid so,' I said, standing my ground.

She took a moment. 'Well, I think it's pretty shitty.'

As I mentally packed my panniers and saw the open road unfold before me, I could only think of one thing to say: 'I see.'

Pretty shitty felt pretty good right now. I mean, it might cost me their permanent resentment, any prospect of promotion and I had to agree to be 'on call' should the demands of men in suits so require, but, crucially, I was free. I had six weeks to go and cycle a David Bowie song lyric.

Countdown to Mars

T-minus 10 …

10. With all that said and done, what's left to say? Bowie has already conquered the world and I don't need to flagellate my private parts on a bike seat designed for a small marsupial. Grow into middle age gracefully, keep the career, leave it there. But the wheels were too far in motion.

9. Friends were more excited than I was. My three-ish training rides were entirely different to cycling across a continent. How do you prepare to ride a lyric a 24-year-old had written while simultaneously shopping for slacks and shoes?

8. I found myself doing things I hadn't done for many years, or ever, like hanging around in a plumbers' merchants asking for lagging to protect my bike and saying things like, 'Yeah, mate, six mill oughta do it,' without having the faintest idea if this would actually 'do it'.

7. Buying blow-up pillows which, at best, could accommodate half a human head. Writing 'to do' lists I had little intention of doing, and proudly dismantling my bike without any idea how to put it back together.

6. Bowie had 'Life on Mars?' on his setlist, but my packing list had barely got beyond a spare inner tube and a compass, and even after three YouTube tutorials I wasn't sure how to use either. Fortunately, Lucy provided a 'kit' with useful things like plasters, bandages, even a penknife. Funnily enough, that's how Bowie's name came to be, christened as he was after a Bowie knife because it cuts both ways.

5. Mum was right, I couldn't sleep by the side of the road. At least not without a tent. I consulted an outdoorsy website. This one-man number I was eyeing was 'fantastic', apparently, but you have to question the 'fantastic' nature of a

tent that was discontinued two years ago. Perhaps it disinte-grated in rain, or was highly flammable. Maybe they'd found it attracted menstruating bears and several unsuspecting campers had been heartily dismembered. Well, maybes aren't definitelies, so I found one on eBay and bought it anyway.

4. I visited Stanfords map shop where I learnt how big France and Spain are, even when shrunk to 1:25 inch scales, while the poor staff learnt I couldn't refold maps as I left them in a crumpled mess near the Eastern Europe section.

3. I procured two *Aladdin Sane* lightning-bolt stickers and proudly applied them like go-faster stripes to my panniers. I used bungee cords to tassel my camping gear into a big blue IKEA bag but got them tangled in the spokes and nearly lost an eye when they pinged back out.

2. Someone who'd done a long-distance bike ride advised me to get chamois cream for my backside, but at £14.99 I thought it too pricey and scoffed at their suggestion.

1. And, in a final homage to Bowie and our bicycling youths, I took the train home and recreated my old paper round. Tipping anything lying around into my panniers: door stops, tea towels and a handful of Dad's crap records. It was a breeze. I was older, wiser and those bloodthirsty dogs had long gone. By the time I'd whistled up the hill a second time, I had no fear of the Pyrenees, no fear of cycling a song lyric; all I had to do was figure out what the song meant, and I had around three thousand sprightly miles to do so.

Lift off!

3. FROM IBIZA …

On 29 March 1974, David Robert Jones fled London, crossing the channel on a ferry, and ditched England as his home. On 11 September 2016, I did likewise, leaving London to look for the meaning of a song, and in doing so, abandoned all sense of reality. On a glorious autumn morning I loaded up and turned to face the strangest journey I would ever undertake. The night before, in between bouts of unbridled panic, I'd tried to get into Bowie's head. It quickly became apparent that Bowie's head was a difficult place to get into, so I resorted to farting around on the internet trying to find out what the lyrics to 'Life on Mars?' meant.

I wasn't alone.

'The million mice reference further pushes socialist/communist ideas. Giving them homes both in the Mediterranean Isle of Ibiza, all the way to Norfolk, in the Northeast of England, it adds tension in the form of real places. This is not Mars. This is Earth,' Atwood Magazine opined.

Good to know, as I didn't have a map of Mars but did have a couple of southern Europe.

I suddenly realised Bowie wasn't being particularly complimentary about the folk who go on holiday to mass tourist destinations like Ibiza and the Norfolk Broads, and I was setting out to go to both. Sorry, David.

I had more apologies to give – to Lucy. I'd stolen any chance of us having a holiday together and packed it into my panniers. She knew whatever the hell I was doing was important to me, but what was it going to do to us?

'Sorry,' I mumbled.

'Don't worry,' she offered gently.

'I am, really.'

'It's OK, you should do it.'

Throwing in a few lip wobbles, kisses and drawn-out hugs, she came up for air and wiped away the snot I'd dribbled on her shoulder. I waved goodbye and stuttered into the punch of early morning sun. Hoisting my steed, which weighed about the same as three shire horses, onto the street, I didn't so much slip a disc as Frisbee throw my entire spine across the neighbourhood. The random bits of clutter I'd 'trained' with had been a lot lighter than this camping gear, cooking equipment and hefty stack of European road maps I'd bought, but hadn't unfolded for fear of not being able to refold them.

The 6.6 miles to London City Airport thankfully didn't require their use, and I swooped past the Olympic swimming pool into a slalom of East London suburbs. This felt good, I brashly thought. The kind of misplaced confidence a hedgehog experiences as he coolly strides onto a motorway moments before he's a gooey pulp of spikes stuck to the underside of a BMW. Next was the moment I hadn't trained for all my life: dismantling my bike to the airline's satisfaction. In a blaze of grunts, spanners and calling the saddle a 'twat', I turned the handlebars, removed the wheels and hacked off its pedals before shoving it all inside a giant plastic bag, which was masking-taped to within an inch of its life. The look of wild surprise from the lady at the check-in desk, which I took as acknowledgement of a job well done, only served to boost my false confidence. I was redirected to oversized luggage, where a burly airport worker helped me ram it through the security machine like a postman desecrating a *Yellow Pages*. Plastic shredded, metal scraped; I watched my new best friend disappear towards the plane's bowels.

Interestingly, for a man of the cosmos who dreamed of space, Bowie had a foible. He hated flying. 'Can't do it ... if it flies, it's death ...' he said. 'I've had a premonition I'll be killed in a plane crash.' No wonder he had a disdain for mass tourism. As I settled into a seat the same width as my bicycle's, wedged between a woman who kept saying 'innit' and a plump man drowning in linen, I could see why.

We crept up on the White Isle like a curious mouse. A mouse made of metal, carrying twenty tonnes of aviation fuel and my bike in millions of little pieces. A sweeping pass revealed alabaster buildings tossed like dice across the landscape: package hotels decorated with bright towels, chic cliffside villas, tumbling mountains carpeted with pine, the white blanket of the old town – all the way to a water park filled with a tangle of colourful flumes.

In arrivals, the mice in their million hordes came in all shapes and sizes. More linen-clad men, presumably on their way to Man from Del Monte conventions, designer track-suited teens, retired clubbers, hippies and superstar DJs given away by headphone cans eating their diamond-studded ears. But I'd been here before.

Eighteen years ago, a group of schoolmates and I had come for sun, sea and sex. We got third-degree sunburn, drowned in an ocean of peach schnapps and all eight of us left as pristine virgins. If attracting the attentions of girls was difficult then, what chance did I stand now as I embarked on the most practical half-hour of my life? Being the kind of man who gets lost on step 1 of IKEA instructions and for whom step 5 comes a wasted Saturday afternoon later, drenched in sweat, chastising instruction booklets and kicking leftover pieces of wood across the room, reassembling my bike was clearly not going to be easy. After half an hour of gently chiding nuts and bolts, I seemed to be winning. Wheels were touching the ground, handlebars pointing forwards and pedals whirring in circles. I puffed out my chest and looked around for impressed girls. All I saw was the saggy backsides of old men taking glamorous young wives to hire cars with air conditioning. Nothing had changed.

As everyone drove away, I tried to make sense of why I was here. I spied a woman manning a tourist information kiosk. Maybe she knew.

'Hello!' I announced with an over-pronounced Iberian lilt.

'*Hola!*' she said without the need to pretend she was from another country.

'Do you know if David Bowie ever came here?' I queried, dropping the lilt.

'To Ibiza?' she said with a lovely roll of her Zs.

I nodded enthusiastically.

'No,' she said with a damning finality that wiped out my entire reason for being here.

Of course Bowie never came here. Or at least showed his face in public; he couldn't after dishing out his lyrical swipe to the masses – there would have been a lot of angry tourists throwing espadrilles, glow sticks and Man from Del Monte hats at him. With time to burn and tyres to bake, I rolled my bike onto the airport's steaming drop-off area.

The heat took me by surprise, the kind of surprise you get when you tentatively nibble around the edges of a microwave pie, concluding that it's ready to eat, only to find the filling is the boiling blood of Hades and offers life-changing injuries to the roof of your mouth. Immediately, I was sweating grotesquely, my lungs drowning in humidity, and I hadn't even set off yet. When I did, there was more discomfort. As I choked on the acrid fumes of taxi exhausts and boiling air danced skittishly above my hair, dreams of meandering highways and fragrant clementine groves were quickly vanquished by the E20 motorway. And it wasn't taking any nonsense from someone who listens to greatest hits albums.

'OK, you little weasel. I'm going to keep the temperature around 27 degrees, but it'll feel like 40. Get right. Get peddling. I'll throw in the occasional hard shoulder. Sometimes it'll be next to the fast lane, sometimes the slow lane. You figure it out. Oh, watch out for cars, they'll be going fast. Real fast.'

If real fast was screaming past my sweat-speckled cheeks at 120 km/h, the E20 was a road of its word. The sensation of being fanned by hulking Jeeps and Mercedes moving at light speed brought a confusing mix of mortal fear and cooling relaxation. The late afternoon sun circled viciously above, forcing me to glug greedily from my bidons, which I'd earlier filled with airport toilet water. I'd only been peddling twenty minutes when, in a particularly shoulderless part of the road, I swerved to avoid a pool of brightly coloured vomit festooned around a cat's eye. It seemed people still drank peach schnapps.

With near death and the regurgitated contents of someone else's stomach, the E20 had been fun. But as the hard shoulders grew wider and the speed limit fell below instant death, the Balearic beast began to soften her stance and flaunt her native colours. I eased into the revolutions, passing low-rise farmhouses, rusty terracotta roofs and tumbledown carpenters' shops as valleys of green ran away to clusters of pine huddled on hilltops.

Bowie *should have* come here; it was rather pretty. Sadly, as this pleasant nirvana revealed itself, so did a rumble from my belly. Those two hastily imbibed bottles of airport tap water seemed to be strumming an increasingly unpleasant bass line, one desperately out of tune with my first day on the bike. Like the sun's retreating rays, I was fading fast, but, more troublingly, in need of a toilet even faster. Then salvation: among the burnt copper pastures and gnarled tree branches, a sun-beaten sign – *La Playa Campsite*.

La Playa was Ibiza's original hippy campsite, one Bowie might have found himself visiting if his Beckenham bohemian phase hadn't transitioned so quickly into his rise to stardom. In the fifties, Ibiza was attracting counter-culturists, writers and artists before the hippies flocked here in the sixties. It was a slice of paradise where they could converse, listen to music, ingest hallucinogenic drugs and inflict tie-dye on each other. The rock and rollers came too. In 1964 The Rolling Stones brought their buckets and spades and Pink Floyd supped a cocktail or two. The locals were savvy to this. The tricky-to-fit-in-your-address-book Maria Fuencisla Martinez de Campos y Muñoz set up the super club Amnesia. A place for pioneers, free-thinkers and, later, eunuchs from Yeovil.

Minds were expanded, feet danced till dawn, people kissed the sky and vast amounts of LSD were consumed. Wanting to fit in, I arrived looking like I'd been raving for 36 hours straight, sweat pouring from the orifices of orifices, matched with a washed-out look that suggested my mind was already on Mars. The young idealist manning reception would catch my drift. She'd dig my vibe. She certainly looked cool: her raven hair tucked behind pixie ears; her brown eyes emboldened by tortoiseshell glasses. She was young. She should have been brimming with the liberal, socialist joys of youth. But no, she was a pernickety capitalist vole. A very unhippy, unhappy receptionist who demanded an exorbitant €18.50 to sleep on mother nature's earth.

'I'm sorry, I only have twenty euros,' I said, passing a note.

She didn't have change and hesitantly handed me €2 back.

'You don't have fifty cents?' she badgered.

'Sorry,' I said with a casual shrug, suggesting with a tired smile that perhaps I could bring it tomorrow.

'I won't forget,' she said, whipping off her glasses to reveal the cold, dead eyes of a crack-shot sniper.

'Chill out,' I muttered when she was out of earshot.

'What was that?' she snarled.

'I'll bring it tomorrow,' I cowered.

The vibe was deep here.

As I dragged my bike through a jumble of tipis and hand-painted caravans, a passing Spanish man sporting dreadlocks and little else exclaimed, 'Woah, bike!' as if he'd never seen a bicycle before. 'Kinda crazy,' he added, ramping up his incredulity at the common object that had been around for about 200 years. He ambled away with a blissful smile, presumably to point at other things, like books and cars, and accuse them of being mentally unstable too.

I erected my tent under a canopy of spruce, and an ocean breeze drifted kindly through a chain link fence.

Camping here was a fitting beginning, I reasoned with myself. Bowie's first ever gig was also on a white island campsite. Well, the Isle of Wight. In 1958 he'd played skiffle with his friend George Underwood at Scout Camp. Indeed, if you strained your ears tightly enough, through the sound of Spanish guitar dancing from a tipi, bass pumping along the shores and a woodwind instrument being played badly, you could channel Bowie's hippy phase.

More instrumentation sang out. My stomach. Ah, yes, I had to pay the ransom for the airport tap water – and fast. That done, my stomach let it be known that it was now hungry. Putting on a brave front, I wandered back to the receptionist from hippy hell and asked if she had any restaurant recommendations.

'Ours,' her obvious reply. 'And maybe you find fifty cent?' she added meanly.

This was how I found myself ignoring the busiest, most popular dining option on the beach in spiteful favour of Restaurant Martina. The waiter, in spite of no one else being there, seemed desperately reluctant to acknowledge my existence – a bit like girls when I was eighteen. It was uncanny. Minutes of unreciprocated eye contact, before I spent another five trying to look cool and then in a final attempt to get noticed, a further fifteen waving my arms around like a Morris dancer after too many Digestive biscuits.

Finally, he walked over and placed two menus down. He must have thought my imaginary friend had nipped to the toilet. When he realised they weren't coming back, he said with a smile, 'Oh, you're on your own,' before adding a chuckle and really rubbing it in by taking away the surplus cutlery. Individualism. Lead, don't follow. Eat alone. It's what Bowie would have done. The bang average four-cheese pizza not necessarily what he would have ordered. After hurriedly drinking an ice-cold beer, then several more, I pored over my place mat, a badly out of scale map of Ibiza. Someone had seen fit to place a giant dolphin across it. Perhaps it was a tourist attraction, maybe I'd visit tomorrow. A little tipsy, I began singing the lyrics that referred to the same big brained, ocean-dwelling mammals that featured in another Greatest Hits song, 'Heroes'. But sat alone, I felt like the greatest tit of them all.

As I trudged back across the beach, the flamenco dancer and traditional guitarist that played in the popular restaurant I'd skilfully avoided began to soothe my frayed edges. I stumbled back into the campsite, I drunkenly looked for the night sky, but it was blocked by around 36 dreamcatchers and a cluster of clanging wind chimes. With a sigh, I flopped into my tent and, with fibreglass poles groaning at my bloated presence, concluded I was a long way from Mars.

The next morning, I woke not to find the millions of rodents Bowie promised; indeed, not a single mouse stirred. Even that dreadful receptionist was nowhere to be seen. Having already established Bowie had never been here, my aimlessness apparent, I took a stroll through the green pine of the campground not entirely sure what to do with myself. Just go with the flow, like the trust-fund bongo bashers still asleep. A walk along a red sandstone sea wall plummeted into a secluded cove. It was dressed in feathered strips of seaweed that resembled witches' hair. This is nice, I thought, trying to sunbathe in the dead locks, but I found it difficult to relax, restless as I was for my quest to begin.

I looked around to see the un-golden sands littered with unusual flotsam – a rusting engine and a prosthetic leg. Not a beautifully carved wooden one, but a rather modern one. I wondered if I could make a link to Bowie, mulling over 'legless' jokes from his cider-swilling hippy days and quickly discarding them. Suddenly, a scooter pulled up in a cloud of dust – at last, someone to ask about Bowie! A chef wearing his whites – *Viva España!* A local taking a liberating dip before he went to work – the spirit of Ibiza! He removed his helmet, shook out tousled locks and strolled to the sea's edge. Then, with a flourish that was more Bucks Fizz than Bowie whizz, whipped off his whites to reveal some funky Speedos. At least, that's what my British conservatism expected. He had actually unveiled a sizeable bronzed penis. Not even a *tortilla Española* to hide his modesty. So, as I mentioned, David Bow—

No, wait. He was coming over, his appendage swaying like a grandfather clock pendulum. His cock halted half a metre from my face.

'*Qué hora es?*' he asked casually.

He wanted to know the time. To be fair, he could probably have used the willy as a sundial to find out himself. My first cultural exchange secured, but none the wiser about the meaning to 'Life on Mars?', I figured it was time to go and check out that dolphin.

With a bike on an island, you're not really going anywhere, just doing laps, so I gave Bowie's hippy life a whirl and spent the afternoon pootling about trying to find some camping gas and some Starman. A quick look at my Star Map revealed the first of my loosely scrawled notes. One of his gold discs was hanging in the Hard Rock Hotel, one of a series of themed hotels and restaurants that are a haven for things covered in melted cheese and lazily curated cultural tat. But it was miles away. And it was hot. And I was a counter-cultural hippy. And hippies do things like sitting in the shade and tunelessly tapping bongos, so I did what any self-respecting free spirit would and badgered the barman for the Wi-Fi password.

I wanted to find out more about 'Life on Mars?' and how Bowie, straining to escape his suburban shackles, had written the song before taking it to the Spiders to work with. On first listen, they were impressed.

'I remember leaving there in St Anne's Court, Trident Studios, and coming home and saying to a couple of friends that evening I met in a local pub, I've just played on what I consider to be the best song that I've ever had the privilege to work on,' said pianist Rick Wakeman to BBC Radio 2. The drummer, Woody Woodmansey, speaking to the *NME*, was no less effusive. 'We'd heard him plinking and plonking in his bedroom ... then when we got in the studio and we got Rick Wakeman on piano ... we stood there with our mouths open going, "Holy shit."'

I let this revelation wash over me. I was inspired, I was ready to roll, so I grabbed my bike and bowled straight into Senorita Evil Eyebrows. This time she wasn't messing about. 'You have fifty cents?'

Thinking this was no time to be engaging in role play about the kidnapping of an American rapper, I cut to the chase: *'No cambio.'*

'You don't forget,' she said with a vicious wagging finger.

I shrugged. It was an excellent loose-shouldered hippy shrug. This really riled her.

'It's not my money, you know,' she said, visibly furious.

'Ha, exactly – it's not your money, so why do you care?'

In this moment of smugness, she saw the glimmer of a one euro coin in my hand and in some form of voodoo swapped it for a fifty cent piece.

Defeat.

I retreated to my tent swearing in a way most unbecoming of a hippy. Oh well, I'll console myself with an omelette from my freshly bought groceries. Eggs whisked, camping stove primed, gas cannister non-compatible. Oh, do go and fuck yourself, dear world.

It was then that I saw a man grinning violently at me. That man was Daniel. And Daniel was a talker. Fluent in nine languages and with a penchant for drinking my beers, he'd been visiting the campsite for twenty-five years. People had probably tried to explain the concept of hotels to him, but every time they got close, he'd start rabbiting on about something else. Daniel was a DJ, a lover, and a friend of the stars. He had long hair, crooked teeth and an uneven gaze; and he was angrier than a swiped wasp about the music scene in Ibiza.

'It costs me eight thousand euros for a DJ licence and even then, you have to stop playing at midnight and Ibiza is over. Fuck Ibiza.'

'Yeah, fuck Ibiza,' I half-heartedly murmured, attempting some camaraderie. I asked if he went anywhere else on the island.

'I used to go to San Antoni ...'

'Oh, that's where I went,' I said excitedly, meaning that's where the Yeovil virgins went.

'Full of Brits. Drink. Smoke. Drugs. Fuck off. I hate San Antoni.'

He missed the virgins bit.

Bowie seemed shaky territory, but I asked anyway. The reply, luckily not 'fuck David Bowie', but nothing by way of insight into 'Life on Mars?'; instead, I discovered it was Daniel's birthday. And with that he smiled a wonky smile and gulped down the last of my beer.

With Bowie clearly not on the menu in Ibiza, the next morning I pushed my bike back to the campsite gate. This liberal beginning of Bowie's free-love period reached a capitalist conclusion as I asked for my deposit back from the security guard.

'How much?' he said.

'Ten euros ...' I replied.

He rattled around in the money box.

'And fifty cents,' I quickly added.

Compasses are quite frankly useless, to the useless man. A fact I proved by spending twenty minutes attaching a Sat Nav to my bike, which stripped me of map-reading masculinity but meant I wouldn't get lost and be further stripped of it by having to ask for directions. That was the theory, anyway. The bossy device had an alternate plan. *'You see those pretty pine-clad mountains over there? They've got absolutely nothing at all to do with "'Life on Mars?'" or David Bowie, they're actually the long way around, but I'm going to make you ride across them anyway, so you think you'll miss your ferry. You just don't know it yet.'*

I pushed off and revelled in the crisp morning air, enjoying the pretty pine-clad mountains away to the west, the Ibizan rush hour limited to workers' trucks and the odd whining Vespa. As I hit a diversion through mist-blanketed valleys and Spanish wind-mills, the scent of pine grew thick, the bracing air welcoming me into an ever more arduous climb towards the tips of limestone mountains. I hadn't planned to ride over any hillocks and became concerned these thirteen miles might take a little longer than I'd allowed for. A concern shared by the numerous drivers forming a tailback behind me. As my legs burned, I pulled over, waving them through – a courtesy to my fellow road users, and also because it felt as though someone had stuck knitting needles in my lungs.

Time wasn't on my side, nor were the cars, all impatiently over-taking as I spluttered dewy breath over their windows. I *was* going to miss the ferry. What would Bowie do? Changing the face of popular music forever wasn't going to help. Instead, I reverted to type, staggering around like a Brit, wobbling like the man-boobed disappointment I had already become. Then, finally, hills, but the reverse side of them, the down bits. The wobbling now coming from the back, as the heavy panniers gave the bike a loose-hipped shimmy, the kind your groovy dad pulls out on the way to a wedding dance floor after six pints of mid-strength bitter, four sugared almonds and your nan's sherry.

I barrelled into the valley at lightning pace, cool air rushing all around me, birds soaring across my path. It was terrifying. Somehow, I didn't end up as an imprint on the side of a white van or a blood-splattered mess in the scraggy gutter, instead getting a sweeping view over Ibiza Town's whitewashed buildings and an industrial plant pumping out what I assumed was the remains of dead cyclists. I pulled over to gather my bearings outside the fume-battered Pacha nightclub. Ah, Pacha, another of the original super clubs where eighteen years ago I'd paid £25 to dance self-consciously to music I didn't like and shit myself every time a girl came near. Teenage memories were quickly pushed away, though.

'Oi, Oi. Bowie!'

Two 'lads', a bit sweaty, a bit Britty, had spotted my Ziggy Stardust T-shirt.

Daniel's words came back to me: 'Full of Brits. Drink. Smoke. Drugs. Fuck off.' I had to respond, and quick; this was an olive branch for the sorely neglected hero of this trip. I shot back a double thumbs-up – one for each of their 'Oi's. This seemed to satisfy them, as they stumbled off laughing and giving me the wanker hand gesture.

I resumed my exit, heading south on Avinguda 8 d'Agost, and with great leaps of giddy excitement passed a fellow touring bike rider. This was organic ecstasy, nature's MDMA, the joy of knowing that you're not the only idiot going around in circles on a bike. We aimed weird sailor salutes at each other and pointed to each other's bikes, laden for life on the road. His seemingly packed just as badly as mine with tie-dye, fisherman pants, bandanas and other bits of hippy paraphernalia exploding from panniers. But boy, did he look the part with his natty vest and wide-brimmed hat, a real Travelling Wilbury. With my colourful spandex get-up, he must have thought I was a sporty cross dresser.

With a spring in my step, and an added push in my pedal, I found my way to the boat with minutes to spare. As I hoisted my bike aboard, its preposterously overloaded back end meant it violently twisted 360 degrees, skittling a man's stack of Louis Vuitton luggage. He looked at me as if to say, 'You, sir, are an arsehole.' I apologised, regathered control of my bike and jumped on board. None the wiser about Bowie or 'Life on Mars?', I set sail from Ibiza, in a roundabout way, to the Norfolk Broads.

4. A STAR MAP IS BORN

Now, the good news. Bowie had been to Barcelona. And, not just once, but twice. Told you he was everywhere. But in 1987, sixteen years after 'Life on Mars?' was written, he was in danger of being washed up too. He'd made a textbook mainstream crossover from his earlier avant-garde records, thrusting him into the hearts and minds of the middle-of-the-roaders' affections. *Never Let Me Down* was an album that sought to fuse all the styles and influences he'd tried so far, to chase down commercial success. The album wasn't lavished with praise; fans poured scorn on it, some proclaiming it as his worst ever album, while *Rolling Stone* said it 'didn't bode well for his present, or future'. It's an album that hasn't fared better with time. The first two tracks – 'Day-In Day-Out' and 'Time Will Crawl' – open with DB yelling the song's name, hinting at the lack of creativity to follow. It labours under homogenous eighties production, which although of its age, feels without its own Bowie zig, or zag, desperately beige. 'Zeroes' references Prince's 'Little Red Corvette' by lifting the song's name, while superfluous guitar flourishes bookend the lyrics rather than drive them, making it a pastiche of his purple peer. The theatrical 'Glass Spider', with its spoken-word narrative, was probably designed as an enigmatic stage show opener but sounds like an offcut of Jareth the Goblin King gibberish as it slides into angsty Peter Frampton wig outs and Bowie wailing 'Ja, Ja, Ja' in nightmarish vocal ad libs. Even the biggest hit, the perky but disposable 'Never Let Me Down', feels a false saviour. At best, it's kitsch and fun, but if you're not in the mood – and many rarely are – it's bland eighties excess. Bowie later conceded it was a bitter disappointment and perhaps at the age of 40 was at a muddled middle-aged crossroads, like me.

As the ferry approached the mainland I retreated to the ship's bowels. Lorries grunted to life and car engines hummed as the ship's metal ramp unfurled like a red carpet, letting us bolt into the blue of a Barcelona afternoon. Sweeping across the port bridge, a hotchpotch of terracotta roofs sped away to the horizon, interrupted by Gothic masterpieces and the hazed swarthy green of the Collserola Mountains. With the sun casting shadows along the port wall, I banished the sea wobbles by gazing adoringly at my towering presence on the concrete. I looked great, I thought, until I nearly bowled into a stationary truck. The steamy rush hour was in full cry, awash with map-toting tourists, siesta-fulfilled locals and zig-zagging scooter drivers. As buses skirted and taxis sweltered, cyclists were smartly given the entire central reservation to whizz up and down while frustrated commuters listened to blaring radios and drummed impatiently on steering wheels.

I'd taken the liberty of booking an Airbnb, attracted by the host Alex's rave reviews ('The perfect man!', 'Muy Bueno!'). Upon arrival, I feared Alex's hosting skills had gone to his head. His directions led to an address on the wrong side of the road, and when I found his casa, I discovered that my room, with its yellowing walls, naked lightbulbs and generously stained sheets, was little more than a downmarket sex dungeon. I stashed my bike on his landing while his Stegosaurus-sized dog fixed me with a look that suggested it knew its way around a knee joint.

It was time to test Alex's credentials. 'Hey, Alex, do you know where the Mini Estadi is?'

'Use Wi-Fi.'

Fortunately, I had the Bowie bit between my teeth – and the internet – and discovered the Mini Estadi was only ten minutes away. After scribbling out the Hard Rock red herring, this was the true beginning of the Star Map, my inaugural biro jotting – where Bowie played his first ever gig on the Spanish mainland, the accompanying live show for *Never Let Me Down*, the pompously bloated 1987 Glass Spider tour.

'Life on Mars?' didn't even make the setlist, deemed irrelevant at this point with Bowie still keen on playing new material. But boy, was it an extravagant affair. Spoken-word song introductions, blinding visuals and backing dancers were all embroidered together for the largest touring set ever. It took 43 trucks to move and 300 people four days to build. Bowie thought of it as taking a musical on the road, albeit with a crappy album in tow. With casts of characters and twists of outlandish theatre, he threw dancers, pyrotechnics, 20,000 light bulbs, an infamous 60-foot fibreglass spider and half of Spain's kitchen sinks at it. Fans loved it, but like *Never Let Me Down*, it was a critical flop.

I had to see it.

I tested the waters with Alex again. He begrudgingly admitted the stadium was close and suggested a taxi, but he failed to inform me there'd be 90,000 people hanging out there as Barcelona were at home in the Champions League. The Camp Nou was swarming with football fans, all of them not looking for the Mini Estadi, which lay in the same complex. More importantly, both were locked to anyone without a ticket.

If Bowie had intended his show as theatre, mine was wretched pantomime. Ticketless, I skulked around, kicking empty cans of Mahou beer and wondering if my trip was washed up too. I was about to admit defeat when the gods intervened. My mopey face had attracted the interest of a Christian. Not a man with defined religious scruples, but a man of the same name without any at all. Christian was a real snollygoster: sharp features, bespectacled and with the trustworthiness of a shark who pops up next to you in the ocean and tells you he's already had lunch. Christian wasn't a man to be dunking babies' heads in holy water, no. Christian was a tout. His tentacles were quickly deep in my pockets. I sensed that having bartered him down from €150 to €50 in one swoop and his fleeting look of mock anguish that said, 'You're really screwing me here, amigo,' meant the only one getting a pneumatic rogering was me. But the trail of space crumbs had been light so far, so I took a buggering for Bowie.

Once inside, I waved down a steward.

'*Donde este* … the mini stadium?' I asked, meeting him halfway with the language.

'*Aquí mismo,*' he replied, pointing to the Camp Nou.

'No, no. El Mini Estadi,' I said, upping the ratio to three-quarters Spanish.

'The football match is in there,' he said in four-quarters English, correctly identifying me as a moron.

Trying to get into the empty stadium next door should have been easy, but I let myself and David down by following the smell of hotdogs into the full stadium instead. Bowie, a fixture in his school football team, would have been impressed with Barcelona, who walloped Celtic 7–0. The real winner here, though, was Christian, who sat down next to me to let me know with a delighted smile that I'd paid way, way, WAY too much for my ticket, which usually went for half the price I'd paid, but not to worry, as he'd charged the two Chinese women next to me €150 each for theirs. They gave me the peace sign.

As the crowd funnelled out, lustily singing Catalan songs, I nodded to the still locked Mini Estadi, where Bowie's own tunes would have been sung 30 years ago, and took solace in a three-scoop ice cream which didn't bode well for my belly's present or future, either.

🚲

The next morning, only ten hours had passed in the present year, but three Bowie years had whizzed by. The second spot on the Star Map was just up the road at the Estadio Olímpico de Montjuic – Barcelona's Olympic Stadium. In 1990, Bowie was back for his Sound + Vision World Tour. Although this show was more pared back, Bowie, craving commercial success, had an idea. He'd set up a premium hotline so the fans could choose their favourite song: 1-900-2-BOWIE-90 if you want to call (ask permission from your mum).

This was leapt upon by mischief makers requesting his novelty song 'The Laughing Gnome' be played (it wasn't). But 'Life on Mars?' was back on the menu, played fourth in the setlist. However, with the hits came the middle-of-the-roaders and more trouble in the form of disgruntled fellow musicians. Bowie had made the show all about him, and the only other band member allowed on stage was guitarist Adrian Belew, with the rest behind a curtain. Belew remembered in David Buckley's book, *Strange Fascination*: 'Every now and then, I'd duck back just to interact with them for a bit. I would see Rick Fox, the keyboard player, eating a sandwich.'

Food was on my mind, too. It was only a short pedal to the Olympic Park and the day was as handsome as Bowie's cheekbones. The Sunday reverie saw early morning dog walkers drifting between towering marble statues and ponderous water fountains while the city swirled beneath. The internet, not Alex, said a free tour started at 10am, but on arrival the gates remained firmly locked. I wandered off to find that breakfast – a full Catalan – served by a grease-smeared woman who looked like she'd been chasing the ingredients only moments earlier. Two tubes of sludgy pink pulp masquerading as sausages, a tomato that looked like a pig had been keeping it warm with its arse, eggs drowning in pools of grease and a bowl of white bread that seagulls would squawk 'no chance' at. It was without doubt the worst breakfast I'd ever seen. And one I polished off in under five minutes.

I made it back to the Art Deco stadium twice as heavy and thrice as regretful. As its marble towers gleamed in the morning sun, childhood memories churned of the 1992 Olympics and an archer sending a flaming arrow into the cauldron as Freddie Mercury roared 'BARCELONA!' with the kind of explosive 'B' reserved for shouting bastard at elderly drivers who've just pulled out in front of you. But this wasn't just a place for men and women to run quickly and throw things far away from themselves, this was a place for musicians at their peak. A sign inside recounted all the greats who'd played here.

> Springsteen. Jackson. Prince. The Stones. David Bowie. Metallica. Van Halen. Springsteen. Jackson. Prince. Metallica. David Bowie. The Stones. Van Halen.

So good they'd written them all twice. Or to fill the sign. The free tour hadn't materialised but there were lots of chirpy teenagers pottering about in blue polo shirts for something called Open Camp. It was an 'activity morning' where you could pay fistfuls of euros to step onto the track and compete in Olympic events. Could you pay to sing Bowie songs too? According to the woman at the counter, no. She suggested I complete six events and pay her €35. Short of time and athletic ambition, I paid €5 for one – the 100 metre sprint. I mean, how often do you get to run in a stadium where Bowie had sung 'Life on Mars?' just moments after you've eaten a platter of ultra-processed food?

Obviously thinking the same, a Middle Eastern man – early fifties, cannonball belly, button-down shirt, chinos and tasselled loafers – saw my grease-smeared lips and shot me a look that said, 'I got you, bike bitch.' To make a short event long, five minutes later, and merely fifteen since I'd mopped the last smear of pink sludge onto my fork, I was on the starting blocks of an Olympic racetrack where Bowie had freewheeled around the stage 26 years earlier singing his greatest hits.

The starting pistol was raised by one polo-shirted youth and another said, 'GO!' A false gun and a false start, surely. The Kuwaiti chap wasn't waiting around to see; he was already steaming down the track like they were giving away free corduroy trousers at the finish line. I slumped out of the blocks, the protests from my gut drowned out as a roar rose from the crowd of tourists. Was this how Bowie felt, the exaltation of an expectant crowd? The chants demanding 'The Laughing Gnome'? The battle of the bellies took shape, the greasy upstart versus the oil-rich fine diner. Surely the odds wouldn't be on an out of shape Middle Eastern man in beige pants winning – he was winning! I lugged my processed slop harder, closing the gap, hunting him down, and sure enough Bobby Beige began to fade. I sensed glory, the roar of the crowd willing me onwards. I pumped my cyclist's legs and took him on the line, snatching the world record for having just consumed a breakfast and immediately doing a 100 metre race with indigestion in 15.3 seconds.

I would have offered some words of consolation but I was too busy consuming all the air of Catalonia and wondering why I wasn't experiencing Sound or Vision. As I choked on that Bowie pun, one of the youngsters helped me off the track. 'Do you know David Bowie?' I wheezed desperately. He placed a sympathetic hand on my shoulder and gave me a look that suggested I was too old to be doing things like this. And like late-eighties Bowie, I was left to contemplate my next move.

Aside from wasting half a day eating questionable foodstuffs and racing Kuwaiti men in venues Bowie played at, I actually planned to do some cycling today. But attacking a city such as Barcelona in the midday sun turned out to be the least terrific idea I'd had so far. Gothic architecture was wasted on me as I drank the fumes of tour buses and hugged delivery vans as they pelted around the city's baking boulevards. The heat choked my overworked lungs as I darted under bygone fiesta decorations and sun-bleached *avenidas*. Barcelona's city transport department had decided the best way to keep the roads calm was to plonk a set of traffic lights every 25 metres. This meant I'd gradually work the crank to get my heavy cargo moving, build momentum, then bring it to a juddering halt eight seconds later and start the whole process again. I was looking for the ocean, but by the time I hit a patch of dead-end industrial estates, I was exhausted and having to use all my limited navigational nous. This involved swearing at the useless fucking Sat Nav and asking a yellow-uniformed postman to point me in the direction of the N-II, the main route linking Spain to France.

Luckily, the N-II was an ocean breeze. The steady tailwind on the Costa Daurada seemed to be doing most of the work and I was spirited along at a raucous pace. I gathered a head of steam and hair of sweat as I was propelled through scrappy seaside towns. Their rundown appearance easily explained by the fact that someone had decided to build one of Spain's national highways right in front of them. A lifeguard sitting alone in his highchair surrounded only by seagulls illustrated the road's problematic positioning.

Happily, Spanish drivers had been nothing but courteous so far, although one disgruntled pistonhead had seen it fit to pepper a speed camera with a hail of bullets. As I swept across the swishing watery borders of the Costa Daurada and the Costa Maresme, my mind drifted from death by stray bullet back to filling my stomach with something more nutritious. Having cleared 30 miles, what would be my first proper cyclist's lunch? After finding a super-market and failing to grasp the concept of weighing and stickering my fruit, I had little old ladies' tuts for starters, till workers' eye rolls for mains, and empanadas, bread, ham, cheese, tomatoes and bananas for dessert.

Refuelled, I ploughed on, noting that the ever-present wash of coastline was home to two distinct groups, hang-ten surfers and hanging loose naturists sitting on towels waiting for a breeze to tickle their testes and titsies. The seaside towns and swollen glands flashed between tall grass and speeding trains until the N-II swept inland, abandoning the sea views and pneumatic-breasted Germans for the less titillating B-682. Siesta time was over, and it seemed the best course of practice would be for everyone to get in their cars and immediately congest the nearest roundabout. This provided excellent practice for forgetting to look left and getting honked at by Spanish motorists as their Catalan grievances echoed behind me; 'Sí-agradable indicando, knobhead!'

With two Bowie stadiums, a 100 metres title and around 60 miles under my belt, this was the furthest I'd ever pedalled. It was time to stop trying to pat myself on the back while cycling and wind things down for the day. A sign indicated that Lloret de Mar was near and would provide a plethora of seaside accommodation and a dearth of girthy penises. But after navigating the last of the roundabouts without so much as a beep, a new kind of Spain unveiled itself.

The First World War poet Rupert Brooke once said, 'There's some corner of a foreign field that is forever England', and he may have been sitting in the Costa Brava slugging cans of warm-as-piss cooking lager when he wrote it. This was a modern kind of England, awash with blokes whose bellies spilled from their garments like trifle jelly. Rule Britannia was not out of bounds here. Want a fried egg with everything? You're in luck! A replica of the Queen Vic pub from EastEnders? You bet! A Bowie themed bar pumping out 'Life on Mars?'. Keep your glitter to yourself, gender bender.

I cycled on.

The immediate downside to not stopping was an upside: a grotesque climb. The narrow road and beady heat making for a perspiration-heavy finale. With a few last grunting revolutions, I crested the brow, pausing to drench it with sweat, then the road fell away to reveal a leafy enclave with a campsite.

Fanning euros at the receptionist, I found a sandy square and devoured a bag of cookies in the time it had taken me to run

100 metres that morning. Between bouts of tent putting up and cookies going down, the campsite showcased its unsullied beauty. Pine spruce pinged in a haze of lime and burnished trunks of trees replaced tree trunk legs falling flabbily from Speedos. The glistening sea stretched outwards and made a gentle whooshing as it returned to the shore. Myself aside, there wasn't a prick to be seen.

Exhausted, I thumbed my map to see that I'd only covered five centimetres of Spain. With a sigh I hugged my empty bidons and went searching for water. I found a short man aggressively cleaning his dogs under a spluttering tap. He motioned that the water was good to drink. This guy looked tough: leathery skin, lean body and a bent boxer's nose. The kind of man whose advice about taps you take. Perhaps if I drank enough, I'd develop a mad stare like him too. We began exchanging athletic small talk, something I was definitely qualified in having done half a day's cycling. He introduced himself as Joseph and told me he liked fighting and music. Swerving the fighting talk and sensing some Bowie chat, I asked what music he liked.

'Only good music,' he said, scratching his stubble noisily. He reeled off a list of classic performers. 'Hendrix, Dylan, J.J. Cale.'

'Bowie?' I chanced.

'Of course, only good music,' he replied as if I'd not listened to a word he'd said.

I sensed my opportunity. 'I'm doing a cycle trip for him!'

'OK,' he said blankly before crushing my fingers with an earthquake of a handshake and retreating to his caravan. Nice guy, couldn't give a shit about my trip. I needed to get better at this if I was to find some semblance of meaning. Having scared off my potential music buddy, I hunted for a cold, contemplative beer. Back in the village, an upscale seafood restaurant seemed happy to serve me frosted lager as long as I sat my unkempt carcass outside. Returning a few brain cells lighter, Joseph and a female companion appeared out of the darkness with a Tupperware offering.

Yolanda was Joseph's kind-featured wife and had made a dinner of chicken noodle soup, which they invited me to eat with them. I met their two rescue dogs, a foam-faced Alsatian called Bob Dylan and a skittish mongrel called Wilky. It was a sign. A supremely tenuous one, but one I was desperately willing to take. Because a mere four songs from 'Life on Mars?' on the *Hunky Dory* playlist is 'Song for Bob Dylan'. This furry four-legged troubadour didn't have a voice of sand and glue, but was excellent at catching tennis balls with his rabid face.

As we dined together, I learned that they lived happily on the campsite for four months of the year. But I was knackered, so I chucked Bob a mucus-coated ball or two, gratefully thanked them, and headed to the washroom to brush my teeth. The humidity that had been steadily growing outside was torn asunder by a raucous bout of thunder. Lightning bolts fizzed down in a stage show to rival Bowie's 1987 extravaganza while rain drummed apocalyptically on the corrugated roof. Eventually, a wash of cool air broke the tension and the troubled clouds breezed away to reveal a clear sky straining under the weight of faraway stars. I was to reflect on a satisfying first day of proper cycling where too much food, wind and men's genitals had crossed my belly, face and eyes, and I was asleep before you could say, 'Didn't mention "Life on Mars?" once at dinner.'

5. ¡HELLO IGGY POP. HOLA SURREALISM!

With the lyrical jumping off point of Ibiza ticked off the list, and Barcelona navigated with faint flashes of Bowie, I just had the Norfolk Broads bit – and roughly another 2,950 miles – to go. Before I set off along the coast in search of further stardust, I rose with a stiffness in my legs to discover a pressing issue – I had a saggy tent. A puddle the size of Luxembourg had gathered on the roof but fortunately hadn't penetrated it. I cajoled and provoked the little lake, quite chuffed my second-hand canvas home had remained watertight. As I gave it one last prod, the whole lot cascaded in through the door and washed across my sleeping bag. That added hour of drying meant Joseph and Yolanda were able to come and chat before taking their dogs for a walk. As I told them the lyrical idea behind the journey, they seemed most approving.

'I don't know what it means but it's a beautiful song,' said Yolanda.

'*Muy bonito,*' added Joseph like a tough guy with a broken heart.

'What's your bike called?' asked Yolanda enthusiastically.

'Oh, I don't know,' I replied, foolishly not having thought of one.

'Good bikes should have a good name,' she said wisely.

Yolanda was right. What would be a good name? Steve? Ronald? I did quite like Ronald.

No, wait! I had an idea. Performing some linguistic gymnastics, I took the bike's brand, Ridgeback, kept the I and the G, added a G and a Y, and lost a R D E B A C K.

'Iggy!' I replied with a satisfied nod.

'That's a good name,' said Yolanda.

Joseph's furious nodding suggested he agreed and had another name for his list of musicians who played 'only good music'. With a hug, handshake and promise to seek them out if I returned next year, Iggy and I were ready to roll.

Every great explorer needs a sidekick, so it was unfortunate Iggy had me. The choosing of this particular name wasn't without coincidence. Iggy Pop was the skin, bones and veins frontman of The Stooges, a rambunctious bunch of misfits making waves in the early seventies punk and alt scene. Bowie, when searching for his own identity, had admired his rampaging stage presence and befriended him. They first met in New York when he turned up outside Iggy's apartment. 'I could see that he had some ideas for me,' Iggy said to *Rolling Stone* in 2016, 'He was always like, OK, who are you and what are you thinking about? And he appreci-ated oddballs …' This was the start of a friendship and musical ping pong over many decades where they shared ideas, recorded, played, sank into drug-fuelled despair together, and later saved one another.

On that existentially gloomy note, my skinny legs worked the crank and I began to navigate the winding seaside roads that tee-tered precipitously over the azure coast. With the sun watching from upon high, a cool breeze buffeted my brow as I sprinted inland at Tossa de Mar, dipping past abandoned campsites swamped with graffiti. Yesterday I'd lazily used the ocean as a means of direction, but heading cross country meant perusing a map. The green squig-gly lines darting upwards depicted an area of outstanding natural beauty. What it blithely failed to address was that it was an area of outstandingly large hills.

The road to El Gironès was a never-ending asphalt monolith that wound around clusters of pine and recent rockslides which littered the hard shoulder. I climbed endlessly, and arduously, zig-zagging back and forth like a disorientated crab, unsure which end of the beach to make for. As I attacked the climb with gusto, it attacked me right back, sending pain flaming through my quadriceps. In what seemed like half a day, but was in fact only three-quarters of an hour, I'd drunk my entire water supply. Soon I was in the lowest gear possible, my legs spinning wildly like a hyperactive hamster on a wheel. For every fifteen revolutions my distance gained was roughly fifteen centimetres. I took a rest, a banana and some inspiration from my overheating iPod. Iggy Pop on shuffle! The first tune that played, 'Spanish Coast'. A sign that hopefully wasn't prophetic: the lyrics, caught in a swirl of sixties-style sound, suggested death by the same coast was imminent.

As I wheezed into the climb again, the once desolate Squiggly Mountain became vastly populated by road cyclists freewheeling downhill in spandex catsuits offering jaunty greetings and smug grins. I think they did, anyway. Sweat and factor 50 sun cream were busy infiltrating my eyebrows and pooling in my eyes like soapy lava. Finally, the hill plateaued to reveal brown and green plains thrown across Spain like a patchwork quilt, while puffs of cloud marked the sky like tobacco smoke. I rewarded myself for not going up hills anymore by taking a break and unattractively gobbling another banana by a drab filter lane. A combination of sun-baked dirt and knots of brambles provided a thorny throne and just enough time to realise I'd crashed a party for 246,000 biting bugs. They didn't seem to mind, desperately trying to break the barricade of my cycling shorts to realise the dream of being ants in someone's pants.

Having gone hard early, come mid-afternoon I'd ejaculated all my body's water in tears, tantrums and sweat. In my infinite wisdom I hadn't acknowledged that: (a) if you're thirsty, stop at that roadside café where everyone else in Northern Catalonia seems to have gathered; and (b) more of (a). In cycling this is known as bonking. Something your mum might use to describe David Bowie's nocturnal habits. Bonking in cycling terms is when you go bonkers for lack of food, drink and energy. Or something like that. You basically find a giant metaphor, preferably a wall, and cycle really fast into it. I was out of food and water and was slowly losing my mind to the point where the gleaming edifice on the brow of the hill was definitely a supermarket stocked with cheese sandwiches and drinks beginning with 'w' and ending with 'ater'. Racing towards my saviour, it was with much disappointment that I discovered it was a mechanic's garage. No pasties, cured meats or sweets, just spanners and little men in overalls with twirly moustaches.

Even if I'd wanted to cry, I couldn't, due to my severe dehydration, so I filled the next eight miles with swear words and whimpers until a service station finally appeared. Never had I been so glad to be thoroughly robbed for water, crisps and king-size Snickers. A mutually pleasurable mugging that had me simultaneously inserting foodstuffs into my gullet while thumbing euros at the clerk like he was an exotic dancer called Oklahoma. I greedily took the rest of my treats round the back of the garage and scoffed the lot, hoping it went straight to my hips, thighs, calves and any other muscle group that would get me through the rest of the day's cycling. As my powers of observation returned, I spied a pile of shattered glass and noted that it would be wise to cycle around that later. I also noticed the car park was home to a travelling community of eastern European truckers intermittently urinating in scrubland.

This wasn't on the Star Map.

As I refilled my water bottles next to a metallic blue HGV, a godly voice boomed from the gods, 'HELLO.'

'Oh, David, is that you? Thank God. This was a terrible idea. That thing you said about swimming to the deep end, well, I'm way out of my depth. I'm only on the second day, I'm shattered, I've seen way too many cocks and I keep running out of water.'

'You cycle?' the voice thundered again.

I gazed to the heavens to see a pair of stumpy trucker's legs dangling from some arguably too tight denim shorts. I scanned further and saw a man with a head like a breeze block and a smile like a puppy dog. He hopped down, the ground quaking.

'Yes, I'm cycling,' I said, thinking that my standing in the middle of nowhere with a bike made that plainly obvious.

'Yes, where?' he asked enthusiastically, stepping closer and invading my personal space to the point where a bit of his eager spittle nestled in my eye.

I reeled off the FITTNB (From Ibiza to the Norfolk Broads) story but his puzzled look suggested he thought I was as dense as elephant dung. I had an idea. I pulled out my phone and played him 'Life on Mars?'.

As the chorus broke, my eyes widened in wondrous exaggeration at the song's lyrics. I nodded in an encouraging fashion that said, 'You see?' His grin grew, and grew further still, growing so much it threatened to swallow his head whole. This would have been some feat, possibly a world record, considering its planetary dimensions.

'I like this very much,' he offered with furious nodding.

'Do you know what it means?' I offered with pleading hands, hoping to get the trip wrapped up early.

'Do I wear jeans?'

'Oh, no, I mean ...'

'No, it is jean short,' he said proudly, pointing to his denim hot pants before hoisting himself into the cab and shoving several folds of pimpled arse-cleavage in my face. He dropped back down with his phone. This was fantastic; he was going to hit me up with his favourite Bowie song. A roadside call and response. The drums rolled, a thrashy riff kicked in. Didn't sound like DB, probably not on the Greatest Hits. The trucker began to nod aggressively. I did too. He was big. Then as the chorus dropped so did a long, lolloping tongue from his mouth.

Huh.

He moshed his head as if he had flowing tendrils of rock star hair even though he didn't have any. He sensed my confusion.

'It's Gene Simmons,' he exclaimed. 'From Kiss!'

We both laughed and patted each other on the back, then after he spent a few minutes rolling his tongue back into his mouth, we shook hands. Bowie and Kiss had just shared an unlikely double bill in a Catalonia car park. Refuelled and re-spirited, I picked up my bike and he heaved his short shorts back into the cab. As he leaned from the window, he gave me the rock hand-horns sign. 'Yeah!' I yelled, pumping my fist in the air in brotherly bonhomie. And then, revitalised by make-up infused heavy metal, I hopped back on my bike and cycled straight through the big pile of shattered glass.

Somehow my first puncture didn't materialise, someone up their rejoicing in my efforts to spread the gospel of David via crappy phone speaker. I rejoined the N-II where a crosswind was busy galloping across syrup-coloured cornfields. As it beat me stealthily around the jowls, a dark, foreboding presence rose on the horizon. With every grimacing revolution the Pyrenees grew from the fallows, their serrated peaks snarling like hungry teeth primed for attack. If that was an ominous sign, an actual road sign appeared – twenty kilometres to Figueres. And then a kilometre later, another, also saying it was twenty kilometres to Figueres. Then two kilometres later a third, informing me I was still twenty kilometres from Figueres. Was I in a vortex, was this Bowie's doing, or had they made too many twenty kilometres signs? Either way, this could be a long twenty kilometres.

When I finally arrived, Figueres town centre was fairly small, which was fairly great as I was enormously tired. I lugged my bike into the sun-blushed streets and headed for the old town where mazes of whitewashed walls leaned in like old friends in warm conversation. Having knocked on the door of a hostel, I was told by a neighbouring barman that the owner would be back shortly. That'd do just fine. I plonked myself on a barstool, welcomed the newly named Iggy to this shambling mess and downed a couple of icy beers before wobbling him up the stairs and over the threshold into the hostel.

I made myself at home: aired my shorts, horsed down some pasta and had a brief flirtation with the city night. As a sepia haze followed me along the mellow streets, I chased the scent of sizzling garlic to a small plaza where families dined on tapas in swirls of laughter as bowtie-wearing waiters danced around their tables. More than satisfied with my resting place, I was almost back at my hostel when I happened upon a staircase hewn from marble. As my gaze followed the steps towards the black and silver sky, I noticed a dark and infinitely contorted figure stood like a surreal dream – the next stop on the Star Map.

6. DREAMING OF DALÍ

'Where are you going, then?' said the sheep as he passed the chorizo.

'I'm cycling from Ibiza to the Norfolk Broads,' I replied to the fluffiest one.

'Cool, bro,' chirped the black one in the passenger seat.

'*Si, muy cool!*' said a matted hippy sort, jamming out 'Space Oddity' on a battered twelve-string.

As the rustic pick-up truck rattled over the mountain pass, with the biggest sheep drumming his hooves on the steering wheel, I sat back, nestled against a hay bale with a group of furry folksters. They'd kindly picked me up and were now spiriting me across the Pyrenees. The sky was blessed, and the breeze felt good as it slipped between my hair, which, miraculously, was as thick as it had been in my teenage years.

'Say, I don't suppose you guys know what "Life on Mars?" means, do you?' I said.

'Why of course, it's—'

BANG, BANG, BANG!

The meaning, and my sleep, were interrupted at the insistence of a Figueres tradesman's hammer. My eyes blinked at the fractured morning light fighting through the hostel shutters. It was all a surreal and furry dream. But this was part of the city's surreal, beating heart. An hour later I strolled back to reality and was standing in front of the statue I'd glimpsed last night. In speckles of early autumn sun, *Homage to Newton* by Salvador Dalí truly revealed itself.

Its open stomach, flayed limbs and suspended heart held a dreamlike appearance as splinters of sunlight stole through its bones. But this was typical of the Surrealists, artists who brought irrational imagery to the world prised from their dreams. Dalí believed his best ideas appeared in his sleeping subconscious. He even tried to harness the power of dreams using what he called the 'slumber with a key' technique. While the rest of us wolf down cheese to get the desired mad dream effect, he swore that holding a key while resting your arms over the edge of a chair above an upturned plate was enough time to ignite the burners of creativity. It was this half second of unconsciousness between falling asleep, the key dropping and the clang of the plate that stirred the surreal inside.

While Bowie was an incredible influencer, he was a man of many influences, too. And not just music. His world from a curious young age straddled the avant-garde, the great thinkers and art, including Dalí, whose surreal sculptures and paintings had captivated him. Due to its combination of abstract lyrics, isolation and longing for other worlds, 'Life on Mars?' itself was labelled by BBC Radio 2 as 'a cross between a Broadway musical and a Dalí painting'.

This was a lot to try and figure out before breakfast, especially as my brain hadn't been working on much more than correlating the peak time to consume a banana and how to avoid ant-coated pavements. Bowie saw ants, too. Before his 1976 Isolar tour supporting his *Station to Station* album, he didn't bother with a support band, instead screening Dalí and Luis Buñuel's revolutionary silent film *Un Chien Andalou*. Surreally, it featured not only ants crawling in and out of a man's hand, a razor slicing open a woman's eyeball and dead donkeys sprawled across pianos, but also a man cycling in a nun's outfit. That's a wild party by anyone's standards. My commitment didn't extend to trawling Figueres' fancy dress shops for religious garments, but I was willing to explore the Dalí museum in case it shone a light on Bowie's other-worldly lyrics.

The Dalí Theatre-Museum, to give it its full title, stood like a Disney Castle with Humpty Dumpty eggs perched on its turrets. Glass onion domes glistened and pink and gold studded walls housed the contents of his mind and the bones of his body. My gormless gaping led me to enter the museum just as the tour buses did. Something actively worth avoiding for the sole purpose of not getting trapped in the world's slowest penguin waddle. In a hurry to get going, I was instead swept along with a tide of shuffling, skin-shedding French pensioners, getting merrily bumped between bumbags, browning teeth, walking sticks and bingo wings.

I snatched an official pamphlet, keen to find out more about the museum's artistic treasures, but it appeared exhausted by Dalí's oeuvre. I learnt this ranged *'From impressionism, futurism, cubism etc …'* That's right, Just plop an 'etc.' on the end! If the official guide had given up, what hope for the rest of us? And there was more, including a warning that due to the idiosyncratic nature of Dalí's work, there was no route to follow. *'It does not have, nor does it wish to have, any systematic function or chronological sense.'*

But such logic would have missed the point. The museum was a delight. I got lost in self-portraits of streaky bacon, melting clocks and giant telephones spread across nihilistic landscapes. Even the death march with the coffin dodgers was a calming affair until one of them backed up at the grandeur of the – don't try and say this if you've got little lungs – *Fifty Abstract Paintings Which as Seen from Two Yards Change into Three Lenins Masquerading as Chinese and as Seen from Six Yards Appear as the Head of a Royal Bengal Tiger.*

'C'est magnifique!' the woman gasped, rubbing her varicose veins across my legs.

Like Bowie, Dalí was an outsider who became a popular artist. And it wasn't just an admiration from afar. Their lives became tangled up in each other's, by their art and their loves. Their mutual respect became clouded by Dalí's muse, the sixties French singer Amanda Lear, who became romantically linked to Bowie. Which wasn't a surprise, as young Bowie tended to be a smash with all men and women. Indeed, when Bowie was in bed with Lear, Dalí would call most mornings. Bowie would playfully answer the phone and wish him 'good morning' in a comedy Spanish accent before handing the receiver to Lear.

Alas, although captivated, I emerged without finding the meaning to 'Life on Mars?'. Unless it was the feeling of deep resentment towards the gift shop assistant who charged me eight euros for a bookmark.

If that was a dreamlike start to the day, what nightmares lay ahead: the Pyrenees, border crossings – French people? The N-II was anything but surreal as I launched back along its baking lines and a cheek-ruffling gust buffeted me back to reality. As if to confirm how quick the wind was rampaging in the other direction, a man possibly in his mid-hundreds flew past in a cloud of Fabergé deodorant, bearing a *tricolore* flag. France was close, its appearance obscured by the hulking mass of snarling rock barricading the road ahead – the Pyrenees. I ventured forth, bullying Iggy towards its jagged peaks, the midday sun clawing at my scalp as the fragrance of pine trees was overtaken by fumes spewing from trucks. I glanced at the map, scanning for an easy way around the smudges of mountainous yellow. About 50 kilometres west was a settlement called Marsa. A worthwhile re-route, there's probably life there, question answered, journey over, stick your surrealism up your bum.

As I blabbered to myself, a stream of people began popping up by the side of the road. It was just like summer in England, I reminisced, where delectable fruits could be purchased from wholesome farmers in country laybys. But this was autumn, there was no such crop. The woman's tiny black and white top didn't tally with your stereotypical Catalan fruit seller. She seemed to have misplaced her fragrant pyramid of satsumas and, wait, was she wearing panda ears? I stopped and offered a friendly bonjour all the same. She responded by flashing a toothy smile and her breasts.

Panda-monium!

I'd been exchanging pleasantries with a lady of the late afternoon, dressed as a panda. It was a strange choice of costume. Confused but too tired to question this new species, I burned on in a blur of tiring muscles and prickly sweat, spotting a steady stream of sexy woodland animals as I went. These included but were not limited to: a rabbit with six-inch heels, a beaver and a red squirrel who darted up and down trees juggling acorns in a bizarre mating dance. Well, maybe not the last one. I felt like a grubby David Attenborough.

Looking at my map, the aggressive contouring suggested I was mid-Pyrenees and approaching the border town of Perthus. In my laborious climb, I'd skilfully accrued a long line of fans – French drivers. As a ragged line of retailers chucking out booze, fags and Ray Berry™ sunglasses appeared, my pace slowed to a couple of pasty femurs rotating like failing pistons. For every six revolutions, I barely gained a metre in altitude. As if to rub brackish water in my eyes, a rotund Frenchman offered a sarcastic *'Allez, allez!'* as I passed in super slow-mo. So slowly, in fact, that I could identify he was a cigarette-chuffing wanker. But he was right to be mean. Le Perthus is one of the lowest Pyrenees passes, reaching an elevation of only 250–1,300 metres, depending on who you believe (I'm with the 1300 metres guy). Finally, with a few last lung-squelching pants, I shambled across the border. *Adios España, bonjour Franca,* home of the velo, hopefully more David Bowie tales and fewer women dressed as frisky herbivores.

7. THE PASSENGER

As Spain fell away, the mountain pass peeled around the Pyrenees like a clementine, unveiling France's verdant plateaus below. I wasn't faring so well. This was no swift delivery of sausages like Bowie on his butcher's bike. The headwind was brutal, physically pushing me back up the hill and forcing my cycle helmet to tilt at jaunty angles. I had to throw this rabid wind off my scent. A detour (that the Sat Nav offered) was the solution (of the Sat Nav) and I wound up in the French village of Maureillas, a deathly silent community of sandstone summer houses and very shut shutters (good one, Sat Nav).

I took this as an opportune moment to switch from Spanish to French maps. It seemed the French were a little underwhelmed by the name of the N-II, thinking a jazzy D900 would be more appropriate. But it was no more exciting, the bland dual carriage-way mysteriously empty and fervently wind battered. The wind seemed to take particular delight in howling about your ears for five minutes, then stopping dead, only to reappear below and give the underside of your chin a good seeing to. I was getting blown after all. And so was French litter.

First, a pilchard tin whistled past my spokes. Who eats fish by the side of the road? There was no time to answer, as a fizzy pop can bounced with deadly intent towards my face. I ducked left as a pineapple logo whistled past my eye socket. I veered to the safety of a supermarket car park. Disappointingly, Pollestres wasn't the place where Bowie's seventies stage costumes were manufactured, but it did provide me with my first cultural exchange and rare possibility of a Starman anecdote. Sadly, as I placed my bounty of cheese, meat and fruit on the checkout, my French wasn't up to the barrage of questions fired at me and I ended up clutching six plastic bags I hadn't asked for. I took a table for one behind a large sign advertising washing detergent and ate my saucisson baguette, its cheese slices trembling in the breeze. I'd become surprisingly adept at picking some of the worst places to have a picnic: sunless car parks, glassy backsides of petrol stations, ant-infested verges and now wind-rushed supermarkets. Hark at the glamour Bowie's lyric had bestowed on me.

Afterwards, I dived straight into post-work traffic, so around 3.30pm for the French, and a weary hour later I was riding through the breezy university town of Perpignan. Boy racers played thudding hip hop and hard shoulders lay immaculately jewelled with coloured glass. Someone must have heard my wimpy cries of loneliness, as now I had company, too. A grey-green cricket – an actual insect, not a woman in a skimpy costume – had hopped onto my handlebars, intent on cadging a lift.

Cricket: 'Salut.'
JB: 'Oh, hi.'
Cricket: 'What you doing?'
JB: 'Cycling FITTNB to find the meaning behind "Life on Mars?"'
Cricket: 'But you are a fat man on a bicycle.'

This didn't stop him stretching out his gangly green legs and sitting tight through the spaghetti-like roads that twisted into the brackish

French countryside. With the sun slumping and the salted scent of the ocean catching my attention, I floundered onto a greenway of spindly reeds. A thicket of grass bristled and a drunken man with sagging cheeks peered out, barely able to comprehend the Sports Direct Roadshow wheeling past with a talking cricket leading the way. With mental faculties clearly in disarray and the legs not too far behind, I slowed, becoming increasingly unsteady of mind and wheels.

Cricket: 'What eez wrong with you?'
JB: 'I'm wrecked.'
Cricket: 'Non, you are pathetic and 'av begun to smell like damp
           towels.'

He abandoned bike with a click-clack of his legs and left me to my mental unravelling. As a haze of ocean appeared like a desert mirage, I was confident I was on the home straight. Indeed, the reassuring sound of breaking waves made me so self-assured that I proceeded to begin guessing where I was going, which is obviously one of the stupidest things in the great pantheons of navigation you can possibly do, and is how I arrived at a headland with no bridge to the campsite I was hoping to retire to. In the distance I heard a voice.

Cricket: 'Moron.'

I didn't need him anymore. A bicycle tourer was barrelling towards me. I hadn't spoken to anyone since the plastic bag debacle, but this man with a cork hat and similarly loaded bike would surely provide cyclic assistance and directions to the campsite. *'Bonjour!'* I trilled. He cycled straight past, heading home to the hamlet of aresholes where he clearly resided.

As the sky turned pink, then purple, like a fruity tea infusion, I arrived dispirited at the village of Leucate. It seemed a pleasant enough place to spend the night, a sea-swaddled cluster of bunga-lows and wind-blown beaches where locals played boules around seaweed-dressed lobster pots. Real French people doing real French things. I don't know if sunstroke was setting in, but I came over all warm. In celebration I bought three drinks from a bearded man in a fish restaurant, my attempts at French as surreal as anything in the Dalí museum. Taking sympathy, he directed me in flawless English to the campsite.

'Just to the left, you will see,' he said. And at the risk of sound-ing like Yoda from *Star Wars*, see I did.

I couldn't spot anyone at the reception so I snuck Iggy into a shaded corner and pitched up. Next to me, early evening shadows were cast by families dining in awnings while kids stole the last vestiges of daylight, gleefully booting footballs. I followed some-one into the keycode-guarded toilet and showered, washing away the wind, twigs and crisp packets that had lodged in my hair. The downside to free showers was that anyone who came in suspected me to be an odd, wind-burnt toilet attendant. I ignored French peo-ple demanding I hand them paper towels and browsed the campsite news board. On a tattered piece of A4 paper was a warning that the campsite lay in an area where earthquakes were known to occur. Handily, there was a set of instructions should this situation arise.

1) Keep calm
2) Head to reception
3) Stay in your tent

I know I'm crap at French but there seemed to be some logic flaw there, especially if you'd arrived naked, bits-a-jiggling at reception, only to remember point 3.

Regardless, I proceeded calmly back to my tent as a little boy whizzed past on roller skates *'Bonsoir, monsieur,'* he offered with a cheery Gallic bounce. That's more like it. As I lay my tired legs down and tried to ignore the possibility of an earthquake, a chorus of cigarette lighters clicked gamely to life. Lucy sent a text saying, 'Just looked up your route on Google Maps, you're making good progress!'

A little smile slipped out.

As I felt my eyes getting heavy, I tried to gather my last impressions of Spain and my first of France: dreams, Dalí, baguettes, boules – David Boulesie.

Sexy panda: 'Night.'
Freeloading
  cricket: 'Night.'

And I slipped into the surreal.

8. ISOLATION

I awoke to reality, and dozens of French people clattering past my tent to empty their chemical toilets. A week and 350 kilometres in, my legs felt like mashed-up human waste too. After the excitement of climbing a mountain (the highest bit, remember), the adrenaline was wearing off and the novelty of the idea was drowning in lactic acid. Most of all, I felt alone. Alan Yentob in a 1997 BBC interview, *Changes: Bowie at 50*, found a similar story. 'From the beginning Bowie was attracted to outsiders, to the displaced ... or just lonely, like the girl in his classic "Life on Mars?"' So, if the song really was about the alienation of this girl, sung through a slew of surreal images, my trip was certainly offering me an insight into her dislocation. This morning, I was laughed at for being different – ordering tea in comically bad French – and as a result ate breakfast in a sea-blown huff. Although I hadn't happened upon much Bowie thus far, inadvertently I was living the themes of Bowie's anomic (not gnomic) heroine in 'Life on Mars?'.

An individual who's anomic is someone lacking societal guidelines to follow, who then becomes alienated and struggles to find meaning in life. The word is derived from 'anomie', an idea popularised by sociologist Émile Durkheim, who in his study of suicide argued such dislocation could be a factor. The girl in 'Life on Mars?'

is no different. She feels like she doesn't belong. Her sad yearning manifests itself in isolation as she wills to escape her universe. In *Hunky Dory*'s liner notes Bowie said it was, *'A sensitive young girl's reaction to the media.'* Adding in his 1997 interview with Yentob, 'I think she finds herself let down, I think she finds herself disappointed with reality ... that although she's living in the doldrums of reality, she's being told that there's a far greater life somewhere, and she's bitterly disappointed that she doesn't have access to it.'

While my work ennui meant I was looking for a far greater life, my escape also meant I would spend nearly two months away from my girlfriend. My isolation was self-inflicted, an element of Bowie's rooted in his childhood. As well as fighting suburban orderliness, his mum's side of the family had a history of mental illness, including his half-brother, and hero, Terry. Although Bowie didn't really understand, he felt it made him different from other children – adrift, isolated, on the outside of everything. Some of his songs nod to the push and pull of Terry's influence and struggles: 'The Bewlay Brothers', with its scattershot of schizophrenic and difficult to penetrate lyrics depicting a brotherly relationship; 'Aladdin Sane', a play on words about insanity; and more, such as 'All the Madmen' and 'After All'. He was writing sympathetically and insightfully about a subject before it was even understood, and 'Jump They Say' alluded to Terry's eventual suicide when he was hit by a train aged 47. While the spectre of his half-brother's insanity haunted Bowie, he used art to placate his fears. The metaphors of aliens and distant worlds, a character called Major Tom adrift in space, all rooted in the feeling of being an outsider, someone on the fringes of society who doesn't feel understood by it.

In a 2007 interview for Swedish TV programme *Musikbyrån*, Bowie said, 'My subject matter hasn't really changed over the years. I'm still, in a way, writing 'Life on Mars?' all these years later ... the way that I present songs has changed a lot. And the style for each album has changed considerably ... like finding a different door each time I approach that same subject.'

And then, when asked specifically about isolation: 'A lot of it is. One's interior kind of isolation as well. It doesn't just mean one's social isolation, it can mean how you get in contact with your own feelings. It can be quite personal in that way.'

My tea had gone cold. I tapped out a mopey message to Lucy, which she batted back with, 'You're OK, you're on holiday!'

Some fucking holiday.

As I set off, the gloom that had gathered figuratively now loomed literally. The grey ocean mirrored the leaden skies and an icy breeze ravished my arms. I was having to ask myself some tough questions. Are you too old to be lost? Probably not; I think half of us don't really know what we're doing with our lives. Was I simply cycling away from my problems? It appeared so. Was I going to get indigestion from that croissant I'd just wolfed down? Almost definitely.

Within half an hour I was lost not existentially, but Sat-Navically. I'd ignored my map in favour of a lazy morning guided by beeps and electronic circuit boards. These exact same things spirited me away from the straight lines I thought I'd be following along the D27 – taking the scenic route – as I looped higher on juddering gravel trails and the scraggy land below grew stricken and desolate. The snapping wind and swirling grey appeared inhospitable to life, save for the odd prickly thing.

A pick-up truck growled past, its rear loaded with broad-shouldered men in orange jackets. Big paintball game, possibly. Then I saw a pair of legs dangling over the side. A deer, not a sexy one, as dead as the night. I might have squealed a little as it dawned on me that I was cycling through a sizeable game hunt and the large men were carrying even larger guns. Seeking a return to the petrol-spluttered main roads, I tried conspicuously to avoid looking like an animal as increasing numbers of orange-vested men prowled the hillsides in search of prey. I rode for my life, doing my very best human impression, corkscrewing through valleys of thistles ruled by lawless winds until I reached a settlement.

The smell of fermenting grapes oozed from under splintered oak doors and crept up my nostrils. It was eerily quiet (the French seem good at this), shutters closed (and this) save for a hunched old lady sweeping leaves from her porch with a straw brush (this too). One leaf was causing her untold problems, swirling in the wind and avoiding her attempts to brush it away. Each time she swatted at it with her broom, the gust would spirit it into the air and settle it down nearby. Eventually, she lost patience and went to kick it, but it merely lifted like a magic carpet and landed whence it came. With a gummy curse, she gave up.

I was a long way from anywhere, especially Bowie. France had been tough so far, carefree whimsy had been replaced with an itch of uncertainty. That's why it was quite frankly a delight when, ten kilometres later, I spied two cyclists on the side of the road. They were going to get a monstrous talking to. Pulling up with a mani-acal look that screamed, 'Speak to me about Bowie, pleeeeeease!' I gathered myself.

'Hi there, which way are you going?' I said with all the calmness of a man with two lobsters clamped to his testicles. Four more cyclists swept around the corner.

'Hell-oh ...' said a man with a wide brimmed hat and wrapa-round shades, 'we're from Russia.' I wouldn't have cared if they were from the school of homicidal maniacs, I was just delighted to be talking to someone. So chuffed, I affected my English accent with an awful Russian-baddie-from-James Bond intonation. 'I make trip for David Bowie,' I announced, like someone intent on killing them all with lasers. They nodded, impressed. Just as I was about to go for the jugular and ask if they knew what 'Life on Mars?' meant, wraparound shades began his own diatribe.

'We're from Kazan.'

'The best,' added another, as if he were a manager at the local tourist board.

'The best of the best,' chirped a woman, in case I hadn't understood that the best usually can't be beaten.

The Bowie thread was lost as they vandalised my notebook with drawings of the River Volga, various people's names and someone's address. It was settled, I was to visit someone's uncle in Kazan next month when they finished their cycle trip. I wasn't really sure what had just happened, but I think being talked at about Russian rivers made me feel better. That meant I was in a good mood when I saw the pretty town of Beziers with its cathedral set dramatically on a rugged bluff. As châteaus romanced and the flitting wind serenaded, my lungs filled with a sea-salt breeze, and the glinting coastline of the Cap d'Agde announced itself in a blaze of burning sky. I turned into a campsite and decided my isolation was over.

After a buzzy exchange with the receptionist, I was quickly back to being on my own. Yet after some moules-frites and *deux grandes biers*, I remained dangerously optimistic. I spied another solo camper, a cyclist. Bigger tent. More gadgets. Mountain bike. Better looking. More muscular. Cooler clothes. He didn't know it, but we were going to get along GREAT!

He was obviously just biding his time before looking up and saying, '*Bonjour, mon ami*, let's talk about our heroic cycling adventures over a bottle of exquisite Bordeaux.'

But in an alternate universe where I was stealthily watching someone, someone was watching me. A couple in a caravan had spotted my pathetic yearning.

'Is he your friend?' said a man wearing a fleece with too many pockets.

'No.' At least not yet, I thought.

'Yes, because he could not fit in zat tent,' he said, pointing at my canvas coffin and expelling a Germanic snigger. Before I could scream, 'Hey, it's lonely on the road,' he magically produced a glass of red wine and invited me to join them. Andy and Nena were great fun. They were Swiss friends, about my age, chasing the sun along the south of France. After I'd dropped FITTNB on them, Andy dropped his own bombshell.

'I don't know who David Bowie is.'

Even Nena was taken aback. She flicked through her phone and played 'Golden Years', the first time on my trip I'd heard someone else play a Bowie song.

'You really don't know?' Nena said.

Andy shook his head.

'Who's big in Switzerland, then?' I snorted.

'Gotthard!' said Andy proudly, quickly adding, 'They had an album called *Dial Hard* but the singer died in a motorbike accident.'

We toasted absent musicians, unknown or otherwise, finished off the wine with a gutsy flourish and laughed some more about how my tent could barely fit an eight-year-old inside, never mind a man with tits like an orangutan.

By morning my brooding introspection had evaporated. I took a quick look at the long stretch of sand as a white glow began to punch a hole through the grey horizon. By the time I'd forced a ham and cheese baguette down my throat a wholesome dawn was imminent. Andy and Nena hadn't risen, but as I fussed with my panniers, I still had the sensation I was being watched; maybe 'Muscles' had relented at last. I spun around to see a fifty-something man who might actually have been the inspiration for Popeye's nemesis, Bluto, his head a straggly mess of combover hair and his face camouflaged with a thick black fisherman's beard. I could see his brain whirring; he was either thinking, 'Look at this twerp,' or he fancied a chat.

'*Kaffee?*' he said warmly, producing a steaming mug from behind his back.

A cuppa and more human contact seemed most welcome. Bluto's curiosity was piqued by the bike and he wanted to know all about the trip. When I mentioned Bowie and 'Life on Mars?' his eyes lit up. This was the cue for him to talk not about what the song meant, but to rabbit on about his own travels for half an hour. And then a further fifteen minutes on how his musical tastes had changed from rock, to acoustic and now Italian classical: 'You light a candle, run a bath. It's all in the head.'

Having not been near a bath for more than a week, I couldn't relate, but I nodded nonetheless. Having craved companionship, I was now beating people off with a French stick – which is more innocent than it sounds. As Bluto relayed how he started working as an engineer but now gardened, travelled, sewed, baked and fixed cars, my early start was getting dangerously delayed and human interaction becoming a bothersome chore.

'*Immer lernen, immer lernen,*' he babbled like a rabid Scientologist.

I'd later learn that this meant 'always learning', which was a good enough parallel with Bowie's own vociferous thirst for knowledge for me to accept a second coffee and listen to him bang on about his Africa years.

Ten days in and I was starting to wonder if the metaphor was true, if Bowie really was a musical alien. People knew him, liked him, but did they want to talk about him? I was obviously committing some form of small-talk sin, dismissing chit chat about cycle routes, Russian wraparound shades and camping set-ups by diving straight into Starman chat. As Bluto's spiel span off tangentially, much like Bowie's 'Life on Mars?' lyrics, I hung on, half out of English politeness and half in hope that once we'd moved on from him talking about fixing trucks, he'd drop some Bowie wisdom. All while desperately trying not to picture big hairy German men gaily soaping themselves in the bathtub while listening to classical music. Eventually, I came to my senses and escaped, resolving not to be such a desperate needy bastard today.

I had the relative luxury of just 80 kilometres to Nîmes, the next destination on the Star Map, which was completed with a strengthening wind forcing my face into impossible angles, forcing me to relinquish muscle control of my jaw and deposit a torrent of saliva down my top on numerus occasions. By mid-afternoon, however, I was able to fix back to a smile when I realised I was flirting with the outskirts of the French city, which as well as being an important Roman landmark has an even better claim to fame: it is the home of jeans. Not just groups of namesake French blokes who gather on street corners, but the ubiquitous denim trouser that conquered the world, its origins lying in the local cloth Serge de Nîmes. Now, if you're worried that 'The *Jean* Genie' or 'Blue *Jean*', two Bowie songs, were the loose hooks I was toying with to offer this place as an official hotspot, fear not. Bowie had actually been here, a mere fourteen years before, on Bastille Day as part of his 2002 Heathen Tour.

Heathen was his twenty-second album, a whopping eighteen after *Hunky Dory*. An electro-analogue hotchpotch, it was ever-evolving Bowie. One that saw him balancing themes of birth and death. As a 55-year-old who'd recently become a father for the second time, he'd also just lost his mother and was grappling with his faith. An unease was growing, one Bowie outlined in the BBC's 2017 *The Last Five Years* documentary: 'I think because of my orientation towards the apocalyptic ... it rather hones that low level anxiety. Especially the event of a new child, my daughter, really sort of focused my fears and apprehensions.' The album title, with its religious symbolism, nodded to Bowie's questioning of himself and a higher power. But musically he was still surprising, still pushing boundaries, still using that saxophone. It's experimental, awkward, packed with outstanding angular guitar and digital flourishes, the tracks flitting between swirling shades of light and dark; from the gloom-baiting opener 'Sunday' to the 'Life on Mars?' referencing 'silver screen' on slow-burn epic 'Slip Away' and the frenetic sci-fi slingshot of 'I Took a Trip on a Gemini Spacecraft' – a cover of the Stardust Cowboy song that inspired his Ziggy moniker. He even manages to satisfy both shades on 'Everyone Says Hi' – the album's most successful single – a track about speaking to someone who has passed away, set to an upbeat melody. By the time he reaches the album's final reckoning on 'Heathen (The Rays)', he's weighing up his beliefs against his mortality. Writing the lyrics, he was said to have tears streaming down his face. Bowie had scratched his existential itch and seemed satisfied with the vigour at which he'd done so, describing the album as 'fulfilling'.

The city of Nîmes was equally attuned to life, and the need to live it, awash as it was with jubilant individuals itching for the Feria de Nîmes to begin. Every year at harvest the town gets swamped with horses, music and the French getting off their pantaloons on pastis and wine. As I pedalled through the town looking for a hostel I'd earmarked, the ancient settlements, bubbling fountains and palm-lined streets reverberated with conviviality. Bright skies watched on as bunting swung ceremoniously from balconies, and men and women warmed brass instruments on street corners.

I found the lodgings, a converted school with a long sloping lawn that led to a tangle of trees shorn of leaves by autumn's whims. It was quieter than a ventriloquist without a puppet, the receptionist hinting that everyone was in bed mortally hungover. After last night's hospitality the idea of a bit of toe-tapping and a glass of splosh seemed quite appealing. Right on cue, a couple of young lads came out looking like they'd gone toe to toe with several cases of Beaujolais. Georg and Robin, two winsome German students, were tripping around Europe using carpooling to fund their frolics, which had reached a boozy zenith at the Feria. We got chatting and they liked the sound of my trip, but respectfully stated Bowie wasn't their kind of music. Even though they were wrong, they were amiable guides and it wasn't long before I'd convinced them it was absolutely necessary to sample the festival. As we walked in the gold of late afternoon sun, my legs quite at odds with this mode of transport, their hangovers evaporated and they informed me the Feria was a three-day celebration spelling the end of autumn and the bullfighting season.

By now, dazed people were emerging from buildings scratching their heads, looking like they remembered they had children but had forgotten where they put them. They slumped over café tables with cigarettes and coffee as bartenders flung open bodega shutters with a thunderous clatter. This was my first official 'rest day'. A rest day for a cyclist is usually just that. A chance to hop off the saddle, recharge the batteries, eat a good balance of replenishing proteins and carbohydrates and not move much at all, so it was a surprise to me that three hours later I was flailing my arms around like a man excitedly pointing out UFOs as a brass band belted out funked-up French classics.

I recall lots of 'Hey, hey, hey'ing, some 'La, la, la'ing, a bit of hopping from one foot to the other and putting my arm around a 73-year-old Malaysian man and asking if he knew what the fuck 'Life on Mars?' was all about. By copying the locals, who were mostly intent on aggressively drinking anything alcoholic and running on the spot like mad people, we ended up overly tipsy. Someone had erected a TV on the wall – a bullfight was in progress. A matador stood breathing heavily, the shoulders of his teal costume rising and falling as the beast circled the sand-strewn theatre. With a poetic sidestep and gruesome flourish the fighter thrust a sword into the bull's neck. A respectful ripple of applause rang out, the French expertly sombre in their appreciation for the bull and its conqueror.

I was mortified. 'But, the bull ...' I whimpered in an extremely unrested manner.

'I know, I know. But they have a better life than most bulls,' said Georg, attempting some form of consolation before draining the rest of his pastis and immediately ordering three more. Drinks in hand, we staggered to a coliseum of smooth curved stone where the bull fight had just taken place, Les Arènes de Nîmes.

'This,' I said, regaining my composure and raising a rat-arsed finger, 'was where David Bowie played his last ever gig in the Languedoc region.' A fact two German lads who didn't like him would surely appreciate. What they seemed to appreciate more was dancing to ear-splitting techno, and that was how I came to spend the remainder of my 'rest day' propped against a six-foot-tall speaker being slowly deafened while shovelling a baguette stuffed with iffy meat into my drunken face.

By sunrise the Germans had gone, leaving the gentle chatter of birds to soothe my alarmed head. I checked my phone and saw I'd sent a message to Lucy: 'Bull killed, drunk!'

Upon reflection this might have left the impression I'd giddily cycled over a bull in a booze-fuelled rampage. To maintain the façade, I really should have followed that up with, 'Took a few goes but got the sod, eventually.' The second half of my *rest* day was this morning, and although I couldn't envision anything other than reliving Bowie's existential *Heathen* dread, farting in my sleeping bag and trying not to breathe in case I was sick, I needed to learn about his Bastille Day gig. Suffering monumental queasiness and what felt like a detached brain cortex, I rolled back through the empty streets, stale booze and good times still hanging in the air.

As I approached the professional-looking girl at the arena counter I caught my reflection in the glass. I looked like a bag of spanners that had been in a fight with a bigger bag of spanners – in a hedge.

'*Bonjour*,' she offered with a genuinely welcoming smile.

'*Bonjour*,' I said, breathing the contents of a brewery across her window.

'Would you like to visit the arena?' she continued, maintaining her smile in the face of passive intoxication.

'Yes, please,' I rasped, expelling last night's pastis onto her microphone. This was poor. I needed to be on my game, I had things to find out. 'Say, I don't suppose you know about the David Bowie concert that was played here?' I said weirdly, like a nonchalant Texan rancher.

'I don't, I'm sorry,' she offered with a polite shrug. Probably because she would have been about four at the time.

I shrugged back and picked up an audio guide. Perhaps that would know. It didn't, of course, but it was rife with gushing tales of legendary gladiators, wild animal hunts and the previous night's entertainment, bullfighting. I climbed the big slabs of Roman stone and stepped into the arena to find I was practically alone. The early bird catches the worm. But early birds also catch a glimpse of the bull's last frantic moments, its blood still fresh on the sand. I felt a twist of nausea.

The arena was, however, magnificent. Its grey stone moving from light to dark as clouds cast checkerboard shadows across its sandy interior and blue skies warmed its flagstone seating. One of the signs noted the Roman people were interested in 'entertainment and supplies'. I needed supplies. Bacon, cuddles, those sorts of things. Desperate for information, I sat on the stone and drunk-typed 'Bowir Mimes HuLy142002' into my phone.

Did you mean '*Bowie Nîmes 14 July 2002?*'

I did, Google, you blistering smart arse. But it brought success – a French website, Live on Mars written by Christian 2002 had recounted the gig in minute-by-minute detail. At around 10pm, 'Bowie appears like a dream', his voice filling the arena as a strong wind ruffles his hair, a local wind known as the Mistral. It reports Bowie is in fine form. Mike Garson playing the opening chords to 'Life on Mars?', the band striking up and the song moves to 'an unforgettable peak … leaving the crowd breathless'. The 12,000 strong crowd want more. Stamping their feet, 'They want Bowie again!'

I gazed across the empty amphitheatre and let out a little shiver of sentimental nostalgia. I wanted Bowie again. I imagined the crowd listening to 'Life on Mars?' and his voice echoing around the arena. Right on cue, a plume of pigeons scattered behind me and brought the morning to life.

With a bit of Bowie under my belt, I felt more rested. Back at the hostel, I unfolded my map. As the vast expanse of France yawned before me, I noted that the ViaRhôna cycle path followed the Rhône river northwards into a black hole of Star Map destinations. Bowie had not disappointed Christian 2002 on Bastille Day, and as I forced the last of a dry baguette into my sickly face and set out for the nothingness beyond, an element of that story lingered on.

The wind that had irked Bowie as it tousled his feathered noughties mane was the Mistral. Its gusts are known to bluster at speeds of over a 100mph and locally it's called the 'Idiot Wind', not after the Bob Dylan song, but on account of it driving people mad. Wibble. The cold, dry Mistral has irked many a soul, not just singers, and I'd been warned that its strength becomes particularly amplified as it funnels through the Rhône Valley. Of course, I'd blasély plotted my route towards some Bowie bits in Lyon slap bang through what looked like a beautifully picturesque, but now disgustingly windy Rhône Valley.

Bowie was right, the Mistral was a rotter. My ears flapped like excitable castanets as it slowed my progress to a crawl. I laboured along the D6086 with extended glances at the arrangement of flowering shrubs and trees bent double from years of whistling bombardment. As its jet-engine thrust peeled back my eyelids and yanked my helmet backwards, my irritated jabbering seemed to confirm madness would be my next destination, so it was a pleasant surprise when an hour later the landscape gave way to rustic vineyards, sprawling châteaux and the rich, swarthy hills of the Rhône region. This was wine country. This was more like it.

I tailed tractors splattered with tannin and pettily judged farmers on the presentation of their vineyards. Heroically, I fought on, ploughing up calf-burning hill after hill, perspiring unattractively in the stupefying heat of the afternoon. The Mistral, not to be outdone, responded by summoning a storm of alabaster dust from a stonemason's yard that clung agreeably to my prickly sweat, leaving me dressed as a ghoulish apparition. As I circled the sleepy satellite villages of Pont-Saint-Esprit looking like Patrick Swayze in *Ghost*, or, if you believe in the paranormal, just Patrick Swayze. I gazed at passing drivers in the hope one would take pity, whisk me to a château and feed me grapes and wine before driving me half-pissed to the meaning of the song. The Live on Mars blog would probably have been most dispirited.

6.45pm: Man on bike enters town of Pont-Saint-Esprit
6.50pm: Man on bike is faffing around a bit
7.05pm: Man is gazing dimly at a roundabout
7.15pm: Man on bike who looks a bit like Patrick Swayze (in *Ghost*) is saying swear words at his map
7.20pm: Giving up on man on bike, he's an imbecile

The Mistral *had* driven me crazy, and Pont-Saint-Esprit holds a fair history of that. In 1951 its residents were mysteriously struck down with mass insanity and hallucinations. A local postman had the sensation he was shrinking, with fire consuming his body and snakes coiling themselves around his limbs. One man threw himself from a second-storey window yelling, 'I am a plane,' while another begged a doctor to put his heart back in his body because he could see it escaping through his feet. All up, five people died and countless more were admitted to mental asylums. For many years the accepted theory was that bread from a boulangerie had become contaminated with a fungus called ergot. However, the case of the *Le Pain Maudit* – the cursed bread – took a new twist in 2010 when an investigative journalist called Hank Albarelli found a CIA document revealing that during the Cold War the Americans were investigating the effects of LSD. With research facilities a mere 350 kilometres away in Switzerland, Albarelli concluded that someone had breezed over the border and popped the psychedelic into the bread deliberately.

Sounds like a big bag of Hank.

I needed to address the prospect of having nowhere to sleep. Another lap of the roundabout confirmed there were no rustic guesthouses serving an abundance of cheese, so instead I looked for a field without a crop of dodgy fungus. Spotting an open gate into a tufty thicket, I guided Iggy down a lonely farm trail and set up camp between rows of naked pear trees.

Wild camping is one of those things that sounds amazingly liberating in theory: a real poem to nature, the call of the wild, the mischief of adventure, watching the stars shimmy across the sky before waking to birdsong at dawn. But strip away all that romance and you're basically homeless. Every breeze in the leaves, every car engine or train horn knows you're there. Each splinter of light from your torch alerts badgers, spiders and woodlice to your presence. And let's not forget the farmers: big bug-eyed, hairy-nostrilled Breton farmhands creeping up to your tent and poking their gun barrel through the door. Or so your imagination tells you as you lie alone in a French field.

I thumbed out a message to Lucy: 'I'm camping – wild …'

'Cool. Let's go camping next year, somewhere warm!' She hadn't grasped the perilous nature of my situation. 'Remember to text your mum.'

'What, to tell her I'm going to die?'

'No, to tell her you're OK.'

'Oh.'

'Are you scared?'

'Nah.' (Yeah.)

'You'll be too busy snoring.'

As I settled into this natural wonderland, a distant rail line rattled, crows cawed and a restless breeze took flight between the branches. I ravished my quiche with a nervy gulp, jammed in my headphones and passed an uneasy night.

9. WILD IS THE WIND

Surprisingly, I woke alive, which as anyone over the age of 80 will tell you is a good start to the day. Two weeks in, I'd navigated a night's wild camping, learnt how the French reacted to a live version of the masterpiece, and more importantly wasn't pulling pieces of shot from my derrière. Although finding the meaning to a song by cycling a lyric wasn't going to be easy, I felt, at least, it wasn't entirely a fruitless endeavour.

As I stretched my strained limbs under a tangle of damp branches the debate over whether there was 'Life on Mars?' hung in the balance, but there was definitely life on Iggy. Slimy, suckery life. I removed a snail the size of a family hatchback who'd adhered himself with a long trail of bum deposit, and, feeling spirited by the Bowie breadcrumbs, transported myself back to the magic roundabout.

Out of all the joys of last night's wild camp, not being able to wash my stink-splattered body wasn't one of them. Fortunately, local French government departments have a rather agreeable policy of placing public toilets in the middle of roundabouts. Just as I treated my armpits to a good lathering and set about scrubbing the night from my teeth, the door swung open and a lady carrying a mop bumbled in, humming cheerily to herself.

That all changed when she caught sight of this *thing* that had just been dragged backwards out of a hedge and was now stood foamy-nippled in front of her. With an almighty, 'AWOO!' she thrust her mop in the air and I jumped in shock, raking my toothbrush across my gums. I tried to placate her with a bloody smile, but this frightened her even more. As she shooed me into the local administrative offices next door, I realised if I wanted to spend the day cycling along the ViaRhôna – and avoid a custodial sentence – I was going to have to channel some Bowie and mime the shit out of this.

In 1968, Bowie was post-hippy but pre-'Life on Mars?' His '*Immer lernen*' mindset meant his grey matter was receptive to all kinds of performance. He'd became a part-time member of the Lindsay Kemp Mime Company. Kemp was a flamboyant mime artist, dancer and thespian who lived as dramatically as he performed. Under his tutelage, Bowie learnt about characterisation, make-up, sexual ambiguity and how adding theatrical flair would help him stand out. It was also how he met the girl who broke his heart.

Kemp was asked to choreograph a play called *The Pistol Shot*. For the production he chose Bowie and a beautiful red-haired artist, Hermione Farthingale, to dance a poetic minuet. The pair were very soon an item. Bowie's next project would be Feathers, a group consisting of him and Hermione performing poetry, folk and mime. Bowie later conceded this was an excuse to be with Hermione for as long and often as possible. But as he charged forward in his career, the romance unravelled. Farthingale went off to shoot the movie *Song of Norway*, entered a new relationship with a dancer, married and moved abroad. Bowie retreated to the suburbs, tail and libido between his legs. In the wake of his devastation, he penned a string of songs, some, like 'Letter to Hermione', obvious in their subject. But could the girl with the mousy hair in 'Life on Mars?' also have been Hermione? Thrilled with my new theory, I quickly formed the 'Could "Life on Mars?" be about Hermione Farthingale detective agency' and got to work. She actually did have red hair, and her middle-class parents were entirely disapproving of their fledgling relationship. Her father, a solicitor, wasn't overly enamoured with their daughter shacking up with a working-class Brixton boy.

As I got dressed and the bathroom cleaner recovered from her fright, I felt rather pleased with myself. Had I unwittingly stumbled upon the girl from 'Life on Mars?'? Probably not. Hermione denied it was about her and the mystery continued until Bowie briefly reprised the theory in 1990 when he announced the song at a concert with the most plaintive of introductions: 'You fall in love, you write a love song. This is a love song.'

For once, Bowie's mask slipped. But who it really was about, if anyone, has never been made clear. Fiction, or otherwise, the girl with the mousy hair from Bowie's lovelorn youth was an indelible story he would carry through his career. As he journeyed through the sands of time, his perspective, like that of many of his songs, may have changed from its original meaning as he reinterpreted his own art and music. I wondered how I'd view my own youthful-ish journey in ten or twenty years' time. Mid-life madness, me finding my way, or life on earth going the wrong way?

As the whistling Mistral brought me back to the present morning, this indulgence had taught me something: how to perform a mime act to three female French civil servants. My concentric circling of arms – translation: 'Roundabout' – and dove-like hand gestures – 'Fly along the river' – led them to think I was a seagull who'd gobbled some dodgy rye bread and was tripping his beaky tits off. Eventually, Iggy saved us. One of the women spotted him, gently escorted us from the building and pointed out the road to the ViaRhôna.

My inner murmurings on the future were hushed as I let nature swallow me whole. Tiny lanes wove around isolated farmhouses, opalescent streams plinked and plonked under lily pads, moulting ferns shed fronds into the yonder and the Mistral plundered across distant farmland. The path performed a two-step, as it moved away from, then closer to the low thunder of the Rhône. With withered sunflowers peering from behind naked trees, I rolled across bridges as the water sprinted south, the Mistral letting me know it was still in charge by slamming me against iron railings like a school bully looking for lunch money. The path ducked into the shelter of forest and I paused briefly to hydrate. Then, even without the wind's bluster, the bushes began to rustle.

Bears! I thought.

'Jesus!' I yelped.

No, neither. It was Antoine, a cyclist from Switzerland.

'I've just slept in there!' he said, pointing proudly at a bosky thicket.

'Oh, cool. Where are you heading?' I asked, relieved.

'South. Travelling with the wind, like everyone else. Only an idiot would go north. How about you?'

'Oh, you know, here and there,' I said, noticing Iggy's tyre pointing north.

'Heading south, then?'

'Yup.'

'Want to ride together for a bit?'

'Oh, um, yeah, well, I'm just going to hang here. Eat a sandwich, you know.'

And with a wave, off Antoine breezed, the Mistral at his back as he whooshed merrily south. After all, only an idiot would go north.

Peeling a generous layer of map from my face, I decided my stagecraft would have to evolve too. I adopted various positions to tackle my gusty foe. First, the hunch, where I squeezed my shoulder blades tightly and sucked in my cheekbones, but I'm pretty sure I just looked like a deflating sex doll. Then, as the battering continued, I went full foetal, curling up like a frightened armadillo. The mighty wind roared all around, leaving my ears ringing with feedback. I pulled out my camera to capture its incessant howl, cycling no-handed as I did. This seemed particularly brave as I'd never actually learned how to do so, which meant I didn't see the pothole Iggy's front tyre was about to trundle through, which in turn would send me pirouetting down a gentle slope, where with a bound of theatrical drama I thrust my hands forward, maintained my hold on the camera but slid elbow and cheek first across some unforgiving French gravel.

I'd saved the camera, but my palms and face had accrued a healthy slathering of grit and graze, dabs of blood dotted over them like a child festooned with chicken pox. Iggy fared worse: his handlebars twisted; his paintwork scratched. Dusting him down I mumbled, 'Sorry mate,' and peered around to see a quintet of black cormorants emitting gleeful chirps as they thrashed around, much-amused, in the wash of the river.

There was no doubt which way the wind was blowing when I opened a packet of crisps only for the Mistral to deposit a third of them across my face. The rest waltzed off down the ViaRhôna, where a Swiss man gusting along at a cracking pace was wondering why it was raining chicken and thyme flavoured potato cuttings.

Who's the idiot now, Antoine?

It was still me, to be fair, since now I was entirely bereft of food, so it was with great relief that I chanced upon the village of Meysse. I looked for vital signs; nothing. Nothing except a poster saying that Pauline and Alex had hosted a karaoke night on a Wednesday about a month ago. Shutters remained shut. Cobbled lanes went untrodden and shops offering fruit and legumes dispensed none. As the sun bore down, gently reddening my skin, I slumped onto a bench in the pretty village square. I was out of fuel and the Bowie well had run dry – maybe he wasn't everywhere, after all. I pored over my map. Where now, exactly? What now, exactly? And then, like first love's crashing arrival, a lightning bolt smashed to the ground.

10. MAKE-UP & MOUNTAINS

As Bowie set about enhancing his early characters and career, his creativity extended out from his music. He wouldn't follow fashion; he'd create it. And that didn't just mean clothes; that meant make-up. A man wearing make-up in the sixties was unheard of; it was outlandish and it was outrageous. Encouraged by his first wife, Angie, he blurred gender lines, then rewrote them, taking influence from ancient Japanese and Arabic styles that lent him an alien-like appearance. As with other aspects of his career, he picked only the best people to work with. Bowie had a man he called 'My Picasso', a French make-up artist called Pierre La Roche, and it was by sheer coincidence that around a map square to the east, served by a squiggly green line jutting into the Ardèche mountains, was a settlement called Saint-Pierre-la-Roche.

La Roche helped make 1973's *Aladdin Sane* album cover and, more significantly, the iconic red and blue lightning bolt that transformed Bowie's face from androgynous alien to twentieth-century cultural icon. The two-tone blue and red lightning bolt has since adorned everything from copycat celebrities to keyrings, T-shirts, dog bowls and the sides of badly packed panniers. The legendary image was shot in photographer Brian Duffy's studio, where La Roche and Bowie knocked heads to create the friction for lightning to flourish.

Various stories have surfaced as to the bolt's origin, ranging from the signet ring Elvis wore of his Templar of the Christian Brotherhood society, Duffy copying a sticky face transfer and drawing an enlarged version with lipstick, or, in a victory for household appliances, the red and blue lightning flash logo on a Panasonic cooker in the studio. Incredibly, given its status and enduring iconicity, Bowie only ever wore it once, on the day of the shoot.

What if somewhere up there lay a memorial to the designer of one of the most instantly recognisable and enduring symbols in popular culture, or better still the meaning behind 'Life on Mars?' The lightning bolts on my panniers winked encouragement. No, this was stupid. Why would I destroy my legs cycling eleven kilometres up a mountain to see a silly village called Saint-Pierre-la-Roche? Moments later I was destroying my legs cycling eleven kilometres up a mountain to see a silly village called Saint-Pierre-la-Roche.

The Ardèche mountains provided ample reward, the thunder of wind replaced by the gentle progress of water over rocks, while farmhouses lay flecked in poetic tangles of winter berries. Brooks plipped, grasshoppers bounced and butterflies flitted as I glided past village schools and rarely used post boxes. The sound of hammer on rock echoed through the valley as I spiralled ever higher, past horses, donkeys and strutting cocks, each slowly turning to see who this wayward traveller was.

After 30 minutes the valley's blissful charms had worn off. I'd been spinning pedals for nine kilometres and, having had my fill of hill, got off to walk. Almost immediately, the main road forked sharply into a steep grassy bank where a bundle of crates blocked my path. 'Route Barrée!' screamed a spidery, handwritten sign. I ignored it, powering past gnarled farm machinery and some furious frothy-faced dogs. Finally, a further three kilometres later, I crawled, lungs heaving, into Saint-Pierre-la-Roche. The clanging had come from a chocolate box church. I rested Iggy against its side and found a bench from where I could peruse the tiny settlement. Two drywall houses, one black cat, a sweeping vista across the Ardèche, a bottomless quarry of jagged rock, one wally on a bike, but crucially no iconic make-up designers and no meaning to the song.

The *Aladdin Sane* bolt may be the most well-known and enduring of Bowie's looks, but La Roche was central to many more. The sleeve for the 'Life on Mars?' single released in 1973 featured Bowie with a La Roche-designed gold sphere on his forehead and it was also 'Saint Pierre' who gave Bowie the startling metallic-blue eyeshadow in the 'Life on Mars?' video. Sadly, La Roche became something of a forgotten man and passed away in Paris, supposedly from Aids-related complications in 1991, with shamefully little fanfare. And that was it. The fleeting but tragic story behind one of the most enduring pieces of music iconography ever. The conspiracy was over, Saint-Pierre-la-Roche nothing more than a leg-busting coincidence.

Bowie's Picasso had some legacy. A job shouldn't define anyone, consume them either, but his slow fade to obscurity didn't seem fair. Surrounded by nothing but swatches of Ardèche green and cloud kissing rock, I wondered what would happen if I stuck with my job. Would I fade into a shadow of my former myself? The church bell chimed again, sending a flock of birds dancing up the mountain face. I began my chilly descent back to the ViaRhôna as the outraged dogs threw themselves at the fence like it was made of sausages that had somehow wronged them. With shadows growing longer and supplies getting lower, I stopped at a little shop in the village of Baix. Although the door opened with the clang of a bell, the lights and fridges were all switched off. Regardless, I dutifully did my little shop – baguette, ham, cheese, mountain of sugary crap – before my eyes widened at a blue pack of cigarettes behind the counter.

Gitanes – Bowie's favourite.

An old lady emerged and creaked into place behind the till. I enquired about the cigarettes. *'Et un Gitanes, s'il vous plaît,'* I barfed in horrible French. The woman looked at me as if I'd asked to fart on her vegetables. I fumbled around with the not many ways Gitanes can be pronounced.

'*Git-anne.*'

Blank look.

'*Git-aine.*'

Puzzled look.

'*Giiiit-anne.*'

Patience-wearing-a-bit-thin look.

Of course, there was the slim chance her name was Anne and I was repeatedly calling her a git. Finally, something clicked. 'Ah, *Gee-tan,*' she said with a knowing smile before hammering some numbers, seemingly at random, into her ancient cash register. It displayed a rather hefty €22. Had she thought I'd put an offer in on the shop? But seeing this as some kind of unofficial Bowie stockist, I handed over the dosh, thanked her for wiping out my daily allowance and surmised it would be budget sleeping tonight. And by budget I meant hedge.

The Rhône looked a suitable place to have a shower tomorrow morning, so I pushed Iggy across a field of knotweed and under a dell of tightly packed trees. Bushes obscured the road and, confident I was invisible, I slung up the tent and set about ravishing my pricey picnic. Daylight had buggered off altogether by 7.30pm, which meant I had around three hours of guessing whether it was wolves, wildebeest or homicidal farmers making the twigs crack around my tent. Concluding that it was probably the Mistral or a crisp-covered Antoine, I passed out just in time to remember I'd forgotten to pack the tent's guy ropes.

Waking unscathed from a night sleeping on someone else's land is a majestic feeling, only to be immediately spoiled by the dawning realisation that you don't have access to a toilet and you need an immediate poo. As I perched between tall grass and a clump of tickly heather, another slow passing thought became entwined in my bedraggled hair. What is happiness? Is it love, or is love happiness? Having escaped from the silver screen, the toilet philosopher was now dangerously alone with his thoughts. I watched as the sun flitted across a dock leaf, stirring a ladybird from its slumber. It blinked into the morning light, extending its little legs, and pottered off to go about its business. Then, as the dotty bug disappeared over the frozen ground, so did my testicles. Which, as it turns out, was a fine metaphor for my not having the balls to move my relationship with Lucy forward.

I was blaming it squarely on another 'Life on Mars?' lyrical reference, 'Rule Britannia' being out of bounds. I'd worked, but still couldn't afford to take the next step and buy a house. Isn't that the dream you're sold? Glittering lights. Glittering job. Chunter through the gears into homeownership and settle down. Not just drift along renting a poky one-bed flat for three-quarters of your wage where the plumbing looks like it's been carried out by an amphetamine-lashed Mr Blobby. Or where ex-husbands errantly reappear once a month to wail up at windows, and where you sleep next to a clothes horse drying damp underpants 30 centimetres from your face. It was either that or good old-fashioned cowardice. Perhaps I was too gutless to take the next step, to take responsibility and build some foundations of my own.

As I grumbled into the morning sun, not having a bed to sleep in also highlighted the other facilities that I was missing out on, like piping hot showers and plump fluffy towels. But the biggest stink about all that seemed to be me. Without access to a sink, my wardrobe of two T-shirts and two pairs of cycling shorts had begun to kick up an irksome pong. Bowie's wardrobe, of course, contained many iconic changes of outfit. My options were limited to popping on jeans and a fleece, and throwing the compass around my neck as a jaunty accessory. The isolation was probably a good thing; that way it was only me who could acknowledge that I smelt like a decomposing badger.

As I tried to outrun the stench of me, I was dismayed to learn that cycling up mountains to not find dead make-up artists had also played havoc with my knee. It felt like a mechanic had stuck a spanner in, then a calendar of big-breasted women and finally a petrol station pasty, before leaving them to coagulate in one infectious mess. I made exceptionally slow progress and increasingly loud utterances to anyone who'd listen, which meant the occasional donkey, bored stork and unsympathetic ears of corn. My complete physical breakdown was confirmed when I whimpered to the outskirts of the river town of Valence and was overtaken by a permed sixty-something jogger in a ghastly velour tracksuit.

I flopped over my handlebars. I hadn't taken injury into account and hadn't practised a mime routine about having a poorly knee, so when Parc Jouvet led to a train station, I took it as a sign and duly bought a train ticket to Lyon. The one-hour ride would knock out the, oh, three or so hours of painful cycling and give me ample time to recover.

Moments later, and to my utter horror, I discovered there was no train service today. Like my knee, the French were on strike. The ticket I'd bought was, however, valid for the rail-replacement bus service that was going to take, oh, three or so hours. I packed Iggy into the boot and huffily climbed aboard, pointing to my knee and wincing when any locals dared make eye contact. I saved six minutes and arrived in Lyon city centre at 3pm.

Our Starman had been a fairly consistent visitor to Lyon since his world tour of 1978 and subsequent ones in '83, '87, '95 and '97, as well as 2003's Reality Tour. The Star Map had tossed up something else, too: a mural by the street artist Big Ben on Rue Neyret. As I limped towards it, I looked up to see a pair of distinctive eyes staring down at me – Bowie's. They held an otherworldly gaze that said, 'I'm not angry, I'm just disappointed by your ongoing feeble efforts.' The mural had only appeared a month before my arrival. An artistic tribute in the wake of his passing, it was slowly being discovered by Lyon's residents, Bowie's sudden absence bringing him to the fore of everyone's consciousness. As Iggy and I gazed into DB's eyes, a man of similar age to me walked up, his young daughter sitting atop his shoulders. He began speaking to me in French. Apologising that my school-boy learnings couldn't stretch beyond 'hello' and 'a rabbit', he switched to English. I explained what I was doing and was met with an immediate recognition of the song. 'Ah, it is a beautiful record,' he said in a warm, nostalgic voice. Sensing an opportunity, I asked if he had any idea what it meant.

'It's like a feeling, non? It goes up and down, musically I mean, like a story.'

I nodded in agreement. Too busy getting tangled in the lyrics, I hadn't thought of its meaning as musical. But it was wholly fair, the progressive, soaring melody an evocative sonic shorthand that immediately builds a world of wonder and drama. I asked if his daughter was a Bowie fan. He gently explained she had learning difficulties but liked the sounds of his music. I enquired if she liked 'Life on Mars?'. As the father asked, she smiled shyly; he seemed surprised by her answer. 'She likes the, how you say, the piccolo?'

He saw my puzzled look, not for his pronunciation, but the instrument.

'The flute, the recorder,' he clarified.

Smiling, we waved goodbye to each other and Bowie's watchful gaze. I had another question that needed answering. The flute, was there a flute? I'd never noticed it before. I cycled to the Parc de la Tête d'Or, jamming in some headphones and listened on my phone. I'd been so distracted by the lyrics I was cycling that the recorder part was sitting slap bang underneath them, as a gorgeously whimsical side journey. Producer Ken Scott said in 2007, 'I love it when the recorders come in. They just fit in so perfectly with everything else.' And in a triumph for school recorder lessons, it was Bowie who played it. The song had conjured another magic trick, revealing something new, at least to me, even now.

Picking up the river again, I aimed Iggy's wheels in the loose direction of Switzerland, around 200 kilometres away. Bowie had lived there for twenty years, so surely a glut of further treasures awaited. As the Rhône ran away east past sun-wrinkled fisherman, I flashed between corn fields which exploded either side of me in a blaze of gold. Static from electricity lines crackled – lightning bolts above and *Aladdin Sane* ones below on the sides of my bag. This cyclist's high, fuelled by the earlier exchange, was only tempered by the fact that I'd greedily eaten three-quarters of a block of cheese for lunch. The Coeur de Melle promised fruity tenderness but delivered a gumptious film that clung to my mouth like a rejected lover.

My journey took another downturn as the ViaRhôna slipped into a sudden lack of signage and a transition to lumpy paths more suited to dragging humans you didn't like along. Loose rocks juddered Iggy's wheels and rattled my teeth as patchworks of auburn fields unfolded all around. These were provisional ViaRhôna routes, basically bridleways, piles of rocks and a lot of 'No, no, hmm, maybe?' on the part of the planners. I headed back to the roads, grubby of legs and mind, where a town hall, a *mairie*, presented itself. Slithering into reception, I sunk my elbows onto the counter and pleaded in my best French, 'Could I have a camping, please?' I'm sure the reply indicated I could have whatever I wanted if I went away and took my horrible French with me. Darkness was descending in many respects when I stumbled into a campsite and pretty much fell into the arms of the husband and wife who owned the place, he a fleece-bothering Art Garfunkel-a-like, she a bodywarmer-donning Iris Apfel-of-my-eye.

Sensing my frailty, Iris' mothering instinct kicked in and she began piling foodstuffs around me: tuna, sardines, pâté, a frozen baguette, crisps, sweets and grain bars. Looking like I'd cleaned up at the local raffle, I found a picnic table and set about adding half the tinned goods of France to the dead midges already lining my mouth. I can recall the moment vividly now; it was one of those epiphanies when you muse how you'd write a letter to your younger self, tell him not to worry, not to sweat the small stuff, that everything would work out in the end. Well, I would have written that letter to myself six hours ago, offering gentle advice about why eating a whole packet of cheap French cheese while cycling in 35-degree heat for eleven hours straight wasn't perhaps the best idea. At best I'd be asking for sunstroke, certainly some dairy sweats, but more likely something far worse.

Far worse came next. The mixture of questionable meat in questionable jelly had made acquaintance with the questionable discount cheese and were strongly questioning whether they liked each other. Add in half a day in the sun and they didn't, it turned out.

Something fishy was going on. A dash to the bathroom later and something fishy was making an arc from my mouth to any available nearby surface. In a pyrotechnic show to match anything Bowie had ever done, barely digested sardines, pâte and hunks of bread sprinted from my mouth in a Technicolor Armageddon.

Then my arse piped up. It fancied joining the rampaging deposit of liquids. Spinning around, I heaved my cycling shorts down in time for several mugs of boiling shit to evacuate my bum at immeasurable speeds. In a brief moment of respite, I caught my sorry reflection in the water, then spewed all over that as well. Feeling like I'd given birth to Satan, I winced through the darkness, simultaneously holding my backside and mouth so nothing more could pass. The occupants of a solitary campervan hadn't checked to see if I was OK, mistaking my berserker howls for a distant pack of wolves having lively sex. Half-dead, I crawled inside my tent, curled into the foetal position and slumped onto my travel pillow, feeling every inch of its miniscule dimensions as my sad face slipped off the edges. My stomach tossed like a raging ocean of bile and the rest of my body convulsed with shivers until, mercifully, I slipped into a pâte-induced coma.

When you feel sorry for yourself on a solo bike trip in an out-of-season campsite there's little opportunity for sympathy, but the next morning I sought it anyway. Two weeks and 400 miles in, creeping towards October, the dawn had brought the first chill of the trip. I crawled from my canvas hole. The tablecloth of mist that hung over the distant mountains lapped thirstily at the campsite edges. As the chill added to my malaise, the size of the endeavour weighed heavy on my sickly body. Lucy, and sympathy, felt a long way away.

I slunk into the reception and discovered that Art Garfunkel was in fact a cheery man called Jean-Claude.

'Morning, how did you sleep?' he said with an unknowing smile.

My face was like a thousand sad teddy bears. 'I've been ill,' I replied.

His head tilted sympathetically.

'Really ill,' I added for bonus sympathy points.

'Come, come,' he said, ushering me to a seat.

I was fortunate enough to have him boil me some black tea and treat me to the French version of 'Oh dear', which seemed to translate as a warm smile and the occasional 'How can I 'elp?' shrug. As the tea slowly worked its medicinal effect, I realised I had a captive audience.

Before departing from England, a French work colleague, Guillaume, had kindly helped me write a crib sheet of questions that might prove useful. While it still felt like my innards were being feasted on by a 60-foot tapeworm, I wanted to grill Jean-Claude on his Bowie appreciation before he hot-footed it. I whipped out the paper and got to work.

'*Aimez-vous* David Bowie?' (Do you like David Bowie?) I asked, sounding like a cat trapped in an accordion.

'Well, yes,' replied JC.

Correct. Next question.

'*Je voyage en vélo d'Ibiza a Norfolk en Angleterre, comme David Bowie dans sa chanson "Life on Mars?",*' (I am cycling from Ibiza to the Norfolk Broads like David Bowie's song 'Life on Mars?') I exclaimed proudly, torturing the cat a little more.

'This I did not know,' replied JC, clearly not up to date with his clairvoyant classes.

I wasn't expecting much from this next one – no one else seemed to have the faintest idea – but if he nailed it perhaps I could go home.

'*Quelle est la signification de "Life on Mars?"?*' (What is the meaning of 'Life on Mars?'?)

Sadly, JC was none the wiser, holding out his hands and flapping his lips like an excited horse.

A change of tact was required. '*Quel genre de musique écoutez-vous?*' (What music do you like?)

This removed JC from his torpor. 'Total!'

It was as if years of campers asking what coins the washing machine took was worth it to take a question like this from a breezy little nomad like me.

'Classique, modern. Vivaldi, Chopin. I play the accordion!'

He played the accordion!

Did Bowie? I didn't know, or care. This had been a revitalising session. Perhaps JC wanted to adopt me, let me rest a while, deliver a soothing rendition of 'Life on Mars?' on his accordion. I could let him know I thought he looked like Art Garfunkel. He'd like that!

Turned out JC wanted to know when I was off because he had to go and pick up some canoes in twenty minutes.

Time waits for no man, I told myself between tidal waves of nausea and self-sympathy. I solemnly packed my bags and trundled out of Camping Municipal La Val d'Amby onto the slender country roads. Within minutes, I was disorientated and dehydrated. I commandeered a middle-aged cyclist and prodded at the direction I wished to take. He puffed out his cheeks as if to say he feared for my wellbeing, or because he liked doing hamster impressions. Either way, I soldiered on for ten kilometres attacking verdant hills with the vigour of a sedated kestrel. It felt like climbing the Alps in clown shoes, my body protesting at every turn of the pedals.

At the brow of what has to be said was barely a hill, I entered a hamlet and slid off Iggy. He collapsed to the floor with a clatter. A bungee cord pinged like a sad party popper. And my tent, and half a baguette, rolled from the blue IKEA bag across an empty church car park. This was beyond a bonk, *total blam blam*, as isolated as I'd ever been. I think I was actually done.

Then, heaven turned on its lights, the sun breaking through the clouds and warming my face. But all that did was make me squint. I retreated to the shade of the church door and reached for a cure, dropping a tiny chocolate square into my mouth and hoping it wouldn't make a reappearance. I moved on slowly, contending not only with zero fuel but a kneecap that felt as if someone had spent the night going at it with a cheese grater.

The roads remained unsympathetic, veering north into semi-mountainous territory where fast-moving water leapt into pools and craggy outcrops fell away far below, the chorus of nature intertwining with my sorrowful moans. I hadn't quite the energy to rouse a rendition of 'Life on Mars?' so tried to fill my spirits with a game of English cheeriness versus French hostility, in which I would say, *'Bonjour'*, and see if passing cyclists, ramblers and sexual misfits in bushes would reply. This game, which I rather originally labelled 'Yes Bonjour, No Bonjour', while not having the entertainment value to arouse TV executives, did provide me with a source of distraction as my poisoned body nibbled away at the kilometres.

By late afternoon I reached the riverside town of Seyssel, where the ViaRhôna came to its *fin*. Not even a provisional route. You're on your own. Use your maps. Navigate. No more leisurely ambling for you, flimsy Englishman. Oh, and you've not mentioned Bowie once today. Yeah, sorry, David. Just been one of those days. I was really ill earlier, nearly died by a church and then got side tracked by the 'Yes Bonjour, No Bonjour' thing.

Seyssel for its part was semi-charming, its two halves dissected by a grand white bridge with intricately detailed railings which the Rhône sloshed gamely under. Boules were tossed with gay abandon, people thinking that because of their 35-hour week and 16 weeks' annual leave they should really kick back and save themselves for tomorrow's graft. I found myself with a similar mindset and slunk into a campsite. I plunged under the shower, treating myself to a lengthy scrub with some shower gel whose bull motif attempted to remind me of my lost manliness, but left me waltzing around the campsite wafting the scent of lavender. I put up my tent with some manly grunts to try to reassert my masculinity while the builders in the cabin next to me noisily watched cable TV with fags in their mouths. I shuffled under a remorseless sky to my one-man canvas coffin, clambered in, thumbing pitifully at the underperforming Star Map and, at my lowest ebb, I mimicked an injured donkey with a long, drawn-out whinny.

11. GOLDEN (TAX FREE) YEARS

It hadn't all been plain sailing so far. There hadn't been a lot of Bowie, and after 16 days, 550 miles and a week in France, 'Life on Mars?' remained as mysterious as ever. But that had the potential to change because Iggy and I were skimming towards Switzerland in the haze of an early autumn morning. Although having a reputation for being a tad humdrum, Switzerland also had a bit of Bowie about it, and the third country on the Star Map was only a crisp 40 kilometre cycle along lorry-rattled hard shoulders.

With my stomach no longer firing wet projectiles and my knee having quietened down, another body part thought it time to pipe up about its overuse. You know where you're at with tired legs, the familiar tightening of muscles and pooling of lactic acid that says you should probably pull over for a cream bun and a cup of tea. But a grumpy, overused arse was entirely new. As I landed my derriere back onto the saddle a shooting pain danced across my inner buttock. A prickling discomfort, like the scratch of a fingernail tip, or sitting on a drawing pin. The kind of pain you get by wrapping your thighs in man o' war jellyfish tentacles and the uncertainty that follows when a bloke called Martin appears, saying it will help relieve the pain if he wees on them. I recalled the moment vividly now. It was one of those epiphanies you have when you nostalgically muse how you'd write *another* letter to your younger self. Well, I'd have written that letter around four weeks ago when a colleague suggested getting some chamois cream and I'd dismissed it with a snort of 'I know better'.

I didn't know better.

That would have saved me a week of shifting uncomfortably from bum cheek to bum cheek trying not to squash the polyp that had developed like a tender raisin in the dark void of my glutes. This resulted in my having to stand for long intermittent periods, and upon reaching the Swiss border, gave customs the impression I was a nervy meerkat on the lookout for hawks with large talons.

In 1976, Bowie also arrived in Switzerland not in the finest of fettle. His baggage was paranoia, cocaine addiction, holdalls of cash seeking a tax-free home and a marriage on its last legs. It had only been three years since 'Life on Mars?' was released, but in a whirlwind of shape shifting he'd gone from lovelorn balladeer to Ziggy Stardust, lightning-faced Aladdin Sane, dystopian Diamond Dog, a funky Young American and an emaciated Thin White Duke.

At the height of the latter persona, Bowie's daily diet was thought to consist of cocaine, milk, red peppers and four packs of Gitanes – that's an unbalanced smoothie by anyone's standards. It left him with cheekbones you could grate carrots on and a ghostly complexion.

'I haven't a clue where I'm gonna be in a year,' he said to Cameron Crowe in 1976. 'A raving nut, a flower child or a dictator, some kind of reverend – I don't know. That's what keeps me from getting bored.' He probably never thought he'd end up in Switzerland driving a Volvo. Although, according to car nuts, the 262C he owned, was, of course, one of the cooler models. Like Keith Richards, Freddie Mercury and Charlie Chaplin, Bowie hadn't come for the fondue and mountain views; he'd settled there to stack wodges of cash between chocolatey triangles of Toblerone, which is to say, take liberal advantage of the country's banking system.

My paranoia was less of a concern, although I did seem to be getting frantically waved at by a man outside a hotel. The bloke mouthing greetings in a West Country accent was my best mate from school, Lee. We'd agreed to meet outside the Cornavin Hotel in Geneva, where Hergé had written the adventures of ginger journalist snooper Tintin. A few days of company was most welcome and fervent chatter followed; me rabbiting on about my knee and Lee ranting about how the transit system had screwed him for eighteen Swiss francs to take his bike one stop from Geneva Airport. I consoled him with a slightly squashed croissant and pointed at the Tintin model in the hotel window. This jogged Lee's memory. He had a character transformation of his own to unveil. He plonked a natty red wig on his head that looked like the trimmings from an Orangutan hair salon.

'Guess who I am.'

'A big red squirrel?'

'No, come on.'

'CU Jimmy?'

'No, I'm Bowie!'

'Oh, right.'

'I bought it in the local fancy dress shop. Asked for a Bowie wig.'

'And he sold you a Native American headdress?'

'Well, actually, it said punk wig on the front and he pulled out a pen and wrote Bowie above it.'

'Quite clever, really.'

'It is, isn't it?'

We tried on the headdress for size and headed out to explore Bowie's tax haven. Geneva, decked out in a royal blue sky, was modern, clean and oozing with conservative wealth. People looked supremely healthy and dressed with an air of European sophistication, any rough edges or regretful tattoos hidden under smartly cut suits, knee-length dresses and V-neck sweaters. We headed for

Lake Geneva, dancing under tangles of tram wire as a confluence of expensive-looking traffic manoeuvred around the city's cycle lanes.

It was a millionaires' playground. If you're a millionaire, that is. Four-wheeled penis extensions imported from Italy and Germany lay carelessly strewn across bike paths, liable to swing a door open and deliver a metal slap to the larynx at any given moment. But any cyclist worth his bananas will tell you the best things in life are free and the vista was just that. The sweeping lakeside highway housed grand houses with gardens that bounded down to the lake's edge, while to the north, cornfields painted golden brushstrokes all the way to the Jura mountains. We burrowed between both, tailing each other through fairytale villages and apple orchards, catching up with shouts over shoulders and chipper observations.

It was great to have company again. Lee, like me, was also bored of his job. But he had a wife and three kids, so instead of a full-blown mid-life meltdown, he'd invited himself out for a week-end of bike-based rebellion. He too was at the 'Life on Mars?' school disco wearing jeans way too wide for his legs and had been dunked in at the Bowie deep end with eighties cuts like 'Let's Dance' and the dodgy-shirted Mick Jagger dance-off 'Dancing in the Street'.

The day breezed on with some mild grazing and hastily emptying of wallets. Switzerland isn't for the thrifty man. A miniscule baguette and cold beer blowing budgets like a clown in charge of the circus' petty cash. In penance, we cleansed our palate, if not our conscience, by claiming back a few apples from an orchard, the sweet flesh boosting our energy as we drifted along the lake's edge. As the day drew to its close, rays of golden light burst through mountain passages and a long, drawn-out descent let us freewheel at eyeball-watering speed into Lausanne, where Bowie's son, Duncan, had attended the old Commonwealth-American School.

Checking into the city's giant cinder block youth hostel and parting with 67 Swiss francs to sleep in a building with all the charm of a decommissioned nuclear bunker, Lee was keen to see how I was getting on: 'Enjoying it, then? Figured it out yet?'

'Yeah, and yeah,' I lied, twice.

'So, you've found the secret to "Life on Mars?"?'

'Not quite.'

It was true. I'd not had a sniff of anything except my decaying clothing. But tomorrow might be different. We'd wake refreshed, and with Bowie having lived here on and off for twenty years, we'd pedal through his golden (tax-free) years.

It wasn't screaming delusions of cocaine paranoia that woke us the next morning but a swarm of posh kids from the home counties. At just after 7am, it was 'Ra' this, 'Trust fund' that, and 'Yes, I really am a toffee-nosed little prick, aren't I?' Two cantankerous comprehensive-school educated old men slunk into the caféteria as the poshos buzzed around croissants and coffee. Luckily, included in the wallet-splitting fee was a bottomless breakfast. Whether there was, or wasn't, life on Mars, this certainly put life into two Somerset skinflints. In an act of gluttony that would have had Bowie's cheekbones screaming, we knocked back pastries, cold meats, yoghurt, chocolate cereal, biscuits, fruit, tea, coffee and juices, while still in the line. Then we made ourselves brunch, elevenses, eleven-fifteenses, a little after oneses, several packed lunches and a couple of quarter-past threeses. Switzerland was cracking value after all.

Bowie probably hadn't got over his mid-seventies crisis in budget accommodation surrounded by toffs, so we departed to places where he might have. Heading east, the lake road darted through areas of wealth and alliteration such as Prilly, Pully and the appropriately named Dully. The Swiss were rather adept at adding a 'y' to any form of life round here. That man driving the Audi like an arsehole was wealth-y, the lithe, tanned women performing star jumps by the shore were health-y, the chap horsing an ice-cream in the green chinos was a fatt-y. Silly town names like Vevey and Ouchy continued the 'y' theme as we headed for Blonay, where Bowa-y once lived.

(It's Bow-ee, by the way-ee.)

Opposite, Lake Geneva sloshed and sluiced back to France while rows of grapevines laddered their way up and down the slopes. We were looking for his marital home, which, with Lee being a long-married man, seemed as good a way as any to introduce him to the farce. He gamely accepted the ludicrous nature of it all, even when I suggested we split our thighs in two climbing mountainous hills to see somewhere someone hadn't lived for 40 years.

It was like searching for a Bowie-shaped needle in a Swiss mountain stack. The burnished wood of cuckoo-clock houses lay piled on top of one another like a game of drunken Jenga. We sweated higher, past village fetes and toy railway lines, until the thinning air clasped at the walls of our lungs and the road disappeared into plumes of marshmallow cloud.

In preparation, I'd downloaded a grainy picture of a Swiss-style chalet, said to be DB's. The problem was it looked exactly the same as every other Swiss-style chalet. The name of the house, Clos de Mésanges, was distinctive but difficult to pronounce. I asked a man with a dog where the Clos de Mésanges was. The dog was useless, but the man proved more helpful. He pointed to 'Le mechanic'. I tried to work it out. 'Le Mechanic?' I mused, spotting a rail line. 'The train!' 'No, the crane,' scoffed Lee.

Bowie had enjoyed his time here for a particular reason. 'In Switzerland, they leave me alone,' he said to local journalists. That's because no one can find your house, Dave, you big throbbing genius. We continued pursuing more of the prettiest dead ends I'd ever seen, every turn of the wheels met with a sandy chalet trimmed with sprightly crocuses and harebells. As I floundered with a moustachioed man who'd either spotted a rare bird or was insisting it was back up the mountain, Lee came riding to the rescue: 'There, there it is!' And there it was, Clos de Mésanges: a curly number 13 on the wall and a mosaic driveway under a swatch of green pine.

In her book *Backstage Passes*, Bowie's first wife, Angie, described it as 'a commodious cuckoo-clock of a house, *très* Swiss'. And as capitalist hoarding life plans go, she had it nailed, perhaps adding with an evil cackle, 'I got what we wanted, and better: legal residency in Blonay … and an almost ludicrously low tax rate of about 10 per cent.' Bowie, it seemed, wasn't looking through the same cash-tinted glasses. 'He walked through that gorgeous house and couldn't stand it,' tutted Angie. 'He tried to pretend he liked it, but you could see the horror in his face. It wasn't his scene at all.'

But Bowie adapted. He was a nifty skier and had fellow musicians nearby. Even the counter-culturalists were bowing to convention and settling. Staring up at his magnificent home, I mean, what wasn't to like? It *was* a gorgeous cuckoo clock of a house; it even had a satellite dish. I flashed back to my own. A flat so small, we'd christened it Eurocamp. Lucy there working, while I was fanboying around Europe with a ginger wig on my head, playing air guitar outside a house someone lived in almost 40 years ago. Depending on how you view mid-life, and modified punk wigs, it was either cool or not cool. Circle as appropriate.

'Right, can we eat now?' said Lee, making a question seem like an angry demand. This meant a bombing descent towards Montreux, washing away the introspection as we burrowed through chicanes of cuckoo houses like famished woodworms, the mountain air whooshing around our ears with a booming roar. In the ten minutes it took to get down, as opposed to the two hours climbing, I wound Bowie's Swiss sojourn forward four years. It was now 1980, he'd divorced Angie and recorded his 1979 album *Lodger* at Montreux's Mountain Studios. The supposed third album in his Berlin Trilogy, it was recorded here and in New York, not Berlin.

Bowie had begun working with Brian Eno, the former Roxy Music musician and knob-twiddling avant-garde experimentalist. Bowie told the BBC that Eno was something of a musical 'soulmate' and, better for DB's creative exploration, an 'empathetic git'.

Together, they began pushing boundaries and their backing band's buttons. Even on the conservative shores of Lake Geneva, Bowie was making experimental waves, asking his musicians to play wrong-handed to encourage mistakes and see what creative doors it might open. Guitarist Adrian Belew was told, 'Adrian, we're not going to let you hear these songs. We want you to go into the studio and play accidentally – whatever occurs to you.' One of the working titles for the album was, accordingly, Planned Accidents.

Lyrically, Bowie used William Burroughs's cut-up technique, where he'd take existing sentences, cut them into pieces, and then rearrange the fragments to create new, unexpected combinations that would become a new musical language. Often overlooked among its illustrious brothers Low and Heroes, it should probably not be part of the Berlin Trilogy, but, fittingly for me, it could be described as a travelogue of sorts. Bowie conceded as much; he didn't want it to be a 'travel along with Bowie' but he was mighty keen to blab about his holiday stories. The semi-fictionalised Kenyan music backing of 'African Night Flight' was a loose tale of old drunken German pilots who frequented Mombassa bars running contraband missions. 'Yassassin' – meaning 'long live' in Turkish – named after graffiti he'd spied in his Berlin neighbourhood, is a reggae-tinged stand of solidarity with eastern European immigrants. 'Red Sails' was a Chinese propaganda song set to the motorik-style drumming of krautrock bands like Neu! and Can, while 'Move On' was a simple motif of nomadic yearning to escape and make new discoveries. Like me after a day in the saddle, it was a bit of a hot mess, albeit one stuffed with creative and cultural leaps, where failures made successes, and where we could whirl through DB's observations on travel and culture.

Eno and Bowie didn't stop there. The album's disparate nature also tackled the nuclear arms race and domestic violence, while 'Boys Keep Swinging' was, bizarrely, Bowie's answer to the Village People's 'YMCA'. At least Lee and I had the wig if we wanted to do a tribute show.

So far Switzerland was a gold mine for Bowie tales. We ate our pilfered breakfast-buffet morsels from a wooden sun lounger facing Lake Geneva, revelling in the niceties of middle-age as dappled light danced across the promenade. As the sunlit lake punched out a glittering Morse code, I felt that, even if I wasn't getting closer to the song's meaning, I was getting closer to the themes of Bowie's work.

We pedalled on past colourful iron saxophones and microphones statues, not the result of a spilled cargo of musical instruments, but a celebration of the Montreux Jazz Festival – a natural calling for Bowie who eventually played here in 2002. And it was his friendship with festival director Claude Nobs that led to a collaboration with the man sculpted into the giant bronze statue we were now standing in front of.

Farrokh Bulsara of Zanzibar, like David Jones of Brixton, had changed his name to something more intergalactic. Freddie Mercury, as he's more commonly known, was, of course, the enigmatic Queen frontman. He'd amassed his own army of devotees who were paying tribute with flowers, photos, candles, handwritten notes and anything else they didn't want in their handbags. Our Native American wig-wearing tribute was to get his famous clenched-fist power pose badly wrong while leaving a group of Chinese tourists wondering if he collaborated with the Rosebud Sioux Tribe of the Rosebud Indian Reservation, South Dakota.

We left Freddie in peace because just a short ride away was the Montreux Casino – the former home of Mountain Studios, owned by his band, Queen. It had been a playground for many other big, slobbering riffs, too. Deep Purple's 'Smoke on the Water' was born here in 1971 after a daft fan set off a flare, burning the casino to the ground and causing a timely plume to drift across the lake. Rebuilt in 1976, Bowie recorded not only *Lodger* here but a slew of late eighties and early nineties lesser-celebrated albums including *Never Let Me Down*, *Black Tie White Noise*, *The Buddha of Suburbia* and *1.Outside*. Now, the studio's last remnants were hidden inside under the guise of the Queen Studio Experience. We clambered the steps with a clickity-clack of cleats, only to be confronted by a picket line of mean-faced doormen.

One stepped forward, first name 'Stephan', middle name 'The Bureaucratic', last name 'Wanker'.

He was on us immediately with a barrage of hostile questions.

'Where are you going, sir?'

'Why are you walking that way, sir?'

'You can't tell me to fuck off, sir.'

To be fair to the wasp-faced jobsworths, we clearly didn't fit the target demographic. Surrounding us were skin-shedding fogies with a combined age of 14 billion. They creaked around slot machines as flashing lights winked seductively, encouraging them to hand over their pensions and the remaining hours of their lives. What they needed was one of Mercury's rousing BE-DE-DOH-DAYs, and it lay up a set of glitzy stairs. With a hop, skip and Bowie jump, we shook off the redcoats and entered the studio. Inside lay a deluge of Queen memorabilia: drum kits, records, handwritten lyrics, electric guitars and glittering costumes. And it was in this studio that Claude Nobs helped the planets align so two musical giants could record the call and response classic 'Under Pressure'.

On the wall was a note from Queen drummer Roger Taylor which said, 'It's one of the best things Queen have ever done and it happened so casually when David visited us at our studios in Montreux.' A 24-hour bender fuelled by Lavaux wine and cocaine gave birth to the timeless riff by Queen bassist John Deacon. Or was it? The conflicting mix of stimulants and depressants led to confusion. Deacon credited it to Bowie, Bowie credited it to

Deacon. Deacon had gone to lunch and forgotten it, until Roger Taylor remembered it. Then, recently, Brian May, speaking to the Mirror Online, said Bowie had come back from dinner and tweaked it. Either way, it's a behemoth in the rock-pop pantheon.

'It was very hard,' Brian May said in 2008. 'Because you already had four precocious boys and David, who was precocious enough for all of us. Passions ran very high. I found it very hard because I got so little of my own way. But David had a real vision and he took over the song lyrically.' The song was going to be called 'People on Streets', but Bowie decided it should be 'Under Pressure'. During the session the famous frontmen recorded their vocals separately. At least that's what Freddie thought. When he heard Bowie's vocal, Mercury was astonished at how perfectly it chased this own. Mercury's flamboyant scatting DEE-BO-BAYs building to a soaring crescendo about giving love one more chance, leading to a pleading refrain that echoes across the lake's glittering expanse until Bowie casually stubs out his cigarette, slips in through a slide door, bypasses the dead-eyed slot machine addicts and steals the whole goddamn show with a euphoric finale.

The reason it worked so seamlessly? Well, cheeky Dave was listening in. Eventually, the sound engineer let Mercury know, to which he replied, 'The Bastard.'

We stepped into the frizzy haze of afternoon sun, hyperventilating on stardust and duelling vocals. A celebration was in order, an ice cream seeming a fun way to pay over the odds for some frozen dairy and sugar. We tried to use some Bowie charm on the girl with a luminous smile handing out waffle cones. Lee grinned, I made a joke – and we still paid 30 euros for a couple of scoops. Feeling confused that we felt happy to have been robbed, we spirited along the promenade as jazz spilled from cafés and quirky hotels whisked past in blurs of pastel paint. The sun began its journey home, throwing rays across the lake's privileged settlements as gilded families enjoyed its blessing. Stuffed on the Starman, today had been good value – ice cream aside – and as the sky dissolved to pink then purple, we ceded a little more by sneaking back into the hostel and stealing a free shower.

With Bowie having lived here on and off for twenty years it was worth sticking around for a couple of days before heading back to France. Fortunately, another old school friend, Chris, who worked here, had agreed to put us up when he returned from holiday. He'd left specific instructions on how to break into his apartment block's garage, which amounted to little more than waiting for a car to pull up and running in after it. As we crouched behind a dumpster, a shiny phallic booster was our cue for what the driver probably thought an unlikely carjacking by two cyclists with really expensive ice cream smeared around their mouths. Leaving our wheels to rest, we killed time and money in Lausanne. The downtown, which was uphill, was a pleasing arrangement of Italian, French and German architecture arranged higgledy-piggledy on top of each other. There were 'people on streets', or more accurately people whispering 'cocaine, cocaine' on streets, which would have added an authentic 24-hour whirlwind to proceedings.

Chris was due shortly with his pregnant other half, Laurie, so we turned our attention to the local pubs. The likeliest candidate was Rockies Rock bar, where inside a gloomy basement lay a set of attractive Swiss scenesters. The refreshing taste of beer that excited our palettes meant we quickly turned our tight-fistedness into open-walletedness. Several drinks later, Lee turned to me, his face full of drunken enlightenment.

'I think I know what "Life on Mars?" is about.'

'You do?'

'Yeah, it's about a girl who's pissed off with life.'

'You think?'

'Yeah, like you.'

'I'm not pissed off with life.'

'Yeah, but you're searching for something, aren't you?'

'Am I?'

'Well, either that or you're having a mental breakdown.'

My first 'night out' hadn't reached the levels of Bowie and Mercury's Mountain Studio ding- dong, nor produced any musical hits except a mild existential drumming against my temple. Laid out on a camp bed in a haze of self-loathing, I mulled over the mad decision to take the trip. The girl in Bowie's song had expressed 'being pissed off in life' in her teens; I'd waited until I was 36, a time when traditionally you might settle down. Oh God, was all this nosing around searching for something the message of the song, that there is no resolution, that the *journey* was the point?

Such booze-tinged woe was marginally soothed by the splendid view of Mont Blanc from Chris' balcony. Something I promptly devalued by airing my sleeping bag, cycle shorts and T-shirts all over it. Today was another rest day and a chance to replenish the body with nutrients (and figure out if I was having a mental break-down). The wheels would remain still; we'd shake out the cobwebs with a walk around Lausanne.

As the sun hustled the morning shadows away, Laurie led the way and was particularly knowledgeable about Swiss life. We strolled past well-heeled street cleaners dressed in tidy uniforms scrubbing water fountains. She told us the minimum wage had recently been voted against to be the highest in the world. Chris chipping in that Swiss citizens still earn on average £31 an hour. It was no wonder people were desperate to work as casino sheep herders. Conversation leapt from pedantry to bureaucracy, where Chris, as an unmarried man, was having to fill out forms to adopt his unborn baby. Laurie began to outline the hardy process they were going through.

'Because we are not married we have to both pay and request our birth certificates from the UK. Pay to visit the British embassy in Bern to swear and get a document each. Send all these documents to a Swiss office and get an appointment to see someone there. Then, we have to sign some legal contracts should Chris and I split up. After that, I had to confirm Chris was the father. We paid more money for another document needed by the hospital and then, even more money and forms for the baby's birth certificate.'

After Laurie took a moment to kick a seagull and drink a bottle of whiskey, we continued walking in the pleasant afternoon sun. Laurie, having caught her breath, said, 'That's why there's so many shotgun weddings at the town hall. If we got married, we'd only need one document for the hospital – a marriage certificate.' She glared at Chris. Sensing his unease and that Bowie wasn't the kind of guy you associate with admin, I suggested we get back to chasing stardust.

In 1982 the Clos de Mésanges was sold, and, a wife down, Bowie upgraded to the recklessly large fourteen-room Château de Signal set high above the Sauvabelin Forest. With Lee departing this evening, I suggested one last adventure.

'Right, tell me the address, I'll put it in the Sat Nav,' said Chris as we piled into his car.

The Star Map was being rather vague, offering three possibilities. Chris rolled his eyes. Good, he was up for it. A short drive later, Lee and I were faffing around on foot in the salubrious surrounds. Chris, meanwhile, was googling it himself, coming up with number 22 Route du Signal. Numbers 18 and 20 were clearly signed, but 22 was unmarked except for a hulk of tangled foliage that rendered the property unviewable. A cocked head here led to a shrub there; standing on tippy toes, it was a brambled no-go. A tower of ravenous giraffes would've struggled to dismantle these leaves. We spied an electricity pillbox, Lee cupped his hands, I clambered up and yes, I could just make out bricks, mortar and a spire. It didn't stop there; I yelled out all the things I could see: gravel, grass, a gargoyle, a birdbath. Chris, tired of me calling out building features, retreated to the car. There was only one thing for it. We'd ring the doorbell, perhaps chat to the owners, inspect the grounds, see if Bowie had left any clues about 'Life on Mars?'.

I pushed the doorbell.

'ERRRRRRRR …' said the doorbell, followed by the crackle of static.

''Ello,' said a terse voice.

'ERRRRRRRR …' I said, performing a canny impression of the buzzer.

They weren't meant to answer this quickly. What was I supposed to say? Lee looked at me. I racked my brain for signs of intelligent life, and then it slipped out.

'*Ou est le* Bowie?'

Well, it shouldn't have been that.

In a final act of wretched schoolboy stupidity I'd asked, 'Where is the Bowie?'

Lee took this as his cue to run away giggling. I swiftly followed. Chris, having already sensed we were morons, had started the car. We hopped in and had barely reached the first junction when a police car tore around the corner in a wail of siren and blue light. The Neighbourhood Watch were on it out here.

The search was over, for now. We dropped Lee at the airport and Chris and Laurie retired in preparation for their adult jobs. My holiday from my Bowie holiday was drawing to a close. Back at Chris' apartment, the extravagance of spreading my map on a floor would be one of the last luxuries afforded to me. I scanned the contours of the Star Map as it roamed northwards in a canvas of tightly formed whirls and green and white splodges blocking my re-entry to France – the Jura Mountains. I casually plotted a lazy line straight through the middle, circling Frasne as tomorrow's end point, mostly because it sounded like a rubbish anagram of France.

12. MARRIAGES & CHEATING

It was time to reacquaint myself with an old friend, Iggy. He wasn't talking to me as we set off for one last stop before we left Bowie's Swiss years behind. Lausanne's centre was quiet as we bumped along its cobbles towards the Place de la Palud. This was the medieval town hall, the place of the shotgun wedding and, more resonating for this story, the scene of David Bowie's second marriage.

After the 1990 concert where he mentioned the romantic theme of 'Life on Mars?' – 'This is a love song' – I thought I might be onto something. Stepping inside I was greeted by a lady in a frilly blouse, glasses appointed perfectly on her nose. I asked if she had any information about David Bowie, the town's former resident. After confirming that he'd lived in the Sauvabelin Forest and that the Neighbourhood Watch was indeed shit hot, she continued more truthfully.

'Yes, there was a big article about him in the paper when he died.'

'And do you like him?' I asked.

'Yes, very much. He was a big personality.'

'Do you have a favourite song?'

Say 'Life on Mars?'. Say 'Life on Mars?'. Say 'Life on Mars?'.

'No.'

She just loved them all.

Even as Bowie's first marriage crumbled on the banks of Lake Geneva, his next nuptials would be recorded in this very building – the same place where all the anti-adoptive parents had rushed to bring their would-be spouses so they wouldn't have to wipe out rainforests filling out reams of Swiss paperwork. Bowie didn't have any bureaucratic worries; he married the Somalian supermodel Iman Mohamed Abdulmajid here in 1992.

I had a more taxing conundrum: short of getting a Swiss girl pregnant and telling the pitchfork-wielding parents I was going to stick around for nine months, I wasn't sure how I was going to get official access to the wedding room. I didn't really have the time or looks, so thought it wise to borrow the voice of a royal butler, explaining I was a BBC travel correspondent and it would be most wonderful if I could see the marriage certificate, ma'am. Somehow it worked. She pointed me in the direction of a switchback stone staircase.

With freedom to explore I peered goggle-eyed through tall windows, snooped around weighty oak doors and waltzed along prissy corridors. If I'd been able to locate the 'APPROVED' stamp, I could have sped up Chris' adoption process, too. Before long, a short balding man dressed far too snappily for a day's hole-punching stopped me in my tracks. He said something in French.

'*Ou est le* Bowie?' I offered, again.

I was frog-marched back to reception where my frilly bloused heroine came to the rescue. She explained to my administrative nemesis, with some high-level chiding, that I was looking for details of David Bowie's marriage and he should escort me to them. With a scornful come hither of his hand, the little zealot marched me back upstairs. We'd barely walked twenty metres before he handed me huffily to another man. Luckily, this man was a lot taller, and more helpful. He reached into a gilded wooden box and pulled out the kind of large medieval key they use to lock people away in damp dungeons for many, many decades. With a satisfying click of the lock, he waved me in. Inside lay a simple mahogany chamber, brushed with lime velvet curtains and a diamond chandelier that rained crystals. Across its jacquard carpet stood a ceremonial table and two hand carved chairs. The place where Bowie, perhaps for the only time, bowed to convention. I took the weight off, sat in one chair, then the other, and, curious to see how Bowie's big day had panned out, found an online account of a Swiss civil servant who was present at the ceremony.

> The Swiss Embassy in London addresses to me a file that shows that a certain David Jones did the formalities to get married in Lausanne. Beside his name, he is inscribed 'Bowie' and under profession 'singer'. Rather fond of classical music, I had never heard of Ziggy Stardust. The week before the wedding, I attended a concert at Wembley Stadium in front of my TV in honour of Freddie Mercury, to which David Bowie participated. I was overwhelmed by his performance and his clothes. On the wedding day, the groom arrives alone in the Place de la Louve dressed as a young dynamic executive. As for his fiancée, the Somali dummy Iman Mohamed Abdulmajid, she goes straight down the street accompanied by two friends. When the fiancés entered the room, I was in a daze. The cherry on the cake, the wife, at the end of the ceremony, jumped on my neck and kissed me. She had stars in her eyes. As for me, I also have when I recall the scene.

Despite calling Iman a dummy, a stunner and accusing her of giving him a love bite, I think it is a lovely memoir. A moment later the key holder returned; was he the same starry-eyed witness? I was ready with my French crib sheet, just in case.

'*Aimez vous* David Bowie?' I enquired, waiting for a long gushing response that would prove Swiss bureaucrats are in no way boring and their country has been misrepresented by nonsensical sweeping stereotypes. Finally he would be free from the infuriating restrictions of meddling red tape to declare his love for Bowie.

'*Non.*'

As I stepped outside the town hall, it wasn't friends and family throwing confetti waiting for me, but Iggy and my conscience.

'Haven't settled down, have you? Lee, Chris, even Bowie did it.'

'Er, no. Got some camping gas, though.'

'Good one, dickhead.'

With that rebuke ringing in my ears, from cash to Queen, marriage and more, I filed the Bowie admin years under my belt and headed for the Jura Mountains.

I set off at pace, the thin heat bringing a steely determination to my face. I bullied my way up Lausanne's slopes and, feeling chuffed, wiggled my bottom – much better now thanks to some chamois cream – in the hill's general direction. Grinding a dizzying path upwards through the levels of the city, the backwash of bluebell-trimmed hills quickly spilled into sweeping pastures, while lonely mountain farms sat below darkening skies. I was back to isolation again. The gradual inclines that had led me from the city transcended into short, sharp quad-battering hills. After a particularly violent struggle to the crest of one of them, the effort was tempered by the sight of a giant thoroughbred horse sporting platinum-blonde pigtails. Equines are notoriously stubborn gits, so I bet that hairstyle would've taken some convincing.

The smug smile was still plastered across my chops when I finally encountered some downhill. I hunched over, making myself as aerodynamic as possible, and propelled myself at the village below. With one eye on a roundabout bursting with blushing autumn leaves, the other was distracted, my gaze drawn to a yellow and black blob spiralling from the heavens. It was hypnotic; what was it doing, where was it going? Its intended target was locked on. Its intended target was me.

First, it dive-bombed for my helmet, then swerved at the last moment and shot down the neck of my T-shirt. 'Ugh,' the strange noise emanating from my mouth as I desperately clawed at my helmet straps. Then the yellow and black bomber began frantically jabbing his arse about trying to pierce my chest. As I abandoned bike and peeled away my T-shirt like a hopeful holiday lover from Yeovil in a two-star Thomas Cook hotel (self-catering), the stripy bastard finally sat down and stuck it where the sun doesn't shine. The 'Ugh' became an 'Argh' and the wasp calmly flew off to the pretty ponytailed horse to let him know revenge had been a dish served with a sting in its tail.

Meanwhile, my T-shirt-swinging lunacy had attracted the attention of some parents on the school run. By way of explanation, I pointed to my reddening naked chest and shook a fist at the sky. The children's eyes were shielded and quietly ushered away from the scary man who was possibly the local paedophile.

A long, laborious afternoon followed, climbing looping hills silent except for the clunking of gears, the clang of cowbells and the throbbing in my chest. Inching back towards France and a Star Map stop inspired by the *Hunky Dory* album sleeve, the atmosphere began to thicken, emulsifying with low pressure and amorous insects. Every gulp of air was washed down with an aperitif of small black flies. If they avoided my gaping cakehole, they succeeded in splatting against my jacket with increasingly vocal *PHUT!* noises. The border guards, sensing my haste and unaware I'd been in a state of undress near a school, waved me through. I pedalled for the clouds, cheek to jowl with snaking lines of HGVs as it started to rain, big thumping water bombs that bounced off Iggy's panniers and my helmet like bullets.

Can you outrun rain? I tried and failed, getting a mild to middling soaking for my arrogance. Weather doesn't really work like that, after all. The gloom grew ever more as I passed the dreary mountain of Métabief Mont d'Or, a long sliver of cloud plonked on its summit like a blob of toothpaste. In season it would be packed with arguing families and handsome skiers; now it looked rather ugly and best forgotten about altogether. I plunged deeper into a grim vale of decaying ferns and sullen pine trees that threatened to blot out the sun for good. My carefree plotting the night before reached peak 'that was a bit slapdash' at the Drugeon Valley, a particular lesson in places not to hang around and admire the view – its withered trees and bruised trunks home to only dead-eyed blackness. If the meaning to 'Life on Mars?' lay here, I was happy to ignore it. As a car headlight lit the rotting fauna, and possibly trolls, I concluded this wasn't an obvious choice to spend the night wild camping.

Racing the fading light, I came to a crossroads and a small village. It seemed everyone had already been eaten by the trees. Where the hell was I? Why was the weather darker than Satan's underpants? Was I scared? Hell no (yes).

Pedalling hastily away from the gloom, I stole from the valley's clutches and met Frasne's fringes at dusk. The town's appeal from the comfort of Chris' apartment was born from the name's similarity to France. I can now vouch that this isn't the smartest way to determine your resting spot after a gruelling day cycling across mountains, collecting bugs in your eyebrows and travelling through valleys where mass murders have probably taken place. It wasn't the miserable light, it wasn't the patchy weather, it was because Frasne was a seismic dump. The kind of town that deserves to be driven straight through at speed, or crossed off maps altogether with a giant marker pen. Everything was shut, possibly abandoned for good, the only flicker of life coming from a building at the end of the road.

Upon closer inspection it turned out to be an SNCF train station. I propped Iggy below a limp *tricolore* flag and pondered my next move. Do I sleep among those bags of cement? Or in the middle of those rotting horse carcasses? I reviewed life's choices with a bag of Haribo Minions. Coursing with e-numbers and blue food colouring, I felt inspired. I felt like cheating. I'd continue the journey north fighting the elements from a warm train carriage. A quick look at the timetable: Dijon, departing in fifteen minutes. Mustard.

13. THE EARWORMS OF THE BURGUNDY CANAL

I awoke feeling most pleased with myself. Iggy and I had found a campsite under the cover of darkness. Technically, all I'd done was trade one French town for another. Why should I feel guilty? I took a stealthy shower, investigated my wasp sting (which disconcertingly looked like the start of a third nipple) and set up my gas stove for its maiden run. Water – check. Pasta – check. Gas – double check. Lighter – bollocks.

I was possibly the only person in France without one, judging by the discarded fag butts dotting the grass like a smouldering art installation. But French national habits dictate you're never far from fire, and before long a caravan door creaked open and a crumpled old lady emerged, fag in hand, rasping and spluttering like a tractor engine. The kind of catarrh croaks that suggested if I didn't act fast, she might pass away before I could borrow her lighter, which would have been a shame, as I had a lot of tea bags left to use. After my questionable caveman demonstration, she passed the lighter with a phlegmy gargle, reacting to my Bowie mime of 'Nice cup of tea' with a Gallic shrug that said, 'Just bring it back, wanker.'

I got my cup of tea, my two cups of tea, and stood as smug as a beaver who'd built the finest dam in all the land. The campsite bordered a leafy park where the gentle trickle of flowing water proving a deft accompanist to the trill of birdsong. Sixteen days in, I was back in France and heading north. Paris, a sure stop off for any international recording artist, lay over 300 kilometres away. Around halfway there, I'd made a Star Map scribble – an origin story – I hoped would bring some autumn light to the journey. In the meantime, it was back to serendipitous roadside meetings. But instead of realising my worst service station fears, I decided the gentle flow of water would be a more picturesque route for such chance encounters.

The industrial sprawl of Dijon's crumbling concrete, rusting barges and waterside graffiti didn't fill me with confidence in the Canal de Bourgogne. There seemed to be a trend of taking a French first name and following it with an English profanity. By way of example, 'Etienne FUCK' was scrawled above the equally point-less 'Theo BASTARD'. To really rub it in, the landscape of rusting things was now littered with brown ducks. I don't know what time French ducks wake up, but I can tell you with precise accuracy what time they open their feathery bowels and spread Jackson Pollock splodges of shit across the canal path. With Iggy's wheels unpleas-antly lubricated, the emerald water sauntered on ahead. This was a chance to retreat from drinking the fumes of lorries and cheerily engage with nature.

Traffic was light, just a slow lane of butterflies who seemed seduced by my panniers, bouncing off the lightning flashes with dopey regularity. Stalking the edges of the water were gangly cranes eyeing a fishy breakfast. These rangy river dwellers were surpris-ingly useless at flying. As Iggy and I approached, they'd launch off with a hopeless flap of their wings and crash clumsily upstream. When God was handing out flying styles, he must have looked at them and thought, You, my beaky wonder, shall be an expert fish catcher, but I'll even that out by making you fly like you've been snorting Shake n' Vac.

The gentle canal paths offered little taxing of the brain as they unhurriedly meandered northwards. The sun had set its stall out, it was going to be a blisteringly hot day. I relaxed into it, remembered what I was doing and started singing the lyrics to 'Life on Mars?'. Which in hindsight was quite possibly the start of my mental decline.

I mouthed the opening lyrics to the chorus, inhaling a couple of butterflies. Then the cavemen doing their thing, definitely ate a dragonfly there. But worse for my mental health was the earworm – no, ear snake – that had burrowed deep inside and coiled itself around my cochlea. Not just a lyric, but a piano riff. The one after between a minute and 1.05 (depending on which version you're listening to), specifically the bit that goes *diddle-ooo*. As the canal snaked towards the River Yonne my mind thought it would regurgitate it until my larynx was a tattered piece of flapping tendon. Cranes, butterflies and dragonflies were all greeted with a perpetually annoying *diddle-ooo*. I could barely entertain another thought without it being barged out of the way by a *diddle-ooo*. If it hadn't been detrimental to my health, I would have punched myself in the face.

Obviously, Bowie's unfamiliarity with the Burgundy countryside meant I'd have to create my own value, so I veered over a bridge and took a late lunch at the next settlement. There lay a pretty scattering of red-bricked outhouses and rustic cottages, but no one in sight. The canal had shafted me. Peering through windows, it seemed to be shut down o'clock, when France traditionally retreats away from cyclists looking desperately for coffee, wine and Bowie chat. Unfortunately for the café owner whose window I had my face pressed against, he saw my strange nodding (translation: are you open?), drinking mime (for a glass of wine?), thumbs up combination (that'd be great because I haven't spoken to anyone since eight this morning and fear I'm going mad – *diddle-ooo*).

The patron, rightly so, opened the door only a few inches.

'*Bonjour, monsieur,*' he said, incorrectly greeting me as a sane person.

'*Vin est possible?*'

'*Oui,*' he said with weary exasperation, pointing to a table and a sign that said, 'We don't host lunatics, but will feed them extremely drinkable red wine.'

As the waiter returned, hunched over, and placed the Burgundy down, I slipped on the 'Ziggy' wig.

'*Je suis* David Bowie!' I announced with a look reserved for escaped psychopaths.

He moved away very slowly, walked expertly up a flight of stairs backwards, manoeuvred round a flowerpot, opened the café door, retreated inside, locked it and pulled down the blind, all while maintaining eye contact and telling his wife to get the shotgun.

Sensing I'd best move my red wine lips on, I wove through the slipping sun as spider webs glistening like gossamer threads gently attached themselves to my bike, arms and face until I looked like an extra from *Ghostbusters*. By the time I'd reached the heavily hyphenated village of Pouilly-en-Auxois, I was so incurably bored – and dehydrated – I began thumbing Canal de Bourgogne tourist literature. Like Bowie, I could now be a vociferous reader. But my learnings wouldn't stretch to German Expressionism, Burroughs and Kerouac. My expertise would be the Tour de Bourgogne. For example, did you know (or care) that the canal is 242 kilometres long, contains 189 locks and crosses a whopping 28 different administrative districts? Or that there would be a zeppelin-sized cloud of midges past the next hedge which would leave me partially blind?

As I wiped bits of antennae from my eye, daylight was sinking into night. The long, repetitive day had led me to slowly deplete my water supplies without means to replenish them. I'd veered towards a village called Saint-Thibault, coming to a halt outside a pretty church, where it seemed all the taps were attached to sinks in people's houses.

British politeness was hindering me. I'll go without, I thought. Will probably die but don't want to disturb these nice people. Luckily, an old man in a beige Mackintosh spotted my dilemma and suggested the Mairie would offer assistance. For the first time in a while I gave the FITTNB spiel. My watery saviour sighed.

'That song, it had, a certain ingredient.'

I let him continue.

'A magical quality.'

He looked longingly past me and away across the burnished fields.

'Yes, I liked him very much,' he said with a gentle exhalation. He stared over my shoulder as if recalling his youth growing up with Bowie's music.

'Very much,' he repeated wistfully, before shaking my hand and going on his way. As he drove off in a cloud of dust, it dawned on me he'd used the past tense, to think of having *liked* someone very much. The weight of mortality leaned in, making me sad.

Bowie, from the people I had encountered, seemed popular almost to the point of being mythologised. They liked his music, liked his story and liked what he stood for, but weren't in the murky depths of trying to analyse his songs. Instead, he seemed to take on some form of mystique, as if his aura outshone who he was; David Bowie wasn't real, he was an idea, and not a year since his passing it seemed he had already entered modern folklore.

I had to push on.

The Mairie was closed, but the public toilets were stocked with as much questionable drinking water as I could stomach, so I set about looking for a bush to sleep in. The far side of a streaky hedgerow seemed perfect, but as I went to claim my pitch a greasy French youth shuffled out of nowhere, sat himself on a bench, took out a pair of crappy speakers and rolled a joint. In the meantime, I pretended to stare at the mustard fields I'd stared at all day. This could be a long standoff. No, wait. He's preparing to move, he's rummaging around in his rucksack … oh, for fuck's sake, he's pulled out a king-size bag of Tangy Cheese Doritos. As it got darker and darker and his fingers got orangier and orangier, I decided he was so far gone he wouldn't notice me whizzing past, whereupon he may, or may not, have muttered 'Christ on a bike' as orangey crumbs tumbled from his mouth.

It's a fine art picking out a camping spot. From the other side of the canal, it looked a fine plot of land. But there are two sides to every hedge. The side I was now on looked across a slow-moving stream in plain view of a tractor bobbing across a muddy field. As the farmer trundled back and forth, I could see the glow of his cigarette hanging from his lip. The second stand-off in as many hours saw the farmer doing the most labour I had seen a Frenchman undertake the entire time I'd been in the country. For what seemed a decade, the red lights of the tractor pierced the evening murk as it chuntered inexhaustibly across the field. Finally, as night fell so did his appetite for graft, the headlights heading for the road, leaving me to blaze up my stove. I mean, I didn't mean to blow my own trumpet, but this caveman, me, like the one in 'Life on Mars?', was really going some. I was man who'd made fire, man who'd boiled water, man who'd made barely digestible pasta. I wasn't living the dream, I was living the themes of the lyrics – I *was* Life on Mars!

I was also man who'd run out of water. And man who, after all his caveman-style prancing, was really thirsty. On reflection I was a rubbish caveman, one who would have been dead in days.

The darkness became complete, the air grew moist and a chill siphoned off the canal. As I carb-fuelled behind a hedge, a hedgehog snuffled by and cows instigated a sleepy singsong of cowbell percussion. *Diddle-ooo*, I added by way of accompaniment. On my last night as a 36-year-old man, I slid into my tent and told Lucy of my wild camping heroics and Dorito Dave. 'Are you scared?' she asked. With my thighs growing in bulk and my confidence increasing, I replied, 'Nah, I'm not actually!'

But I should have been.

14. MIDDLE AGE & MARS

At the age of 37, Bowie was covering, rather appallingly, The Beach Boys' 'God Only Knows'. God only knows, then, why at the same age I was rather appallingly cycling a lyric from one of his songs. Plonked on the bank of the Burgundy Canal, I was feeling fitter of body, if not of mind. Bowie, though, was at the top of his game, at least commercially. In 1984, he'd reached his middle-of-the-road zenith with *Let's Dance*, the bestselling album of his career. In a megabucks deal, he'd switched record labels from RCA to EMI and was fitter of body himself having taken up boxing – a sure sign of a mid-life crisis.

Ripe for a change of direction after his seventies experimentation, the eighties music scene brought new fashion, sounds – and money. Sporting a slick blond crop, Bowie wanted hits. After a bum deal with manager Tony Defries left him broke, he went for the mainstream money grab, teaming up with Chic's Nile Rodgers, whose maddeningly danceable grooves and smoking bass lines had seen hits like 'Le Freak' and 'Good Times' inhabit everyone's souls and feet. Back across the mountains in Montreux they began to make demos, combining blues rock guitar and electronic synths, cutting gems like the saccharine Asian pop hook of a reworked 'China Girl', the Little Richard-tinged 'Modern Love' and the funk-chunk bass of 'Let's Dance'. Bowie, up until then, had influenced other people, but now seeking mainstream cross-over he was the one in need of influence. Rodgers recalls him saying, 'Nile, darling, I think this song is a hit,' playing 'Let's Dance' on a battered twelve string as a folk number. Nile wasn't sure. A song called 'Let's Dance' would have to make people dance. He asked to do his own arrangement, threw in a minor thirteen chord, as he 'knew Bowie liked jazz', then moved it up an octave, brighter being the key. It had gone from folk to funk. Now it would make people move.

It was time for me to dance, too.

Plop, plop, splash.

My head thumped against the canvas. What was that? It couldn't be, could it?

Bears.

Twisting around in a mummy sleeping bag is difficult at the best of times, impossible when it sounds like a four-legged death machine is emerging from the lagoon next to you. As a low snuffling filled every inch of the brittle air, I fumbled for my head torch and emerged from the tent in blind panic armed with a bike pump. All was still.

Plop, plop, splash.

My naked feet stumbled onto a smattering of glassy prickles. The adrenaline meant I didn't feel them cut into the skin of my feet. I couldn't see anything, the sky the bluey black before dawn, the inky water motionless. My headlight scanned the stream and caught a trail of ripples snaking away from me.

Splash.

They turned. The ripples now heading straight for me. I stood tense, a ball of adrenaline primed to unleash eleven and a half stone of skinny-legged fury. My flickering torchlight stalked the convulsing water. The surface broke and two glassy eyes appeared, their gaze burning through me from the wet black.

Then, it revealed itself fully. On my thirty-seventh birthday I'd been woken by otters. Otters. Whiskery-wankery OTTERS. While they continued to plink and plonk through the water, I crawled back into the tent, my feet coagulating in a mess of blood and prickles.

When I finally emerged at dawn, I opened pre-written birthday cards from my family and Lucy by the chill of the canal's mist-laden surface. As I looked at my bloody feet, sure, I was living, or perhaps slowly bleeding to death, but with the otter travelling circus having moved on to scare wild campers elsewhere, I was alone with nothing but goose-pimpled flesh for company. I missed toilets, I missed showers, I missed birthday candles, I missed my family, and I missed Lucy.

As the sun fought its way through the tangle of cold naked branches and its rays set fire to spider webs, I wrestled Iggy from the clutches of brambles and pedalled forth, the only sound the crunch of leaves and the occasional tangle of twigs diggling between spokes. As a special birthday treat, I was also still missing water, having used all mine cooking the previous evening. After 40 kilometres of puffy-tongued parchedness, I pulled into what can only be described as the ugliest town on the entire canal, Montbard's smoking spires and what looked like defunct nuclear facilities just the place to relax. But first, that thirst. I chained Iggy to a boarded-up shop, next to another boarded-up shop, which looked on to several other boarded-up shops, and relieved the only not boarded-up shop, Netto, of its supply of drinkable yoghurt. Humming of fake strawberry flavouring, I trawled the streets. Nothing moved, its inhabitants presumably killed off by large doses of radiation, or so hideously deformed they dare not venture outside. Like a strange vortex, every road I pedalled down seemed to end at the train station. And it's a sure sign that if all roads lead to escape, then the town isn't going to be bothering UNESCO anytime soon.

But it was my birthday, and before I sought out that origin story, I'd give myself half a day off: reflect, recuperate, get rid of the smell of dead ferrets coming from my sleeping bag – things like that. After locating a campsite, I took a lengthy scrub in the shower, washed my clothes and tossed the sleeping bag across a hedge. And I have to say, I rather enjoyed it. A brief moment of respite, a chance to unwind, to revel in the process of simple tasks. Then it dawned on me: I was pottering. That dangerous middle-age pursuit where you find yourself taking pleasure in putting a wash on, airing clothes, rigorously plumping pillows and shaking out duvets. I mean, I was kind of like Bowie, a new man facing a new period in his life. His middle age meant he'd record Greatest Hits certainties 'Let's Dance' and 'China Girl'; I was off to Fontenay Abbey.

Incredibly, Fontenay *is* a UNESCO-listed attraction and is the oldest preserved Cistercian abbey in the world. It lay in a vale of beech trees, where brooks chuckled and, just under a thousand years ago, monks worked their arses off. Cistercian values demanded a life of solitude, something Bowie might have appreciated, less so the lack of women and drugs. More tenuous links abounded when I learnt of Bishop Ebrard of Norwich (a mere thirteen miles from the Norfolk Broads) had fled persecution in the Norfolk city to help build the church.

Then it dawned on me: I was mooching. That other dangerous middle-age pursuit where you find yourself taking pleasure wandering with your hands behind your back, perusing the information boards at a local historical sight then taking disproportionate joy in a cup of tea and a slice of lemon drizzle cake.

I had to reclaim my inner Bowie. I glanced at my phone and wondered if 10.34am was too early to start a birthday bender. I failed with that, too. Instead I spent the rest of the day moseying, tinkering and bumbling – really excelling at middle age. With panniers cleaned and clothes washed, I set about scrubbing my shoes, where my real birthday surprise awaited me – a slug the size of Equatorial Guinea contentedly sucking the briny sweat from my size tens. Montbard was that kind of town.

My plan to leave at the crack of dawn was botched by a family of young campers who wandered over to ask why I was holding my shoe, looking at an exploded slug. They wanted to know where I was cycling to, as well. I drew them a Bowie-shaped picture.

'Cool,' said the husband, all long hair, Jesus beard and anti-capitalist drawl.

'Yes, *very* cool,' said the waif-like wife with her razor-sharp cheekbones and mousy hair.

Their baby was surprisingly low key on my achievements.

I broached the song's meaning.

'Mysterious,' offered Jesus.

'Mmm, mysterious,' agreed the wife. 'And spiritual,' she quickly added.

'Mmm, really spiritual,' agreed a now beard-stroking Jesus.

The baby, again, disappointingly muted on my heroics.

But they were right. The cluster of abstract images painted in the lyrics were 'mysterious' and Bowie's heroine yearning for distant planets was some form of 'spiritual' journey. Through a healthy list of adjectives, they'd nailed the two halves of the song. The first, something we can all relate to, the confused teen yearning for more, the second, the explosion of abstract images she finds herself lost in, the swamp of mass culture facing us, the ever-changing journey we are all on. Maybe this was the transformative song everyone hears in their teen years, the idealistic, liberal epic that always has a place in our heart. The problem was, I was 37, not a 14-year-old girl.

My spiritual journey continued on France's D roads, the D905 as grey and glum as any other: long, flat expanses of dead farmland, cycling space measured in millimetres and intermittent mountains of abandoned grit. It was as if someone had intended to build a family home but wisely concluded that the miserable surrounds would make their wife start drinking rat poison and their children impale themselves on spikes. But that didn't matter, because as I cruised past a sign for Dannemois, I knew I was only moments from how 'Life on Mars?' came to be.

15. INSPIRED BY FRANKIE

Although the song was conceived on a bandstand in Beckenham, there's a backstory to that backstory – a tale of revenge spawned from a triumvirate of different songs. This is spelt out on the back of the *Hunky Dory* album sleeve, a simple message laced with meaning: 'Inspired by Frankie.' With that intriguing tit-bit, I pedalled away from the D-roads and into a picture-book village that might tease the truth from Bowie's cryptic note. And boy, was Dannemois lovely. Its low-rise cottages were dissected by a stream that wound merrily through dainty gardens before drifting casually under a set of silver iron gates.

Sadly, someone had daubed graffiti all over them. But this wasn't any graffiti; the spidery scrawl of words in marker pen said this was old person graffiti. Kind of respectful, sorry I'm doing this, but I'm following Jeanette's lead. And what Jeanette had begun, François, Amélie and Victor had added to: a stream of messages addressed to someone called Claude. But it was all permissible, because where there's a Claude, there's a Frankie and, looping back around, the backstory to 'Life on Mars?'.

Le Moulin de Dannemois was the former home of Claude François, aka Cloclo, a pint-sized blond bombshell and one of the most successful singers in sixties France. In 1967 the songwriting team Jacques Revaux and Gilles Thibault offered François the chanson ballad 'For Me'. He saw its potential and rewrote the mawkish lyrics, calling it 'Comme d'habitude' ('As Usual'). But the real kicker was the music. A slow-build melody wrought with introspection, longing and hope. Suckers for misery, the French lapped it up.

Meanwhile, a young, floppy-haired Bowie, yet to find his outer space, was perched in London's Denmark Street penning tunes for anyone who would take them. While honing his songcraft he took advantage of a trend where European songs had their lyrics rewritten for English-speaking countries. With Cloclo rubbing his mitts, 'Comme d'habitude' found its way to Bowie, who told the story to a German TV programme: 'I had a publisher in London who sent me a French song, "Comme d'habitude", and he said, "Do you want to try and supply an English lyric to this?" So I wrote a lyric for it called "Even a Fool Learns to Love" or some such drivel. It was really ropey, but I thought I'd make a few bob out of it.'

Recording his version directly over the original, so you could hear both sets of lyrics, he handed it back to the publisher. 'He said, "Yeah, thank you – this is really terrible. I'm giving it to somebody else."' With that, singer-songwriter Paul Anka slipped off his smoking jacket, scribbled down some new lyrics, invited Frank Sinatra to sing them on one of the most famous songs of all time and crushed Bowie's dream of writing a big ballad chanson. 'Next thing I heard … it had been rewritten again by Paul Anka and it came back as "My Way". Sinatra had done it!' Bowie groaned.

Bowie was left to search for his own cosmos: 'I was so pissed … I thought, I'll write me own then. So I wrote "Life on Mars?" Ha-ha-ha …' And with that melodic cackle, our genius took the same chord sequences from 'Comme d'habitude', flipped them on their head, gave them an ascending rock twist and started his own god-awful small affair.

With Cloclo's role in the orchestral epic established and Bowie's 'Inspired by Frankie' revenge reeked, I sat myself in the

Cloclo-themed restaurant and took stock. Now I had three songs to over-analyse. Sinatra's 'My Way', a man making a defiant statement of a life lived authentically and on his own terms with no regrets. And François' 'Comme d'habitude' – a gloomy tale of a once sprightly romantic relationship where intimacy has given way to loneliness. Their themes, clear as day, Bowie's brimming with the mystery and spirituality outlined by the French hippies.

Having dodged the themed restaurant nightmare of the Hard Rock Hotel in Ibiza, it felt right to give Cloclo's a whirl and dig into the song's DNA. Here, permed near-dead people forked nouveau cuisine into their mouths as giant promo posters, gold discs and spangly glitter balls lay haphazardly around the room and a giant screen treated us to Claude's fancy footwork. This boy was big, at least in musical standing; he was an impish five-foot-five even when surrounded by his troupe of female backing dancers. The Clodettes, as they were known, not only added razzmatazz to the blond sensation, but also impressively managed to sound like a genital fungus ointment.

I was about to take the official tour. And I was the youngest here by at least forty years. As the clock struck two, walking sticks were gathered, teeth popped back in and cigarettes extinguished. Except for one, our tour leader's. Below her tortoiseshell-shaped hair, she inhaled the rest of her fag before flicking its butt artfully into a bin and walking over with a smile. Cloclo had been something of a housewives' favourite in the sixties and the ones present today, although aged, and possibly deaf, hung on every word of our guide. Spoken exclusively in French, my understanding would be aided through their *coos* and *wowees*. It was left to a boggle of the mind as to what was being said.

'Claude François narrowly missed out on his high school javelin record – *wowee*.'
'Claude François had a penis the length of a telescope – *coooooo*.'

'Claude François once ate a box of French Fancies in under sixteen seconds – *coOo-eEe*.'

But we got to gold quickly when it was translated that Claude wrote 'Comme d'habitude' by his swimming pool, which he'd built in the same shape as Elvis Presley's, who in turn shares the same birthday, 8 January, as David Bowie. If that was more paranormal than normal, a door slammed. 'Claude?' exclaimed the tour guide with expert comic timing, followed by much Gallic nose snorting.

Pushing through the memorabilia – luxury Louis Vuitton luggage, silk robes and crisp tennis apparel – it was obvious Cloclo was a world apart from Bowie, more like a love child of Cliff Richard and Abba. Clabba! I thought with a chuckle. The tour guide spotted my amusement and waved me over. 'Do you know Claude François?' she asked suspiciously, as if I'd taken a wrong turn at Frankie and Benny's.

'*Oui*, of course,' I said, telling lie number 46.

She eyed my green football shorts and cycling jacket suspiciously. 'But why are you here?'

'Bowie, baby!' I obviously didn't say, instead explaining the entire 'Life on Mars?' backstory.

She told me I was crazy in English; I told her she smelt of cigarettes in French.

'I love that song,' she said, giddy with nostalgia. 'It was the first song at my wedding.'

I didn't need an invitation, bursting into the lyric that inspired the trip. She joined in, completing the Ibiza to the Norfolk Broads couplet in a rasping trill before screeching the immortal question about 'Life on Mars?', thereby getting the sequence of the song completely wrong, angering a dozen hearing aids, and adding the sound of a cat being shot in the face to our spontaneous duet.

Two of the worst singers in the planetary system singing 'Life on Mars?' in Claude François' bedroom. If it wasn't before, Bowie's revenge was now complete.

That called for a celebration, so we visited Claude's wardrobe. The abundance of flamboyant garments proved that men can never have too many of some things, especially if those things are frilly silk shirts and cummerbunds. We finished in the toilet, which, ironically, is what finished off Claude. As his career spiralled ever upwards, he found himself in a rare moment of relaxation in the bath. A light bulb flickered – not the idea for a new chanson, but the one illuminating his blond hair from above. Irked by its stuttering glow, he stood to fix the squiffy connection and with a lightning flash different to Bowie's, the story of Claude François was no more.

The French fogies recoiled in horror as if they'd been told there was a decade-long ban on croutons and massive pensions. I was gripped, pressing for more detail. 'Was it really an accident – or suicide?' I said, raising an eyebrow in the shape of a conspiracy theory. Our tour guide stamped her foam-heeled shoes and threw open her arms with a dramatic flourish: 'Non! Accident.' That killed my theory dead in the water. Bit like Claude.

As French grannies flooded the gift shop eager to thumb euros into Cloclo's cummerbund, I commandeered the tour guide. With 'Life on Mars?' being the centrepiece of her romantic life, I went for the jugular: 'What do you think the song is about?'

She smiled and offered a simple reply: 'Happiness.'

With Frankie's 'My Way' a man doing right by himself, Claude's 'Comme d'habitude' a sad man's descent into self-regard, Bowie's 'Life on Mars?' was the hopeful sunshine in the room.

As I went to buy a seven-inch record of 'Comme d'habitude', the host, quite taken by my story, regaled it to another version of herself, but double the age and nicotine stains – her mother. Impressed by my tale of Dave'ing do, or liking the idea of seeing my Lycra on her boudoir floor, she refused my money. 'A gift,' translated her chain-smoking-again offspring. As I gratefully pushed the origins of the song into my pannier, the tour guide took a final drag on her fag and waved me off with a big winning smile, some 'happiness' to take back to the diabolical D-roads creeping towards Paris.

16. DIRTY LOVE

If Paris is the city of romance, then its satellite towns are the clumsy fumbling of teenage foreplay. The downside of mapping your way around motorways is the long, sweeping minor roads connecting unremarkable settlements. The French seemed to have recognised this and decided that although you can't polish a series of turds, you can plot a bundle of half-arsed cycle paths through them. Although well meaning, they invariably allowed nothing more than to build up a healthy dollop of speed before being met with a badly parked car or a frightened-looking man with a Zimmer frame.

With each kilometre of poisonous exhausts, the number of lanes increased and the standard of driving decreased. Paris was a major key for Bowie, in terms of introducing himself to non-English audiences, recording some of his most celebrated work and, on a personal level, romantically. I tried to imagine what it would have been like to dream up a song that brought 'happiness' to people. Was it, as Bowie mentioned, a love song, or was it a love song to escape and wanting more from life? It had been almost three weeks since I'd seen Lucy and now I was heading for the home of romance without her.

Such musings were routinely interrupted by drains, potholes, reversing cars and people hollering in tracksuit bottoms. Without noticing, I was in the guts of the city. Citroëns and Peugeots snaked across delivery vans, while hipsters on fixies and vintage racers jostled with spluttering buses and rollerblading gendarmes. A girl on a shopper bike, her tweed jacket billowing in the wind, arrowed in front of me, sending a score of pigeons down Rue de Rivoli. Even at its grimiest there was a certain romance to Paris, and Bowie wanted that as part of his folklore.

Always the non-traditionalist in his music career, he gave us a glimpse of the real David Jones when he proposed to Iman by serenading her with Doris Day's 'Paris in April' as their boat sailed under the arches of the Pont Neuf. Even now, Paris is no slouch in the romance department. As I loitered by the Seine, the modern way seemed to be to announce your undying love by attaching a padlock to the same bridge as an unbreakable declaration of affection. This may or not be the reason for the recent upsurge in hardware store owners suddenly buying yachts and walking around with chunky gold teeth. Even the street hawkers had cottoned on, the poor bloke selling selfie sticks yesterday's man compared to the gent who'd invested in the romantic bond of the bright green padlock. But why stop there? Love knows no bounds, especially if you have a marker pen. People had scrawled their deep devotion on the bridge itself, 'Jacques loves Angela,' Pink Floyd-loving Cedric wished Michelle was here, and what of Beatrice? Well, someone had misread the situation and jotted, 'Fuck you Beatrice.' Their level of emotional distress emphasised with the use of capital letters and three exclamation marks!!!

With Beatrice off doing bad things to boys, I wanted to find the ninth arrondissement but couldn't get to grips with the twenty that made up Paris. Someone had told me they fan out from the city centre in the shape of a snail shell, and I seemed to follow this a little too literally, taking a slow circular route past renaissance buildings while the soot-laced air left a black snotty trail that looked like a gastropod had slithered across my moustache.

I was looking for the place where David Bowie played his first ever foreign gig. This took place on New Year's Eve 1965 at Le Golf-Drouot. If you were anyone in France, this was *the* place to play, its mini golf and tea bar had Parisians flooding under its blinking neon sign.

Jacques Brel, Edith Piaf and The Stones had already performed here when Bowie came to town at eighteen. After much wrong turning and missing of junctions, a row of beech trees exploded in autumnal yellow either side of a crossroads. I scanned the building numbers, and to my consternation saw that 2 Rue Drouot was now a McDonald's. Regardless, I stepped inside and looked for traces of the small stage, low ceilings and wisps of tobacco smoke Bowie would have seen as he waited nervously to wow the French. Assuming the stage would have been downstairs, I took the opportunity to use the facilities. Again, I closed my eyes, evoking thoughts of how Bowie's world was expanding, how his mind was inspired by textures, influences and scenesters smoking Gitanes, only to open them and see a homeless man urinating noisily in a sink.

Pissing tramps aside, Paris was a treat. I pulled up next to the Seine and flopped onto a bench as families glowed with the *joie de vivre* of a perfect autumn day. I was joined by a quartet of beret-wearing Americans who looked like they were enjoying life, and food. As they sat furiously palming crepes into their mouths, I thought, Oh, well, if you can't beat them, join them in a race to death by heart disease and diabetes. I pulled out a Mars bar and, as I peeled away the wrapper, couldn't believe I hadn't thought of it yet. With a little chuckle I said to myself, 'Is there life on Mars bars?'

Just as Bowie's mind was expanded by his first musical adventure abroad, my appreciation of new experiences was also growing: I'd booked a hotel room. The sight of a weather-broiled Iggy caused some consternation among the management, and

I began to wonder whether he was welcome in the three-star L'Ouest Hotel. After the lady pointed out he was rather big and muddy, we agreed he wouldn't cause any mischief and was allowed to stay on the condition that he bedded down in the luggage room and didn't expose his genitals to the Japanese family at reception. I revelled in the luxury of hot water that didn't stop after twenty seconds, and as grey sludge gurgled into drains, I felt my energy restored at the prospect of a city with significant Bowie milestones.

Outside, a ferocious downpour had sent torrents of water cascading down the streets, whisking cigarette ends from filthy gutters into pools of silty drain water. My attempted stroll to Montmartre was cheered rather than dampened as people dined convivially outside cafés. An umbrella's throw from Le Golf-Drouot, Bowie was drawn to the area's cabarets, like Le Chat Noir, 'Where the artists mingled with the bandits, where powerful words married to beautiful melodies transformed the popular song,' as he said to *Rock & Folk* magazine in 2011.

I paused outside its glowing red lights as sinews of sleaze, sophistication and jazz coiled around one another. It was the kind of walk only a free man can take, a man who has cycled over a thousand miles and has earned the liberty to stretch out his aches and pains with a dollop of culture; it was the kind of walk that quickly ends up in a pub. My eye was drawn to a series of vinyl records that decorated the wall of a scruffy establishment called La Divette. It took four trips to the bar and the same number of glasses of strong lager to ascertain that among the numerous Elvis, Doors and Brigitte Bardot records there was no Bowie. I drained another pint to make sure and offered the barman a boozy *merci*. I took his nod as a quiet mark of respect for my ability to clock a thousand miles and still not have the stamina to handle four pints without my eyes rolling round their eye sockets like marbles on a kitchen worktop.

Outside, the rain had ceased but my chipper mood hadn't. I bowled down the Rue Royale as neon winked and streetlights swooned all the way to the Eiffel Tower. After those beers my confidence stood just as tall, so when I spied a bright blue TV screen through some saloon doors, I'd found my next destination. Karaoke! Cue me up, *serveur*. I'll be ruining some David Bowie, *merci* very much. I breezed in with a floppy smile that alerted the barman to my state of inebriation. He rolled his eyes and continued filling the fridge. Fingering the menu for Bowie back catalogue, I couldn't see any among the frites and spritzers. I spun around with a grin so relaxed it nearly slid off my cheekbones and squinted at the song title on the screen. Someone was about to sing 'Pas de Signal'.

A minor French classic no doubt, perhaps a Claude François number ripe for adaptation. But where was this absent crooner? Come hither, shy pop minstrel. After being relieved of too many euros for a tiny lager, I siphoned a few sips and pointed to the screen.

'Karaoke, *non*?'

The barman looked at me, the screen, then the TV controller. He picked up the latter and began jabbing a finger at the rubber buttons. The screen flickered, the song remained the same: 'Pas de Signal'.

Something was amiss. Did the French hate karaoke? Had they boycotted it after Sinatra's overhaul of Cloclo's song? My drunken brain worked furiously, interchanging words, deducting then adding them like a rat-arsed Inspector Clouseau.

'*Signal non pas.*'

'*Non pas signal.*'

'*Pas signal.*'

'*No bloody signal.*'

Drunken bingo. This was cable TV. There was no signal. My certificate was in the post. I was a certified moron. The barman hammered the buttons one final time, slammed it violently onto the bar and walked away making the noise of an exasperated horse. As I slid through the open doors I'd staggered in through, fortunately my faculties hadn't become so washed away so as not to get me back to the hotel or steal some of the mini croissants that had been left at reception. I shovelled two in my mouth, their stodgy innards confirming they'd been around since the time of breakfast, or Napoleon, before collapsing with *Pas Signal*.

I came to on 1 October, which fortunately for me was the next day. Outside, a grey swamp of air swirled, helping me to recover my senses. There was a restlessness to me, one at the heart of 'Life on Mars?'. The will to escape, to search for more; more places where Bowie made music. The autumn nip seemed to have penetrated my cycling shorts and arrested itself around my shrinking appendage, making it grumble for the toilet. Petrol stations, hedges and alleyways were all conspicuous by their absence as my bladder pushed and strained to be released. That's why it was quite the surprise when the town of Herblay popped up a moment later. It rang a big silly bell because I'd seen it every day for most of my living youth. Herblay was twinned with my hometown of Yeovil. 'The mind of a city, the heart of a country,' so says our town's slogan. Having escaped my own teenage suburban universe, had I cycled over a thousand miles to end up in a French parallel? Regardless, I felt I should do my civic duty. *Bonjour*, Herblayans/Herbalistas/ Herbalists – your twin town's prodigal son is here and needs your help, specifically your toilets.

As much as I looked, there didn't appear to be any red carpet or ticker tape; there was no reciprocal sign expressing its pride at being friends with a provincial town in Somerset, no buffet laid on, no welcome committee and certainly no loo. Which is how I found myself hosing the back of a handsome conifer tree overlooking the town's central playground. My ceremonial duties done, I was relieved of my position as Yeovil's roaming ambassador and given the freedom of the town to piss right off.

I reset my route east, where scruffy retail parks soon gave way to rippling seas of corn, harboured by elms in matching moss brocades. The horizon-skimming meadows meant you could see Paris thirty kilometres behind, or to the north something far prettier and infinitely more relevant – the village of Hérouville.

17. LE CHÂTEAU D'HÉROUVILLE

In 1976, Iggy Pop was in a mental hospital. Torn apart by a heroin addiction that was close to killing him, he was saved by an angel, of sorts. Bowie himself was hooked on cocaine, flirting with the occult and had a fascination with the workings of Nazism; not exactly light bedtime reading for anyone. Somehow, he'd made the album *Station to Station* and introduced us to his latest character, The Thin White Duke. This was the forgotten album – not by the fans, it's quite brilliant, but by Bowie himself. Sat somewhere under a mountain of Los Angeles cocaine, he couldn't remember making it. Before he took it on a world tour, he had gone to Iggy's parents' trailer in Detroit and asked if he wanted to come along. Pop recognised what Bowie was doing.

'The friendship was basically that this guy salvaged me from certain professional and maybe personal annihilation – simple as that,' he said to *The New York Times*.

The damaged souls toured then fled to Europe, seeking a place to get straight and get recording again. Although it was Berlin that would become synonymous with their healing, there was a little side road along the way that helped give their demons the slip.

The D928 is rather underplayed, given its role in what many consider to be the creative peak of Bowie LPs, The Berlin Trilogy.

It was also in France, not Germany, where swaying wheat fields gave way to a knot of stone barns and a castle with a Greystone church watching over them.

I came to a halt outside two hulking iron gates draped with weeping willows and an unruly ivy that strangled them both. Behind, under a bruising metallic sky, was the faded remains of the Château d'Hérouville, a tumbledown cluster of crumbling buildings guarded by an army of forest. And it had some history. Bowie first recorded here in 1973, his album *Pin-Ups* a raggedy collection of covers celebrating mid-sixties English rock. And three years later, in desperate retreat, it was here, through twenty miles of retail parks and pee-stained twin towns, where the infamous Berlin Trilogy began.

The Château d'Hérouville was the world's first residential studio, and unofficial rehab clinic for Pop and Bowie. It was the vision of charismatic French film score composer Michel Magne, who imagined a place where artists could record with creative freedom, whenever they wanted; free from prodding record executives and the underbelly of city life. At first a two-bar trickle of musicians arrived, then a tub-thumping stream of legends: The Grateful Dead, T. Rex, Fleetwood Mac, Cat Stevens, Rick Wakeman, Pink Floyd and Marvin Gaye. Even the Bee Gees' shrill squeals knocked corn off its stems in the neighbouring fields.

Strawberry Studios, as it was initially known, was quickly nicknamed the Honky Château when Elton John's 1972 album of the same name was recorded here. It grew a reputation as France's answer to Abbey Road. But it was much more than tourists getting run over on zebra crossings; Magne took it from being a ruined Roman staging post and artist's retreat where Van Gogh once painted Val-d'Oise cornfields, to a state-of-the-art studio with swimming pool, table tennis, pinball and sweeping gardens peppered with bowing trees, water-filled moats and limestone turrets that strained for the skies.

The real calling card, though, was the acoustics. Bowie gushed to Pop that it was the best place to record a rock and roll album in the world. It became legendary, tales and tunes spinning from its gates. In June 1971 the village held its own festival, a Gallic Woodstock. Rumours swirled, the line-up eventually confirmed: The Rolling Stones, Jefferson Airplane, Pink Floyd, Led Zeppelin and the Grateful Dead. Sadly, it was rained off, but the Grateful Dead turned up and played to the villagers, mayor, chief of police and fire brigade anyway. Things got wild, people got riotously drunk, the punch bowl got spiked with LSD and the entire fire brigade ended up bombing naked into the swimming pool.

The word was out.

More artists pulled up outside the iron gates, a pornographic film was made, a cover version of 'Life on Mars?' by French artist Alain Kan recorded. But while Magne was a visionary, he was a poor businessman. His generosity brought vintage wines but spiralling debts, the dream slowly becoming a nightmare. In 1974, Magne left the studios in new hands – the musician, director and sound engineer Laurent Thibault taking over. The bands continued to arrive but the château was haemorrhaging money. In 1984, Michael Magne tried to return to his dream but wound up in a tangle of debts and legal papers. He killed himself in a Pontoise hotel room just a few miles away. In time, squatters moved in, a fire raged through one of the studios and the landscapes Van Gogh once painted were lost to invasive trees and bindweed. The château fell silent.

This all changed at 2.30pm when a bespectacled man wearing a navy fleece and a swathe of floppy hair crunched down the gravel driveway and wrangled a key in the gates. Bowie himself had been known to gild the lily when it came to extolling the poetry of his own work, so should it matter that I'd told a mountain of lies to secure entry to the castle where he once recorded?

The dark saloon car with suspicious blacked-out windows that screeched up next to me said it might. These suspicions grew louder as a portly man with a close crop of grey hair bustled out and ambled towards me. When I stopped flinching from the certain pummelling my face was about to receive, I realised, to my relief, he was smiling.

'So sorry I'm late. You must be James, the BBC travel journalist,' said the man, furiously pumping my hand.

'That's right,' I hesitantly answered, tossing another fib onto the pile.

'I'm Eric, the mayor of Hérouville.'

'Eric, how do you do?' I enquired, trying to sound like a musical correspondent but reverting back to royal butler.

'And you must be Jean,' I said, offering my hand to the man with floppy hair.

I'd already lied to Jean in a series of emails. He was one of the new partners hoping to resurrect the château's fortunes. Eric was an unexpected surprise, as town mayor he thought it only right he greet 'major international journalists', but fortunately not to check their credentials.

'So, you work for the BBC?' asked Eric.

'Mmm, yeah, sort of,' I mumbled.

They beckoned me inside where we made acquaintance over coffee, their friendliness coaxing me into forgetting about my façade as I babbled in a very un-BBC way about the nature of my journey. My giddy eyes betrayed me as they darted excitedly from turrets to giant oak doors and swirling staircases. Eric, clearly unaware of my civic indiscretions in Herblay, was a particularly charming host, fond of colourful language and keen to show me around.

In the midst of the château's own history, Bowie was arriving at a different juncture in his. A couple of years before, he'd been twitching at a new direction and had been at pains to get that point across. 'I've rocked my roll. It's a boring dead end. There will be no more rock 'n' roll records or tours from me. The last thing I want to be is some useless fucking rock singer,' he said in a 1976 *Playboy* interview.

By way of a warm-up, they concepted and recorded Pop's album *The Idiot* at the château. Pop said to *Uncut* in 2006, 'He made an Iggy album first, but watched the engineers there in the studio, learned how they worked, thought about it, had a chance to get to know the desk, and have daydreams about his own record while he worked on mine.' As changes of directions go, even for Bowie, the album he was about to record was unprecedented, a long way from the space balladeering of 'Life on Mars?'.

Low was Bowie's unrealised vision for *The Man Who Fell to Earth*, Nicolas Roeg's sci-fi/arthouse movie in which he played the titular Man. As ever, Bowie was smart with his collaborators. Along with Brian Eno, he had Iggy on backing vocals, Dennis Davis' sublime drumming and old cohort Tony Visconti. The latter bringing a new toy called the Eventide Harmonizer, which, while sounding like a child's keyboard you'd find in the back of Sunday newspaper magazine that you can pay for in handy instalments and get a second for just £29.99, actually, according to Visconti, 'fucks with the fabric of time'.

Eno had toys, too. He brought his infamous 'Oblique Strategies' cards that would throw up a series of challenges to push the music even further. Some choice examples:

'Are there sections? Consider transitions.'

'Emphasise the flaws.'

'Eat a pack of custard creams in under thirty seconds.'

One of those is made up.

From the above, it sounds totally bonkers, anti-linear, non-narrative career suicide. If you add in Tony Visconti's four-year-old son tinkling on the piano being the inspiration for the song 'Warszawa', it could be accused of disappearing up its skinny backside altogether. But *Low* is truly visionary, bold, uncompromising, one-of-a-kind music. Its electronic soundscapes, groundbreaking use of percussion and glacial vocals created the 'new musical language' Bowie was seeking. Only half the tracks have lyrics, mostly about Bowie's post-LA state of mind, like 'Breaking Glass', whose lyrics reference his cocaine psychosis where he drew satanic pentagrams on his hotel room floor. Whereas others were inspired by the sound textures of Berlin, like 'A New Career in a New Town', whose musical arrangement has an undeniable propulsive optimism to it.

Naturally, and brilliantly, the record execs were mortified, pulling the album altogether from Christmas promotion. When it was finally released in January 1977, Bowie didn't promote it either, instead going on tour and playing keyboard for Iggy. At the time it baffled critics, some even savaging it, but maybe they just weren't ready for the future. It remains his most creative, influential and, many fans argue – sometimes me as well – his best record.

As Eric and Jean led the way through dust-strewn arches, plastic sheeting and rotting ladders, we paused at the dizzying sight of splintered oak steps and wooden balusters that twisted around a wrought-iron staircase. Eric proudly announced this was where the Bee Gees recorded 'Stayin' Alive', the stairwell acoustics so impressive the band lugged all their equipment mid-stairs and hit record.

'Everyone who visits must sing it,' teased Eric.

'Yes,' I said. 'I heard they were asked to go "higher and higher", which led to Robin Gibb climbing to the top of the stairs and asking if this was high enough.'

Eric paused for a second, worked out I'd countered his dreadful joke with an even worse one, then slapped me on my back so hard it sent the wind scuttling from my lungs.

From upon high, it was back to Low. Bowie loved the way sound would drench the château's angled walls, high ceilings and big windows. Its Gothic feel reminding him of his own Haddon Hall. 'The studio itself was a joy, ramshackle and comfy-feeling,' he noted. But with such an illustrious and tragic history, there were bound to be ghosts. Legend has it that Chopin's haunted the grounds and our musical guests felt a few bumps in the night.

'It was a spooky place,' said Bowie 'I did refuse one bedroom, as it felt impossibly cold in certain areas of it.' Visconti agreed: 'There was certainly some strange energy in that Château. On the first day David took one look at the master bedroom and said, "I'm not sleeping in there!" ... Eno claimed to have been woken every morning with someone shaking his shoulder. When he opened his eyes, no one was there.'

The sight of a billowing builder's curtain prompted me to nervously broach the subject with my hosts. A smile spread across Jean's face. 'I have not seen or heard any,' he said with a reassuring smile. 'But if there are, they'll be happy with what's happening here.' That was good enough for me. Feeling more than a touch privileged, we slipped through cobwebbed halls and hauled ourselves up a dusty staircase into the castle's eaves. The George Sand studio was magnificent and had fatefully avoided the attentions of the fire, squatters and rain. Its threadbare appearance, just a dusty scatter rug, bracing oak beams and angled windows that let fissures of light illuminate the room, was warm and characterful. The walls were still bedecked with sprawls of white padding – the original sound insulation. It looked as though someone had taken a hammer and tacked pillows to the ceiling. At the back of the studio was a small step where Bowie would have recorded vocals. But there was more. Jean strode across the room, the sound of his footsteps echoing around the empty studio, and stood next to a bulky object cloaked by a black cloth. This was an unusual shape for a ghost. Then, he whisked away the sheet to reveal a perfectly preserved piano.

'It's 101 years old – a Steinway,' he announced with a sense of wonder.

Its elegant black curves and perfect craftsmanship deserved the admiring glances it was receiving. This was the piano that played the first chords of Elton John's *Goodbye Yellow Brick Road*, on which Bowie would have formed the early melodies for *Low*.

'When we bought the castle, the owner begged me to buy the piano too,' said Jean.

'An American investor had wanted to break it down into pieces to sell as souvenirs – for ten dollars each! But the owner couldn't face getting it down the stairs.'

Through the previous owner's laziness and Jean's romantic vision, the piano remains in one piece. I gave it a closer inspection, Eric too. He smoothed his hand across and found a rare dent. 'Bowie did that,' he quipped, making a guitar-smashing motion. Jean smiled and sat down to play. As his fingers floated across the keys, the most amazing sound drifted upwards. Bowie was right, the acoustics *were* mind blowing. The notes breezed from the piano's open lid and gently deflected from the pillows like summer butterflies. I was on the verge of tears.

There's something effortlessly attractive about a person coaxing sounds from a musical instrument; it has the transcendental power that can turn a certified swamp donkey into a heart wrenchingly beautiful Greek goddess. Not that Jean was a swamp donkey, or a Greek goddess, but I was gazing a little too intently at his flowing brown locks and dimpled chin. Caught in the giddy atmosphere of nostalgia and the aching beauty of the piano chords, was I in love with Jean Taxis? I probably was for the ten seconds he played the Steinway.

We walked giddily from the lofty heights of rock history and stepped into the 'garden' – a sweeping pasture of overgrown grass that dampened our ankles.

'This was once a jungle,' said Eric, that had been hewn back to reveal triangles of shade and secretive nooks where the stars would have kicked back in bohemian bonhomie. A lonely looking football sat on the wind-brushed grass. 'That's David Bowie's football,' chimed Eric, continuing a long line of jokes I suspected might not be true. 'And that's the swimming pool Iggy Pop was photographed naked in. The fireman, too – they were high!'

This one was true, and Eric's cue to stitch up a fellow mayor. 'He sent along the local fire brigade to act as security for The Grateful Dead, but in the midst of the party the wine they were sipping had been sprinkled with LSD and they ended up jumping naked into the pool.' He finished with a gutsy chortle showing a carefree attitude towards drink spiking. With civic stuffiness quashed, Eric stopped in front of a little turret surrounded by an old moat, now filled with thick, browning reeds. With a wistful sigh he announced, 'And this is where the rock stars came for some privacy. If the boat was on the other side, you knew people were inside.' He finished with a dirty uncle wink in case I hadn't understood that this was where the rock stars came to shag one another. I surveyed this musical museum, full of ghosts and mountains of melodic history, and felt an overwhelming sense of privilege. All this cycling, the tenuous links, the projectile vomiting, suddenly felt more than worth it.

Without the sins of the city, in Hérouville, Bowie and Pop were healing. They were even bonding over games of ping pong. Iggy recalls in his 1982 book, *I Need More: The Stooges and Other Stories*. 'Never in my life had I been able to play ping-pong. I never had the co-ordination – literally couldn't play. David said, "Come on, give me a game." But I tried it, and suddenly that day I could play, and I'm playing and we're about tied and I said, "You know, man, this is weird. Really weird. I always failed at this game and now I can play it." He said, "Well, Jim, it's probably because you're feeling better about yourself." Three games later, I beat him and he never played me again. I got good *real* fast.'

Bowie's reluctance to get whooped at table tennis led them to hop on bicycles and take to the country roads. They'd cycle for miles and miles and see farmers with big red cheeks sitting in local bars with long sandwiches filled with ham and cheese. They found a peace, and aided by a couple of bicycles, they got back to making music, but in their own time. This is maybe encapsulated most of all by *Low*'s 'Sound and Vision' – a cheery, brilliant oddity of sunny hooks, funk-fused bass and looping drums, whose lyrics tell the story of a man weaning himself off drugs but somehow having the wisdom through the withdrawal sweats to teach himself patience and let words and ideas come to him.

My BBC accreditation still hadn't materialised, and after two generous hours with the château's new owners it was time to leave. I said an emotional farewell as Jean and Eric confessed they felt lucky to be the next chapter in its history. They crunched down the driveway to see me off, Jean passing me a 'Friends of the château' leaflet, and as Eric throttled my hand one last time he graciously said, 'If you have any more questions, anything you want to ask, please don't hesitate.'

'Anything?' I asked.

'Anything at all.'

'You're not friends with the mayor of Herblay, are you?'

He was, actually.

I was so inspired taking in a different period of Bowie's career, I'd completely forgotten to ask the 'Life on Mars?' question. But after the most exhilarating, interesting and, even at my saggy-faced age, extraordinary day, I felt more in tune with him than ever. 'Isn't it great being on your own? Let's just pull down the blinds and fuck 'em all,' DB said about *Low*. Grinning like a stoned marmoset, I devoured the 25-mile ride back to Paris and did likewise, falling into a cycle-induced coma for ten hours.

18. THE TAMING OF THE BEAST

I'd briefly returned to the capital to make my next move. Buoyed by the cheer of a glorious Parisian Sunday, I pedalled for the Seine, gasping in morning air, gliding past the wonderful Institute of Music and the Louvre as the city slept. Chain cafés, biological cafés and cold press cafés all whizzed by as I hogged the wheel of a man on a shopping bike, a leather pork pie hat atop his head, hefty cigar hanging from his bottom lip and a weathered leather jacket billowing in the soft breeze. We sent pigeons scattering as the sun warmed our cheeks, the delights of the morning all to ourselves. After yesterday's brilliance, I was rejuvenated, a grin as wide as the Seine, all the thoughts that had come at night, banished. That was until my eye caught a glow from the handlebar bag – my phone.

I answered. Caller ID told me this wasn't Lucy's dulcet tones and positive wishes. A more sinister name illuminated itself – HR Susan. I could just ignore it. Pretend there was no signal or I'd been detained at the Herblay mayor's pleasure. My day-to-day life, one that seemed so distant, was calling. The all-seeing eye had spotted my progress and was about to check in. I fell into old ways almost immediately.

'Hi, Susan.'

'Hello, James, so sorry to call you on a Sunday.'

No, you're not.

'How's the trip going? Where are you?'

'Yeah, good, thanks. Paris.'

'*Ooh la la.*'

The small talk was reaching its conclusion. HR Susan readied herself for the killer blow. 'Listen, a new project has come in. We need you to come back as soon as possible. There were never any guarantees. I am sorry.'

I was silent for a second, a million thoughts cascading through my mind: I've come so far, I'm getting somewhere, I've achieved liposuction without surgical procedure. But the Libra in me was here to balance those rebellious notions: Yes, but you're low on money, you should crack on with your career and you'll never shift that flab around your jowls. A few seconds of weak-willed contemplation passed. I folded like a pack of cards: 'OK, let me make some arrangements.'

Whimsy had become clouded with the strains of reality. I knew it was a possibility. They hadn't made any promises, they did say. I'd been caught up in the ride, the journey, Bowie. I should go back, grow up, knuckle down; I could come back and find the meaning later.

Lucy wasn't sure. 'Oh, my god. They're utter arseholes.'

'They did say.'

'They're taking the piss.'

'I know, but ...'

'After all the hours you've worked, the evenings, the weekends.'

'That's how it goes.'

'No. That's not how it fucking goes, not this time. You have to go forward, not back.'

This wasn't the gentle soul I knew; this was the potty-mouthed voice of reason. It was sublime. She'd been so selfless when I'd been so selfish. Now she wanted me to stay. As I daydreamed, she swore. I held the phone a safe distance from my ear as the filthy tirade continued, causing a young mother to walk her two children to the other side of the road. 'Tell them or I fucking will,' she demanded with a wondrous grubby-mouthed finality.

And so it was. By rights, I should have been swinging west and riding the 120 miles to Calais and back into the open arms of capitalism. But by wrongs, and a supportive other half, I pulled onto a sun-splattered pavement flanking the glittering Seine, called HR Susan back and told her I'd made other plans. I'd be finishing the journey. With a slight detour east.

19. THE RAILROAD TO RUSSIA

Imagine a world without David Bowie's music, a place where someone has tried to hide his dulcet tones from your ears your whole life. In 1970s Soviet Russia 'Life on Mars?' had never been heard. The pithily named 'Approximate List of Foreign Musical Groups and Artists Whose Repertoires Contain Ideologically Harmful Compositions' meant his music was banned. This was drawn up by the communist government with a list of reasons why western bands couldn't be played on Soviet radio. You had Iggy's band, The Stooges, banned on the grounds of 'violence', Pink Floyd for 'interfering in Soviet Foreign Policy', and Tina Turner simply for 'sex'. It didn't end there. Madness were poo-pooed due to 'punk and violence' – obviously the fear of a good whipping with a pair of baggy trousers not the desired outcome after a hard day in communist Russia. But best of all, the Village People were blacklisted on the count of 'violence'. What were they going to do, poke your eye out with the feather from an Native American headdress or, worse, tickle you to death with a thick black moustache? Anyway, Bowie's music never stood a chance. But it didn't stop him visiting.

His fear of flying meant he had to expand his horizons in all manner of ways. One of those was to swan back from his 1973 world tour from Asia by picking up the Trans-Siberian Express.

The long rail journey through the frozen landscapes of the Soviet Union to Moscow, and eventually Paris, gave him a window on the world that flooded him with images and ideas. As he read Dostoevsky and witnessed the stark realities of communism, playing off against the bleak parallels of the totalitarian world he'd read in George Orwell's *1984*, his imagination exploded. He began penning songs for his *Diamond Dogs* album such as 'Big Brother', 'We Are The Dead' and '1984' itself. This first trip east bowled Bowie over. He had to show someone. So, in 1976 he convinced Iggy Pop to come and see Moscow for himself.

After Paris, it should have been a straight journey back to Bowie's England for me. But if I was running away from work, why not *really* run away? I'd already done something reckless, why not take it further with a 5,000 mile round trip? While I didn't have the time, fitness or finance to cycle it, the three day/two night sleeper train, an iteration of which Bowie once travelled on, would let me get under the skin of his influences – both nomadically and musically – and see the places that inspired the explosion of surreal imagery in his lyrics and, crucially, the second half of 'Life on Mars?'.

Arriving at Paris Est station I had just over an hour to dismantle my Iggy, pack him up and follow in Bowie's train tracks. A *velo* hokey-cokey ensued: the right bolt in, left bolt out, in, out, drop them under someone's suitcase, shake your handlebars all about. The elbow grease I put in was matched by the bike grease coming off, decorating my arms, hands and, now, not so white T-shirt. Birthday present abominations had nothing on this packaging disaster. Swathes of brown parcel tape swirled at intermittent intervals like a trainee abductor's first kidnapping attempt.

I settled into Bowie's Life on Rails quite easily. I gave Iggy a chipper pat and watched the French countryside roll past in swabs of autumnal yellow. Stepping into the carriage's corridor, all was calm as the train hummed cross-country. It felt strange to be off-bike; I had to walk, for one thing. My leggy amnesia meant my limbs scissored and lurched down gangways where I bumped into one of the female attendants, a provodnitsa, all blonde hair and deadpan glare. I ventured a smile but got a granite-faced look of nothingness in return. I was at ease. Happy, even. I'd binned off work, but felt strangely OK with it. I'd take the consequences later. This Soviet sidestep felt right, both in the spirit of the song and Bowie's own thirst for inspiration and adventure.

In 1973, Bowie's train from the far east hurtled through the night heading for the same destination, Moscow. He and childhood friend Geoff MacCormack had taken a ferry from Japan to the port of Nakhodka, where the Trans-Siberian Express waited for them. If he'd wanted to sit back and watch this strange, barren land slip by unnoticed, he hadn't dressed accordingly. The eyes of the military police were drawn to the wiry, angular alien sporting a yellow leather jacket and large chequered cap which partly obscured a thicket of bright red hair. His superior first-class digs were served by two provodnitsa, like my own. But he made light work of them, giving them a soft toy from Japan and playing music they'd never heard before. His recollections for teen magazine *Mirabelle*, probably ghostwritten, such was their whimsical nature, sounded more becoming of a dreamy wanderluster discovering the joy of travel: 'I could never have imagined such expanses of unspoilt, natural country without actually seeing it myself, it was like a glimpse into another age, another world, and it made a very strong impression on me.'

After playing to his attendants, he was subjected to military interrogations from generals and agents. Around halfway to Moscow, Bowie and McCormack had hopped off to take some pictures at Sverdlovsk when an official in a long leather jacket and tinted glasses demanded they hand over their film. The KGB were onto Bowie. Just as it seemed the Starman might disappear off the planet for good, the train began rolling and they leapt aboard, leaving the baddie floundering on the platform. As the days and scenery began to blur, their monotony grew. In the food cart, their blaring dress sense drew the attention of four Soviet men who began staring at them in an increasingly threatening manner. As they realised they weren't being asked if they wanted second helpings of goulash, one of the Russians gruesomely drew his finger across his throat. They made a run for it.

With 91 stops, Bowie's boredom turned to the frozen wastelands where surely nothing could survive. The alien world inspired him; he jotted down ideas for stage sets, barren communist worlds and a glittering apocalypse that would form the backstory for the *Diamond Dogs* album. As they plundered through the frozen lands closer to Moscow, Bowie peered from his cabin door and saw a group of soldiers. He held out a glass bottle of mineral water and asked if anyone had an opener. One of them took the bottle, stuck it in his mouth and removed the cap with his steel teeth. And with that, Bowie drained the bottle, fixed his cluster of red hair and picked up his guitar. David Bowie was heading for Red Square.

As morning came, the same yellow trees Bowie had seen were now hijacked by metallic skyscrapers rushing towards Iggy and me like totalitarian HQs. I gazed from the window at a broad misty lake, its silver hue inviting birch trees to come closer and admire their reflection. Outside, steam trains lay in shuntings below a grim wall of rain that ruined everything in sight. We inched into the metropolis through long concrete slabs filled with men and women dressed in knee-length overcoats, heads bowed from the deluge. The rush-hour grind as depressing here as anywhere else.

We were into Belorussky Station, and the great exodus began. Outside, I set about reassembling Iggy, the rain drumming a repetitive loop on the platform canopy while an insistent chill gnawed at my bones. Grappling with a pedal spanner, I made the final modifications to my bike, foregoing the fuss of reapplying the mudguards despite the downpour waiting for me. I sensed I was being watched. A pair of flower-patterned pony boots crunched to a halt next to me. Shit, Bowie's KGB nemesis with a sawn-off Kalashnikov? No, it was the provodnitsa dressed in her civvies, her tight white jacket decorated with flecks of cherry blossom. Perched on one knee, ready to spring into the ex-Soviet state, I might have looked like I was proposing to a Russian shot putter. She looked down at me – skinny legs, skinnier arms – and decided she'd be fine opening jars of pickled onions on her own. Then, with all the might she could muster, she cracked the thinnest of smiles, patted me on the head and said, 'Welcome to Russia.'

20. TOTALITARIAN TIMES

Iggy and I were under bombardment. The rain pelting us and the few Muscovites braving the wide, wet pavements. Sleek black cars thronged and sluiced along eight-lane highways as buildings stretched skywards and disappeared into the mob of rainclouds. The city's hulking mass of concrete felt intimidating, but underneath the Soviet shadow, Western ways had crept in long ago. Everything seemed altogether familiar, from the chain eateries and office blocks to the BMWs and Benettons. My plan was to return to those communist notions where everyone is treated as equals – the youth hostel. Distinctly different from DB's double visit in the seventies when he slept at the glamorous Intourist and Metropol hotels, I arrived at the Vagabond Hostel, a faceless apartment block swamped with fat globs of rain thudding from its steps. I hauled Iggy up the brutalist staircase and let him rest, tethering him to a drainpipe. Inside, my soggy arrival caused barely a ripple as heads raised robotically from smartphones, took in my moist presence and returned to looking at news from people they hated at school. The hostel, once the hive of fevered travel chat, had succumbed to the smartphone's glow.

When Bowie stepped off the Trans-Siberian Express in 1973, the same year 'Life on Mars?' was released as a single, he landed on May Day, the Russian celebration of the workers. A parade of Soviet military might was to be held in Red Square, a day when the attention was on bigger, betterer, brutaller. A parade of willy waving that wouldn't be shown up by anyone – unless you were David Bowie. If his music couldn't be heard, he'd be seen. Bowie wore a plume of fiery red hair, a yellow zipper jacket with matching yellow scarf, flared orange trousers and a pair of shoes with three-inch heels. On the Trans-Siberian they'd been warned not to film anything, but ever the rule breaker he's caught on one of Geoff MacCormack's photos rebelliously filming the parade, camera in one hand, fag in the other. In the background you can see Russians staring wide-eyed at the alien who'd landed in totalitarian times like a cosmic cowboy.

My get-up would be much shitter and more waterproof. An oversize fleece, topped with pac-a-mac and billowing jeans that made me look like I was trying to bring Abba's bell bottoms back into fashion. With too much Facebook going on in the hostel and not enough questions from smitten youths about my trip, I took myself for a walk past Tverskaya Street, its imposing parade of brutalist buildings looking like a series of supermarket car parks that had been tipped on their sides. Grey held court as I approached Red Square. It was nearing harvest, and in celebration weather-rattled fishmongers served skewers of dorado that sent pirouettes of fleshy smoke dancing into the sky. If Bowie was living on the edge of his platform shoes shooting the May Day celebrations, things had changed round here. Not only had capitalism staked its claim, it had been usurped by the greatest Western disease known to man. Selfies.

But the square was magnificent. St Basil's Cathedral, built under the orders of Ivan the Terrible, with its cheery iced-gem turrets, felt ironic; he couldn't have made anything more wonderful if he'd tried. As I walked on the cobbles, great slabs of concrete soared and expressionless Kremlin guards stood like granite statues frozen in time: the alien, totalitarian world that had Bowie's imagination in raptures. As light feathered through silver clouds, it did nothing to affect the hue of imperial red from the Kremlin wall, while opposite, running the entire length of the square, was the equally domineering GUM department store. This grand monolith, whose initials spell out Gosudarstvennyj Universáĺnyj Magazín – the state universal store – was where Bowie tried to buy souvenirs but found the shelves threadbare due to communist rationing.

Among the brutalist bluster there was also a sliver of 'Life on Mars?' to be decoded. In that difficult to decipher second half of the song, the lyric about Lennon being on sale again, is the source of some debate. To some, it's seen as a light-hearted dig at his friend John Lennon's song 'Working Class Hero', Bowie lamenting how a revolutionary pop star can only achieve fame through the capitalist system. Or, if you fancy a Soviet twist, it's about the communist Russian leader Vladimir Lenin struggling to inspire his people without the incentive of commodity. Or it's just a ploy of Bowie's to let everyone get their knickers in a marvellous twist and interpret the double meaning for themselves.

The next day, I wound the clock forward three years to 1976 and followed Bowie's route with Iggy Pop. He was keen to show his friend this alien city and spent an infamous seven hours in and around Red Square taking Polaroids, seeing Lenin's tomb and the Kremlin.

Like Bowie, I'd agreed to stop being a lonesome sod and take some company. I'd bonded with Jonathan, an Argentinian raconteur from the hostel, over his insistence that all the best people in the world are left-handed. He even had a T-shirt to prove it, its message translating as 'In few we are perfect, the others are right'. It offered a lengthy list of lefties as evidence: Barack Obama, Albert

Einstein, Bruce Springsteen, Jimi Hendrix, Vincent van Gogh, Kurt Cobain, Bill Gates, Leonardo da Vinci, David Bowie – and Jonathan from Argentina.

Being a leftie myself, I wasn't going to argue. I'd filled my new friend in on FITTNB, and as we walked among the brutalist utopia, I asked what he thought of the man lying ninth on his list of brilliant left handers.

'I like him. He was disruptive, eclectic.'

I nodded in agreement.

'As an Argentinian, not many English people have this good reputation,' he laughed.

I asked about 'Life on Mars?'.

'The first time I heard it, I didn't know a word he was talking about! My English wasn't good. It was just, DA DA DA DA DA ... oh, man!' he chuckled at the memory. 'But with time I started to understand there are different layers. I know it's not science fiction. It's poetic, like criticism of a dystopian world.'

At last, a kindred spirit. And confirmation I wasn't nuttier than a squirrel's cheeks. Jonathan *had* thought deeply about Bowie, and the interpretation of the song, and to celebrate having a full grasp of the English language he was singing its chorus at full volume in Red Square. Unlike the song's meaning, what wasn't open to interpretation was the 'no arsing about' policy of the state police guarding Lenin's tomb. As we entered the stark walls, Jonathan remarked deadpan, 'The meaning of David Bowie is not here.' This drew a forceful *Shhhh* from a guard who pointed to a sign saying no Latin American humour. In the inner sanctum, silence continued to be enforced as international and domestic visitors gawped at the waxy leader. Not so much pickled herring in a fur coat, but embalmed ex-president in a sharp navy suit with polka dot tie. In a triumph for thrifty tourism, and a play on Bowie's lyric, Lenin wasn't on sale again; he was free to look at.

We followed Bowie and Pop inside the Kremlin's walls where a small village greeted us, straining with brutal buildings stacked like concrete shoe boxes between onion-domed churches. Among the religious buildings, tinted windows and flinty-eyed schoolkids was the Kremlin Palace. Jonathan and I took to a bench to take in its hard-edged angles as mustard-coloured leaves drifted pendulously to the floor.

'That is where Bowie made his only ever live appearance in Russia,' I said, pointing to the Kremlin Palace where he was eventually permitted to play in 1996. 'The curtain lifting for the music that had been denied to the Russians for so long,' I added with a sense of drama. Jonathan must have been in stunned awe, as he didn't make a sound, letting me continue. 'But the reaction from dignitaries was rather cold. Some sat at the front with their fingers in their ears.' Jonathan was gobsmacked. Actually, Jonathan was trying to show a guard in a thick military coat his left-handed T-shirt. 'And Bowie was so miffed he vowed never to play Moscow again,' I said loudly to no one in particular.

After succumbing to the new wave of capitalism and buying Lucy a giant pencil (she could thank me later), I returned to feeling old at the hostel. Life without a bike was becoming more familiar. I'd walk into the common area and, with a giant hypocrite sign blinking above my head, ignore everyone and log onto social media. I'd been hoping to discover how Bowie was perceived by Muscovites and had stumbled across a social network specifically for Russians. VK looks identical to Facebook and acts almost entirely the same, except pretty much everything is in Cyrillic. I did a little translating. David Bowie is, for example, Дэвид Боуи, and 'Life on Mars?' Лайф он Марс? I unearthed fan pages that worshipped him and hosted Bowie vinyl parties; there were Bowie lectures, even a David Bowie tribute band.

After a lovely girl called Olga kindly explained the purpose of my trip to a fan group, I began to receive excited plaudits and encouraging words from Russian fans. I quickly became rather pleased with myself. Getting a little giddy, I suggested we all meet so they could tell me about their love for DB and waited for the replies to roll in. It wasn't long before this appeared in my inbox.

> Good evening, James!!! you want to meet with fans in Moscow??
> Sorry, I don't live in Moscow!!!

Mugged off with exclamation marks.

Aside from getting trolled with punctuation, I did manage to strike up conversation with a girl called Yulia who was interested in my trip. We'd exchanged messages prior to my Moscow landing, and upon arrival I'd received a lovely message that said, 'My congratulations with your Moscow arriving! You're a hero!'

I'd taken to Russian social media like Putin to bare-chested horse riding. Yulia was kind enough to answer my question about how Bowie's music came to be banned. She told me that everyone came to his music in different ways. Some knew about him in the Soviet times, getting vinyl records in an underground market. There was a counterculture musician called Boris Grebenshikov who shared DB's music with his fans. Then, after *Labyrinth* was shown on central TV in 1987, many girls became fans. Yulia herself came to Bowie in the nineties after hearing a programme on Radio SNC and finding a record in a music library. She loved it, but couldn't get any others. In 2011 the internet became her salvation. Every album was one of discovery as she supplemented Bowie's music with concerts and documentary films.

Those skin-tight pants in *Labyrinth* did for a lot of Russian girls. But it was Boris Grebenshikov, or BG, as he's known locally, who, after hearing The Beatles, helped spread the gospel of David. In 1972 he formed a band, Aquarium, heavily influenced by both Bowie and T. Rex. Free love and free speech weren't permitted in public, but they were channelled through his band's songs.

BG's artistic tendencies made him stand out as bourgeois and intellectual, everything Soviet rhetoric opposed. He began playing Bowie songs as part of his set in underground venues away from listening ears. Young Russians tuned in and turned on, and soon a black market formed for his records.

I needed to find out more. The young girl at the hostel told me there was a record store half an hour away. This adventure required a friend. I sheepishly made my way outside and apologised to Iggy. 'Sorry for tying you to a drainpipe like a dog who bites people.' He nodded his acceptance and we headed for the road. When I say road, I mean four-lane death-way with blacked-out skull breakers moving at the velocity of fighter jets. Just as I was about to give my life to a speeding vessel, a man in a flapping jacket and flat cap cycled within an inch of my toes straight down the pavement. If you can't drive with the Russians, cycle after them. As buses snarled at junctions and tram drivers juddered around blind corners in a wail of smog and stealth, I swerved around pedestrians and newspaper sellers, before dropping from the kerb into the chaos, shadow boxing with SUVs and provoking decrepit trams whose passengers stared at me without expression. I slowed Iggy to a halt as a Lada chugged past in a belch of acrid smoke, and after swallowing half, the plume dissipated to reveal a sign that spelt out DIG – the record store.

Struck with Russian road PTSD, I made a terrified beeline for the young man behind the counter and said, 'Hold me,' with a pair of trembling arms. Or I would have, if Andrew, the owner, hadn't been so effortlessly cool. He wore an eighties Russian football tracksuit and had an unruly mop of blond Andy Warhol hair. He owned the place with a few mates, spoke excellent 'Queen's English' and even better slang English.

'Got any Bowie?' I asked, feeling old.

'Let me look,' he replied like the cool cat he was.

'Hmmm, don't think so, but there might be some in the crates down there – check it out.'

I mustn't have remembered my age, or any accruement of wisdom, as the words, 'Alrighty, then,' spilled from my mouth like a man destined never to have sex again.

I dug through communist-era records to see what abominations they let those under Soviet rule listen to. Turns out my dad and grandad would have been happy – Abba, Frankie Goes to Hollywood and James Last had all been deemed suitable for Russian ears. With the prospect of returning to the roads somewhat unappealing, I dug through pretty much every record until GOLD! Not Spandau Ballet's namesake, but a Bowie seven-inch from 1987. An American issued 'Day-In Day-Out' from *Never Let Me Down*, a slab of so-so eighties synth-pop where Bowie wails 'Ooo-Hoo' too many times.

Like the rest of the album, it's pretty substandard, perhaps best represented by the fact that decades after his music was available again in Russia, it was still loitering in the record crates. Better still, in the promo video he's dressed in a T-bird style leather jacket and sporting a *Labyrinth* feathered cut while angels hover above a baby, an LAPD tank bulldozes a house and, wait for it, our hero bashes out a guitar solo on roller skates. I bought it for 400 roubles.

I asked Andrew about Bowie, explaining the trip. He liked him, but seemed indifferent to my journey, instead filling me in on the local music scene: how underground venues pop up then close down if the authorities get wind, before reappearing in another part of town. He recommended house, minimal and Japanese jazz as the go-to for thirsty ears. Wanting to sound cool, I replied, 'Cool, man,' sounding horribly uncool. Andrew was so nice, he even winced for me.

'Tomorrow belongs to those who hear it coming' as Bowie's promo message for the *Heroes* album suggested. But with no new music to come, would these words leave Bowie asunder as songs like 'Life on Mars?' become relics to younger generations?

With Russian roads seemingly not the best place to absent-mindedly daydream about Bowie's legacy, I was curious about the cycling, or lack thereof, on the Moscow streets. I'd arranged to meet Vladimir Filippov, the president of the Russian Cycle Touring Club. His club runs tours and free weekend cycle rides and I'd been hopeful of tagging along. But with rain hanging on every street corner the latest had been abandoned. Vladimir said we should meet anyway and so here I was walking towards a man with a brown manbag slung over his shoulder, which wasn't quite the spy/briefcase scenario I'd semi-racistly imagined. Vladimir was a university lecturer who bore a striking resemblance to Christopher Walken and had a Marlon Brando *Godfather* husk to his voice. We popped into another themed café, where twigs and birch branches hung from pots, giving the impression it may well have been a twigs and branches themed café. Vladimir bought some Ivan tea, a traditional Russian drink, and threw a huge map across the table. He regaled me with legendary cycle routes such as the Golden Ring and the road to St Petersburg. He talked gently of how he and his friends used to cycle across the old CCCP on cheaply built Soviet bikes where the flimsy components would literally fall apart beneath them. Keen to find out about Moscow cycling, I asked, 'Surely you don't cycle on the roads?'

'Not really. It's legal, but dangerous, so it's permitted to cycle on the pavements,' he replied. Which explained the chap who'd run over my feet earlier.

In the background of the café, a black and white Italian film was playing out on a large TV. Every now and again Vladimir's eye would be drawn to the screen. I looked to see a beautiful raven-haired woman on a bicycle, whom he was evidently quite taken by. He asked me where I was cycling to and I said only Moscow. As his face dropped, it clicked; he'd brought the map to show me where to go in Russia. This was my cue to deliver the Bowie spiel.

'I'm cycling from Ibiza to the Norfolk Broads!'

Blank face.

'Like David Bowie's "Life on Mars?"!'

More blank face.

'Looking to find out what it means …'

Face awash with joy. Not really; blankest of blank faces. Just then, the Italian lady pootled past on her bicycle and the look of rapture on Vladimir's face wasn't for memories of sailors fighting in dancehalls. We finished the rest of the tea and stood outside rubbing chilly hands and expelling puffs of condensation, agreeing to cycle together in London should he ever visit.

I traced the Moskva River, pushing Iggy along its chilly edges. What was I doing? I was 2,500 miles off-route, floundering around in record stores and asking Russian cyclists for answers. On the one hand I'd escaped and felt this was exactly how I should be living, but on the other I was sharing a bedroom with twelve other people, one with an almighty cough, as the life I'd built was speeding away in another direction.

A jet stream of biting cold air propelled me past Gorky Park through leaf-caked hills to the university, where fairy lights and the eerie red of the Soviet star on the Kremlin cut through the misty surrounds. As I chuntered along the pavement my eye caught the outline of a man bound for the stars. Towering above the static cars was a monument made of titanium, its pedestal a whooshing vapour trail that led to a bust of the first man in space, Yuri Gagarin. This was rather opportune.

'Say, Yuri, while you were up there, don't suppose you happened to see if there was any life on the old red planet, did you?'

'What's that, it's 250 million miles away and I'm a whopper wally bollocks?'

I retired to the hostel, frozen, where young Muscovites were returning from their jobs and diving straight into social media like hungry horses into nose bags of oats. I joined them, totally integrated in contemporary youth hostel behaviour, but it was all fine because I had a new notification from VK.

'There is a café in Moscow dedicated to him. The name is David.B.Café!'

Yulia Shkolnikova, VK hero.

The circle of acceptance was complete, the ban had been lifted and he had his own coffee shop with Gingerbread Starmen and Ch-ch-ch-chocolate chip cookies (probably). Upon arrival, the front wall was dressed in turquoise paint and lit up by his name. Its sparse interior was like any modern café – minimalist white walls filled with maximum millennials wearing spanking new trainers, surrounded by a scattering of Bowie portraits as *Aladdin Sane* played quietly in the background. They sipped lattes and tapped away on Facebook with MacBooks next to Bowie coffee-table books. With the book theme established, I commandeered a bookish waitress and asked if she knew why it was called the David.B.Café.

'I don't know, it's the owner who named it. He won't tell anyone, maybe he's a fan?'

I asked if I could speak with him.

'Sorry, he doesn't speak English – why do you want to know?'

With one last effort I pulled out the FITTNB card.

'You've completely shocked me,' she said, holding her hand against her fluttering heart. She hurried away, returning a moment later. 'The owner would like you to have this.'

She pulled out a David Bowie puppet that did a star jump when its string was pulled.

'It is a gift from the café. Perhaps you could post updates on social media when you make your travels.'

#Verymodernverymodernmoscow

I'd landed at an actual Bowie-themed café. The waitress was lovely, and the owner undoubtedly kind. But it lacked a little of what made Bowie, Bowie. This could have been anywhere in Western Europe. It felt as if his imagery and music were a background aesthetic to modern life, rather than a spirit in which to live it. Russia had changed, at least superficially since Bowie's time. The Soviet era, where his music was previously banned, now pricked by the hipster's carrot cake fork, ensuring his presence in the windows of popular culture.

Outside, rain clouds hung on street corners like naughty youths. Having traipsed to the outer edges of Europe, I felt as if I needed to reclaim Bowie's spirit of adventure. I gathered Jonathan and the young pups from the hostel, and suggested we ditch our phones and get riotously drunk in celebration of Bowie and me being twice their age. Somehow this culminated at 4am with four grown men and one woman jerking their limbs to industrial techno in a deserted club before we all piled into the back of a battered Lada taxi reeking of several too many.

Jonathan made an announcement: 'I have been listening to the song today, and it's true.'

'What's true?' I slurred.

'The policeman beating up the wrong guy,' he said, meaning Bowie's lawman. 'In Argentina there is a lot of that. And now there are billionaires who want to move to Mars. Bowie saw these things before everyone else.'

Jonathan was insightful, Jonathan was right (but left-handed), Jonathan was drunk. 'Probably in the seventies it was the same – in every generation you hear something in the song. I learn more each time. Nothing when I was kid, but now ...' he said with a broad, inebriated smile, 'I will always associate him with you.'

The driver twisted the dilapidated radio dial looking for something to hush us.

'David Bowie?' I chanced.

He twiddled further, landing on James Blunt's 'You're Beautiful'.

'This! This was the music they should have banned,' I slurred, with a self-important wag of the finger. As no one laughed and the car's axle groaned, I pulled the Bowie puppet from my pocket and pulled his string. He performed a tiny leap of rebellious joy. Jonathan saw and began singing along incorrectly to Blunt: '*Our life is brilliant.*' Realising I was flabbergastingly drunk, it dawned on me: Bowie's life was, and tonight, leaking from the gills with cheap Russian vodka, so was mine.

21. EAST TO WEST

In the spirit of adventure, seeing the brutalist worlds Bowie saw was worth it, hearing fans' stories of how they discovered a man's music that was never meant to be discovered was comforting, and knowing there were a lot of other special left handers out there, Jonathan included, felt good too.

Briefly, all our journeys had collided: my railway indulgence, Bowie's 1973 Trans-Siberian experience and his 1976 stopover with Iggy. Back then Pop and Bowie had been interrogated by an albino KGB agent who confiscated a *Playboy* magazine before they were strip-searched at the Russian border on suspicion of smuggling items up their backsides. But whatever ignominy David Bowie's rectum faced, as I boarded the train back west to explore Bowie's creative peak, my body raging with nausea and swimming in Russian vodka, it absolutely couldn't have been worse than Penny and Dave.

'Daaaayve, is this the right bloody traiyn, Daaaayve? We're not meant to be on a bloody sleeper traiyn?' Which, of course, is long-form for Australians.

I'd gotten up to help them find their cabin, before stealthily grabbing some grumpy zeds. Two hours later Penny and Dave decided I'd had enough, peering round my door like a couple of wardrobe monsters. 'Where you from, then?'

Before I could answer, I came to understand that Penny had thrown a six-foot Russian off the metro in St Petersburg, Dave had a gammy leg, they were heading to Warsaw and, like Bowie, they'd travelled on the Trans-Siberian Express. Penny rattled through some more subjects.

'She's a bitch and a slut,' that accounted for Dave's sister.

'Use 'em, get rid of 'em,' her attitude to knickers.

'Useless bastards. Nobody wanted to help us,' the Belarusians weren't popular, either.

I was starting to regret helping them myself.

I managed to spit my story out before the Aussies could ram another down my throat. This got Dave in 'begrudging respect for an Englishman mode'.

'Geez, that's some effort for a bloody pom. How far ya going?'

'Around 3,000 miles.'

'Three-thousand miles for a smart arse song by an English poofter!'

Before I could drive his forehead into my knee, Penny yelled, 'Look, Dave, we're in Warsaw.' In a blur of 'Nice to meet ya's and 'Quick, get the bloody bags off', they departed. But they needn't have rushed. The train was stopping. Men and women emerged blinking from sleeping compartments, children played in corridors, an old man with thick-rimmed glasses stared into the faded fields of Poland.

As the sun broke through and radiated the platform, I hopped off and crab-stepped into its rays, baking my pasty face. Just as one Dave was dragged away by his bolshy wife, another had stepped onto the same sun-splintered platform 40 years ago.

'Warszawa' was another travel-inspired track, appearing on 1977's Low album. Laid on top of an ambient Brian Eno soundscape, its lyrics were a chorus of chanting that Bowie termed an 'invented language'. If the 'Life on Mars?' lyrics were difficult to decipher, Bowie had taken it a step further here. It was apparently inspired by an LP of a Balkan boys' choir Bowie had bought after wandering from this same platform into the city and stumbling across it in a record shop. Was it still there? Perhaps Penny and Dave were digging through the crates right now looking for, 'The sounds of the bloody outback,' or, 'His sister's a slut and she knows it.'

The grumble of an engine broke my serendipity: back to the train. I had new passengers in my carriage, two middle-aged women, a Muscovite mother and daughter. Iggy broke the ice. The mum was an ex-Soviet ballerina whose husband lived in Hannover, and they had professional musicians in each generation of their family. This was my cue to whip out the seven-inch – the Bowie record, not the giant pencil – and explain my trip. She inspected the record but had no idea who this man wearing a white billowing blouse and khaki slacks was. But the sight of a fresh-faced floppy haired Bowie sent neurons fizzing. 'Ooo, Chrisrer, Chrisrer!' she yelped.

Chrisrer? Who was this, a Russian folk legend to rival Bruce Grebenshikov?

'Chrisrer, Chrisrer,' she continued, her face foaming like a nine-year-old overdosing on a Sherbert Fountain.

Was she about to whip out a set of bongos and begin chanting 'Chrisrer, Chrisrer, aww, Hari Chrisrer'? She smiled at my simple genetic make-up and very slowly said, 'Chris Rer.'

Chris Rea!

She had worked herself into a frothy mess over the English gravel-gargling crooner. 'Chrisrer is superb,' she said, folding her arms as if that was the final word on Chris Rea.

I announce my favourite singer, they reveal theirs: *Glasnost* – the spirit of Russian openness. By now I was on first name terms with Lydia (Chris Rea extremist) and Mila (daughter), and after nodding along to some Chrisrer ('Driving Home for Christmas') I felt emboldened to play them some Bowie. First 'Life on Mars?'

and then the distinctive refrains of Robert Fripp's guitar followed by Bowie's voice on 'Heroes'. As his lyrics flowed like stardust from my cheap phone speaker, Lydia strained to hear. I nodded along, a smug plonker from another planet bringing Bowie's music to the ears of Soviet ballerinas for the first time. A woman of few words and multiple furrowed features, she concluded simply, 'Nice.'

As the song drifted down the carriage with Bowie gusting with all his heart, I thought of the Aussies referring to it as 'smart arse' and now the Russian summation of 'nice'. Was I two sausages short of a barbie, was I a ballerina minus a tutu? Perhaps it *was* all a bit 'nice', a bit too 'smart arse'. Maybe the meaning was all in my head. Christ, maybe I should stop asking people. But having come all this way, I wasn't ready to give up yet. Big swathes of Starman lay ahead. 'Nice' can be a first impression that grows into a lifelong love affair. 'Smart arse' can bring repeated listens, new meanings found with every play, or, as Jonathan said, every decade. Russia had caught up with Bowie, it was me lagging behind, but there was still time to solve Bowie's timeless 'Life on Mars?' question, especially with what I was journeying closer to.

In 1976, Bowie and Iggy's train rumbled west along these same rail lines; whether he was also hot-faced by a Russian ballerina singing Chris Rea remains unclear. But as they approached a divided Germany, a smile spread across Bowie's snaggle-toothed mouth. Fans with glittering faces and feather boas had gathered to meet them. They'd reached West Berlin, but weren't in good nick, seduced by drugs and a Hollywood lifestyle that was on the cusp of killing them. I was already in character – booze-related existential dread propping up my paranoid soul. I exchanged 'bye, bye's, '*tschüss, tschüss*' and strangely 'paka paka's – and even a hug with Chris Rea-loving Lydia – then mounted Iggy and cycled into the heart of the city that would become David Bowie's saviour.

22. BERLIN YEARS & TEARS

If there was ever to be a David Bowie annual, and God knows some-one should make one, then Berlin would probably be its centre-page fold out, every single year. Bowie and Iggy had come here to save themselves. They sought a simple life. No hangers on, parties or drugs. To lose their alter-egos and compulsions, drag themselves from death's door and get back to being David Robert Jones and James Newell Osterberg Jr. Or, as Bowie told the audience at a VH1 Storytellers gig, 'Iggy Pop and I were a couple of very naughty boys. We went to Berlin to learn how to be good.'

Coco Schwab, Bowie's loyal assistant and in many ways his guardian angel, arranged a simple home in the unfashionable Turkish district of Schöneberg, the three of them living above a mechanic's at 155 Hauptstrasse. Bowie walked the streets unno-ticed. Nobody cared. He reset and sought inspiration as an artist: painting, writing and visiting the Brücke Museum by bicycle with his transexual artist friend and maybe lover, Romy Haag, to see the expressionists: Heckel, Kirchner and Mueller. He studied the plays of Brecht, read Nietzsche and dallied with local Kosmische Musik. Haag said, 'He wanted ideas. He wanted to swallow everything.'

One night, he couldn't resist jumping on stage at a local cab-aret night and singing a few Frank Sinatra numbers, only to be asked to politely *verpiss dich* – fuck off. With this anonymity, his creative soul was being nourished and his slender legs given a workout; he'd rediscovered the joy of riding a bicycle again. He was just another Berlin resident riding a clunking city bike, its long handlebars looking strange on this slip of a man from south London travelling in time between the two worlds of Berlin. These inspirations dug the foundations for the Berlin Trilogy, his Triptych, and although the albums weren't all recorded here, they were conceived in a city brimming with tension as it fought its own demons, torn asunder by different ideological beliefs with only a wall to divide them.

In the clumsy process of re-assembling Iggy, I'd dimwittedly sheared off a saddle stem thread. The seat was now able to spin an impressive 360 degrees so it felt like I was sitting atop an owl's head. Arriving late at a hostel, the novelty of being back on land, rather than cruising a metre above it, led me to forget last night's festivities and quickly sink three bottles of strong German lager. This added further authenticity when I woke like Bowie in the summer of 1976: paranoid, head thumping like Geoff MacCormack's bongos, and in need of a cure. Under the worship of Sunday drizzle, I took Iggy in search of one.

The city's first light revealed swathes of stubborn grey architecture. My wheels kicked up rainwater as I cantered along the concrete enclave of Oranienplatz where signs rallied for 'Community not Commodity', a hark back to the city's divisions. But if there was any concern I might not find a bicycle shop, I needn't have worried. In graffiti-strewn Kreuzberg they outnumbered people. I popped into one where a lank-haired man stepped from behind the counter, silently removed the offending shards and seamlessly fitted a replacement.

'Great, *danke*. How much?'

He looked for the price on the box of parts. 'Three euros, fifty,' he replied, not having grasped the concept of capitalism.

'Really, what about labour?'

He looked genuinely surprised. 'Fifty cents?' he shrugged.

I liked community not commodity.

Bowie's entrance to Berlin was miraculous in many ways. A first-class ticket bribe from his record label had somehow cured his fear of flying. He touched down at Tempelhof Airport with King Crimson's Robert Fripp, the guitarist on *Heroes* and later again on *Scary Monsters (and Super Creeps)*. I thought it as good a place to start as any. As I circumnavigated the airfield's fence, mist lapped thirstily at its edges. It seemed long abandoned to aliens landing from other planets, its runways now used for genteel activities like kite boarding, jogging, barbecues and dog walking. Sitting in the shadow of the criss-cross of runways was a crescent-shaped airport terminal. In an ironic take on two worlds divided, the hangar was once used by the Nazis and was now a temporary home for refugees seeking asylum. The strange tension compounded as traditional German hall music drifted in on clouds of rain.

Music wasn't on Bowie's mind, at least not straight away. A new career in a new town didn't mean a clean break, because West Berlin was a city to be lived in, and lived in well. As well as being the heroin capital of Europe, the city offered local bars such as Schöneberg's Anderes Ufer just a stumble away from their apartment. Translated, it means 'Other Side', a nod to it being one of Europe's first openly gay bars. A brave stance in the face of provocation from post-Nazi Germany.

It still stands today but is now called Neues Ufer ('New Side'). I'd decided here was a good place to meet Lucy. We'd agreed that Berlin being the heart of Bowie's rejuvenation, less so it being bitterly cold and almost permanently in some form of freezing rain, would make it a great place to reunite for a few days. Four weeks in and 1,300 miles of cycling later, I was late.

I ran in to see a woman behind an antiquated mahogany bar washing glasses. My heart pounded against my ribcage, rattling through bicycle-beaten bones as the excitement of a giddy teenager surged through me. I scanned the bar. Its former patron, Bowie, permeated the wood-panelled walls and there, sitting below a Ziggy Stardust photo, she was. The girl who'd let me take all my annual leave, forgoing a proper holiday together; the girl who'd put HR Susan back in her corporate box; the girl who'd flown to freezing Berlin in October for her summer holiday.

I was so overwhelmed with gratitude; I wasn't really listening to her admonish me for leaving her alone in a bar for over an hour.

'Airport ...' I said, pointing in the direction of the rain.

I'd forgotten how to communicate in whole sentences. Even if I couldn't put one word after another, I was better, if slightly damper, at hugs and chapped-lip kisses. God, how she hadn't missed me. We reacquainted over a beer before I dragged her into the sodden street: 173, 171, 169, 167, 165 ... you get the picture ... 157, 155 Hauptstrasse!

With Iggy, we stood outside Bowie's old apartment. The auto part store that once sat below had made way for a physiotherapist's clinic. We inspected the commemorative plaque outside and eyed his first-floor apartment that reached across to a bay window. To the left was a pebbledash archway and a bunch of orange tulips tied carefully with a yellow ribbon. To the left again, a red iron gate where Bowie would have wheeled out his bike each morning, and to the left of that, a wet dog. But that had nothing to do with Bowie. As a grown man this entrance excited me more than it probably should have. Inside someone had scrawled 'BOWIE WAS HERE' in big black paint.

He was, once.

After dropping Iggy back at our apartment's garage, we eased ourselves into Berlin as messrs Osterburg and Jones had: visiting Kreuzberg's SO36, the infamous seventies hangout where our heroes got punky, its tunnelled entrance plastered with tattered fly posters. Tonight, there was a flea market, and true to its history, the place was chocka with wool-wearing urbanites drinking beer and selling leftfield castoffs. Outside, under the flame of streetlight, graffiti covered every inch of concrete; you had the feeling if you stopped for just a split-second you might also be spray-painted as a policeman with a pig for a head.

We stumbled to Görlitzer Park where drug dealers acted as traffic islands for zooming bicycles, before diving into a bar playing honky-tonk jazz under thick, curdling clouds of tobacco smoke as locals necked liberally poured cocktails. You could see how Bowie and Iggy were naughty boys – and not long after their arrival they were as high as rock and roll kites. One story saw them both sitting in a black Mercedes as Bowie rammed their dealer's motor over and over, before he tore off around an underground car park screaming that he wanted to kill himself by slamming the car into a concrete pillar (the inspiration for *Low*'s 'Always Crashing in the Same Car'), but with a splutter they ran out of petrol and burst into floods of laughter.

But with time, Iggy, and especially Bowie were getting better. Unfamiliar feelings he hadn't felt in a long time began to wash over him. 'It was an irreplaceable, unmissable experience and probably the happiest time in my life ... Coco, Jim and I had so many great times. Some days the three of us would jump into the car and drive like crazy through East Germany and head down to the Black Forest ... just go for days at a time,' he told *Uncut* magazine in 2001.

I'd read somewhere that Bowie and Iggy used to race each other on bicycles to the lake of Wannsee and thought it a neat idea we do similar.

'Wanna go to Wannsee?' I asked poor Lucy.

'How far is it?'

'About twelve kilometres, I think.'

We hired Lucy a three-speed city bike like Bowie's. The sun was high and our spirits loftier still as we breezed the city's cycle paths. As graffiti subsided, architecture grew affluent and foliage plentiful. Roads with silly names like 'Im Winkel' and 'Im Anger' slipped past; with Lucy in tow 'Im Happy', I thought. So happy that as we passed the University of Berlin and swooped under a motorway bridge we'd already clocked 22 kilometres. Bowie must have been really fit, or a liar. As had happened a lot on the trip, I'd drifted away, lost in thought. I turned around to discover I was cycling on my own. Lucy catching up a minute later with rosy cheeks.

'It's not a bloody race,' she groaned.

'Well, it is because ...'

I'd started to string words back together, dangerously so. Lucy's green eyes had a tinge of fire, so I apologised and hung behind her for a minute, then as we edged past the S-Bahn stop of Wannsee, a broad expanse of water flooded our vision. 'Got the camera, Lucy?' I shouted. As she braked, I eased in front of her like a giant pillock and silently, but joyously mouthed 'winner' as she rummaged in her bag.

Iggy and Bowie raced to Wannsee in peak summer; we'd landed in late autumn. The sun was beaten back by grey clouds as the lake's edges lay muted by the yellows and browns. Among three-tiered *schloss* and yacht clubs we found a café, the deserted Seehaase. We opted to 'share' food, something responsible for 99.99 per cent of relationship break-ups. Another race ensued as we pounded through a delicately-flaked apple strudel, my hefty cycle diet meaning I slipped into a 2–0 lead, for which I was promptly chastised. We melted into the warmth of familiarity, pedalled without care, took in the banks of the deserted lake, and although we were chasing Bowie, Iggy and Coco's footsteps, doing it together didn't feel alien, flecked with self-doubt, or selfish – it felt just right.

With the pudding as fuel, we powered back towards the city. By design (fluke) a long sweep around Berlin's western edges brought us to Grunewald, an impenetrable cloak of forest camouflaging another of Bowie's sanctuaries, the Brücke Museum. It was here he fed on German expressionism and the painters whose feelings of alienation echoed his own. Their bold strokes and bright clashing colours were designed to jolt the observer towards emotion. Bowie would stand rapt, or knackered if he'd cycled, admiring Heckel, Kirchner and Mueller, and looking for seeds of inspiration. And it was Heckel's 1917 *Roquairol* painting, depicting an insane and incurable man, that was redrawn by Bowie and used for the *Heroes* album cover and Iggy's *The Idiot*.

But there was one picture I sought that Bowie had taken a particular shine to. As he pored over Otto Mueller's 1916 *Liebespaar zwischen Gartenmauern* – *Lovers between Garden Walls* – for over an hour, a story began to write itself. Its depiction of a kiss under shorn autumn branches the seed for something far greater – a story of two lovers kissing by a wall. I asked the man at reception if I could see the painting, stare at it, see what Bowie saw. He was a tough cookie and German cookies don't crumble easily.

'I'm sorry, zir, it iz in storage.'

I loosened the edges of my wallet, teasing a twenty euro note. Lucy rolled her eyes and walked away.

'What if ...'

He kept the exchange short. 'Zir. It iz not pozzible,' he said, cutting me off mid-bribe and telling me to fuck off with his eyes at the same time.

I settled for a postcard and took out my frustration on Iggy's sticky bike lock, yanking it hither and thither. Lucy eventually stepped in and took charge while I skulked nearby kicking leaves. The city swallowed us into rush hour, and as Lucy gladly deposited her bike back, without knowing it she had suffered a third and final defeat. We did the traditional post-cycle routine of getting merry on German beer and observing the locals. In Kreuzberg everyone appeared to be doing their Bowie years; artists brooded, punks smoked on sodden corners and lonesome musicians carried guitar cases with peeling stickers. That evening, I had my own alienation to face: Lucy was heading home. Among the frozen goodbyes, there was no shortage of lip wobbles, and on the edge of the withered gardens of Görlitzer Park, we kissed, by a wall – heroically risking being graffitied in the process.

What a simple joy to have someone to confide in, to share a moment, a laugh, a kiss. It made everything seem all the more worthwhile. After the hopelessness of the career, the worry and burnout, spending time together had wrestled those clouds away, making them dissipate and fade until all that remained were rays of soft light. Was this happiness? And was I really about to cycle away from it for a second time? Having previously displayed all the emotional maturity of a jam doughnut, was I now growing emotionally? If so, I was still light years behind a certain someone.

Bowie's creativity flourished as he soaked up Berlin's influences. At the age of 30 he was maturing and finding importance in big themes like society, love, life and hope. He was bringing emotion to his work and he was doing it with a bicycle. Every day he'd cycle from 155 Hauptstrasse to Hansa Studios, the hall by the wall. If 'Life on Mars?' was a love song, then 'Heroes', the lead track from its namesake album, was shot through with hope from the hopelessness that divided Berlin.

In Iggy he had a kindred spirit, Bowie not only influencing Pop, but learning from his friend too. Struck by the way Iggy was able to walk up to a microphone and improvise, he again used Burroughs's cut-up technique, taking an idea, sentence, or seed and using it as a jumping off point for his lyrics. As he tried to write 'Heroes' he asked to be left alone. He stalked the Hansa sound room, lit a cigarette and looked out the window towards Potsdamer Platz. In the no-man's land between East and West he made eye contact with a Russian border guard on a watchtower. The place was electric, the tension palpable. This was as real as it got, a single bullet could start a war. As he drew on his cigarette, two people walked underneath the watchtower. He watched. They moved closer. Then kissed – by the wall. Not strangers, but producer Tony Visconti and backing singer Toni Maass. The seed had been planted in the Brücke Museum, the lovers by the wall, and as the guns were primed above these clandestine lovers' heads, they kissed, as though nothing could fall.

Recently, Clare Shenstone, an artist and friend of Bowie, spoke to Francis Whately for a BBC radio documentary. After he pleaded with her to visit Berlin, Bowie and Shenstone explored the city where under the tension and alchemy lay a romance and intoxication that seduced everyone. 'As the light was beginning to go,' she said, 'we walked to the other side of the wall. There were spotlights and you could see the guns silhouetted and we were holding hands, and he took my other hand, and he kissed me. It was so beautiful.'

'Heroes' would become Berlin's hymn, a siren call for hope, the iconic image of two lovers – whoever they were – kissing as Stasi guards shot above their heads. Like the expressionists, Bowie had added emotion to a scene that previously couldn't be viewed without despair. Eager to find out more, I'd contacted the Berlin Tourist board, and they kindly arranged for me to meet Bowie expert Thilo Schmeid thanks to my ongoing credentials as a BBC journalist.

I spun left into Köthener Straße, arriving at number 38, a grand hall, years older than the modern apartment block horrors that had sprung up around it. Drawing on a cigarette was Thilo, strong of beard, physique and handshake.

'So, you're the journalist with the bike?'

Half of this was true.

Thilo was the affable owner of Berlin Music Tours, a child of the GDR, and a self-confessed Bowie nut. He was well-prepared and had a series of photos from the studio of Bowie wearing a plaid shirt and natty moustache, sat behind the control deck with Tony Visconti and studio engineer Eduard Meyer. He showed me Bowie's playful entry to the studio guestbook that reflected his lifting mood.

> *Good morning, could I interest you in a hoover?*
> Bowie 1976.

Hansa had been originally used for high society performances before being commandeered as a Nazi ballroom, then reclaimed as a recording studio. The area around it had been heavily bombed by the British during the war, but miraculously Hansa survived. If the bombers had been a smidgen more accurate there would have been no Hansa and no 'Heroes'. Perhaps they knew.

We crept up on an unassuming panel of deeply varnished wooden doors. One creaked open and a young musician walked out. A sliver of light escaped to reveal herringbone floors and a cavernous hall. Thilo beckoned me in, but my eyes couldn't keep up; beyond the tiled floor lay a stage adorned with red velvet curtains, tall ceilings with swirling patterns and windows that invited fractured light to stretch across the floor. This was Studio 2, or the Meistersaal, where Bowie recorded 'Heroes'. But he didn't do it alone. Tony Visconti was about to add an indomitable touch. He carefully set up microphones around the room, each one further away than the last, so when Bowie sang at different levels the gates, a mic feature that cancels background noise, would open one by one. When he sung with the passion of those two lovers, all the gates burst open, and you'd hear the incredible scale of reverb and depth of emotion in his vocals present in the song. Gulp. My arms grew goose bumps.

I closed my eyes, imagining his voice echoing off the walls with the lyrics that would ignite a divided city. We continued apace, moving into a wood-panelled room replete with piano and a crescent bar. 'This was the original control room, and that window there ...' said Thilo, pointing to the dull brick wall of an apartment block, 'was where Bowie saw Tony Visconti and Toni Maass.' He didn't need to say any more, or do any flappy tongued kissing impressions; I perched on the windowsill under a grey and gold drape. As is customary for pretend journalists, I was lost for words. Thilo stepped in. 'I'm the luckiest man in the world to relive this every day,' he said with a sigh.

Sensing my journalistic integrity was on the line, and that Thilo was emotionally compromised enough to spill the beans on 'Life on Mars?', I asked what he thought.

'It's one of my favourites,' he said with a smile, 'I love the funny story of Sinatra and Anka.'

He moved on quickly, too quickly.

'But my true favourite is "Ashes to Ashes". I didn't understand a word as an East German kid.'

I thought of trying to steer him back to 'Life on Mars?', but his eyes were alive as he recalled hearing it on eighties East Berlin radio.

'I will never forget the feeling the song triggered in me. I will love the synthie intro and especially the outro forever.'

As a reward for telling me his Bowie favourites, I gave him far too many handshakes than is journalistically sensible. Outside, Thilo extracted his well-shaken hand, lit a cigarette and struck up conversation with the Hansa janitor. I gazed back at the hall by the wall, awestruck. What a privilege, I thought, as I mindlessly yanked the key in Iggy's bike lock, breaking it clean in two. I held the snapped key up to the muddled blue and grey sky. In what would be a fitting tribute to 'Heroes', Iggy was quite possibly stuck at Hansa, for ever and ever.

In a 'You won't believe what an egg I am' motion, I waved the broken key at Thilo. As I panicked, the janitor casually extinguished his cigarette, smoothed down his porn star moustache and walked into the studio. He reappeared with the biggest set of pliers Germany had ever manufactured, strode across the road, and with one salient snip cut through the bike lock, just like Bowie's voice soaring above those microphone gates.

'Call the police!' laughed Thilo.

Iggy was free, and after one more throttling handshake so was Thilo's hand.

With the cold haranguing my exposed knuckles, I headed into the gloaming for some sightseeing. First the Brandenburg Gate where I pushed a liberated Iggy around the Platz der Republik to the Reichstag. On a considerably warmer 7 June 1987, Bowie had played this very spot. A series of concerts had been organised for the 750th anniversary of the establishment of Berlin. That's a lot of candles to blow out, so they roped in Genesis and Eurythmics to help. In the shadow of the Berlin Wall, Bowie had the Sunday slot, and as he prepared to launch into 'Heroes', the song he'd written about it ten years before, he addressed both sides of the divided city.

'We send our best wishes to all of our friends who are on the other side of the wall.'

Unbeknown to Bowie, someone had turned some of the speakers to face the East, and tens of thousands of East Germans had gathered by the wall. As he began to sing, they moved closer, straining to listen. This was an unthinkable act where the punishment could have been death. A feeling began to swell, the people filled with hope by the emotion of Bowie's music. They moved closer. The Stasi did not fear the crowds, but the prospect that their civilian minds might be turned by Western music. They reacted aggressively, beating the Bowie devotees back and firing at them with water cannons. Even with over 200 arrested, the crowds refused to be cowed and kept moving forward. And then, they began to sing. At that moment Bowie could hear both sides of the wall singing his lyrics back to him. The Stasi were afraid. The crowd began chanting, 'The wall must fall,' the first time such insolence was heard from the East. Bowie was in tears. 'It was one of the most emotional performances I've ever done,' he said to *Performing Songwriter* magazine in 2003. 'There were thousands on the other side … and we could hear them cheering and singing … God, even now I get choked up. It was breaking my heart and I'd never done anything like that in my life, and I guess I never will again.'

The Wall could stop free movement, but it couldn't stop free expression. Two years later, with echoes of Bowie's inspiration – it fell. I held Iggy, staring at the place it once stood. It began to rain. And as it did, it hid the tear rolling down my cheek.

In 2004, Bowie returned to Germany to play the Hurricane Festival in Scheessel. As he sang, he felt a tightening in his chest. He'd suffered a minor heart attack. It was his last ever live performance. He retreated to New York to recover, and for the best part of a decade wasn't heard from, his career seemingly finished. But the spirit of Berlin still tap-danced through his mind, and in 2013, on his sixty-sixth birthday, a song fell from the stars. Taking everyone by surprise, 'Where Are We Now?' was released.

It was an elegiac love letter to the city he'd once held so dear. Bowie, the man always moving forward, was, perhaps for the first time ever, looking back. The song's lyrics were drenched in wistful nostalgia as he revisited his Berlin. The music built from a simple, and simply beautiful, piano and string demo he'd recorded at home. It landed on the earthly world just before dawn, appearing online as a music video in which Bowie starred as one half of an unsightly double-headed puppet surrounded by props symbolising moments from his career. Some were obvious: a diamond, a dog; some laced with playful nuance like the Song of Norway T-shirt he wore. When Tony Visconti saw it, he instantly knew its meaning.

'That's cheeky,' he said.

Bowie replying, 'I know,' like a giggling schoolboy.

'He never explained why he wore it,' added Visconti. But Bowie fans would know it was a nod to Hermione Farthingale, the girl who broke his heart. She'd run off with a dancer from the film of the same name, leaving him to lick his wounds and write songs about it. Whether one of those was 'Life on Mars?' still remained unanswered. The video continues as a projector draws a visual world of his old Berlin haunt; we follow the journey he would have taken down the wooden staircase at 155 Hauptstrasse to the hallway where, hauntingly, a bicycle sits outside, just like the one he rode to Hansa each morning.

Berlin remade Bowie creatively; it saved him too. During its troubled times, among the rubble and bullet-strewn walls he'd rediscovered his spark, made friendships and felt the simple joy of a bicycle. Eventually, he moved on, another chapter of his life over, but David Robert Jones had returned.

23. WHERE ARE WE NOW?

Berlin and Bowie both moved on but would forever be entwined in one another's hearts. 'Where Are We Now?' was quite apt because after that indulgent 2,900-mile detour, I had the whole of sodding Germany to cycle across. It was time to take stock and think about the 'Life on Mars?' meaning. Moscow pulled back the iron curtain to show how Bowie was inspired visually, Berlin taught me how he brought emotion to his work, and 'Where Are We Now?' had shown Bowie, at least in his later songs, wasn't always so elusive with the stories behind them.

More than a month in, I was meant to be home in a few weeks. I stared at the map; it stared back at me. It looked awfully big. From east to west, I clocked it at around 78 centimetres, but by my reckoning it was more like 800 miles back to the UK. The Star Map, after all its recent Bowie exertions, seemed a little indifferent as to the next destination. Through a yawn it mumbled, 'Well, I've shown you Moscow and the creative peak in Berlin, now I'm going to take the rest of Germany off.'

I was busy trying to remember how to cycle for more than an hour at a time as I headed west. I pumped my legs to get warm as the biting cold stalked me, imploring me to slow down so it could take a nibble. Traversing paths where damp leaves lay ironed flat against the pavement, I reached Potsdam by lunch. This former Prussian enclave's stately parks, palaces, domes and regal architecture were only matched in numbers by the amount of middle-aged men with tight perms. One had clearly been on the *Pils* since breakfast and had set up a boozy saloon in the town's solitary cycle lane, his blotchy face and spaghetti gait a warning of unpredictable movements. As I weaved around him, his mouth fell into a saggy smile that seemed drunker than the rest of him.

By the time I'd rolled into Bad Belzig I was frozen solid and on the same mental level as Willy One-Tooth. Despite its name suggesting otherwise, Bad Belzig wasn't awful, but had little sleeping options and a lottle cobbles. Cobbles usually equate to expensive lodgings and aren't the friend of a cyclist with loosely packed panniers. Having mentally prepared to give up, flop, drink Helles lager and eat a hill of potatoes, this was a test. Bowie wise, we were struggling; there were no cavemen, no sailors, no girls with mousy hair, but plenty of ageing ladies with reddish bobs and fags hanging from the corners of their mouths. There was also a sign strapped to a lamp post announcing DJ Pizza was spinning discs tonight. Decision time: stay and suffer expensive lodgings with the hope DJ Mighty Meaty had some 'Life on Mars?' gossip or hunt down a remote campsite before darkness dropped.

I ditched the cobbles and hit the asphalt and my ass felt much better. Freed from the constraint of commodity, I sought Berlin-esque community, perhaps with a set of badgers. Carving through the fields of the Fläming region I looked for camping spots, a pretty thicket here, a birch canopy there, but each time I saw a possibility, tall wooden structures rose menacingly from the ground. Hunting towers.

As I scanned the fading horizon they seemed to sit in every corner of every field. Whatever. I'd plough on until they faded away, or at least until it was too dark to see them. Having adopted a bullet-evading hunch over my handlebars, I ate the six miles through fear alone. But off season and frozen solid, the camp-site was dead itself. The old lady running the place showed me around with a wise grandmotherly way, responding to my '*Danke schön*'s with '*Bitte schön*'s. She looked at my bike and said, '*Ich schließe gleich.*' I pointed at the remaining lightning bolt sticker and with a sad nod replied, 'David Bowie.' She shot me a look that suggested I'd asked if it was OK to wash my testicles in her teapot.

I'd later learn she was closing for the day and that I had to sign something that presumably said if I was found frozen to death in the morning, I could be fed to the horses in the next field. She also clocked that my waistline was struggling to hold up my shorts and told me to help myself to the pretzels and gummy bears in the common room. Was she plumping me up for the equines? It was a risk I was willing to take as I gobbled gelatinous vegetable fats and salty baked crap to try to kickstart my thermal being. She vanished in a saloon car, leaving me to foist every layer of clothing I had over my head. I looked like the Michelin Man on a ski break. It was going take a big hunter's bullet to penetrate the seventeen layers of clothing I was wearing.

The long grey day, plummeting temperature and wind-rattled hard shoulders had got inside me. I felt distant and alone. The looping nature of the teenage angst from the song, well, it was being writ again. As I climbed into my tent, forgotten thoughts crawled from the shadows, anxious murmurings of returning to work that swelled, then came crashing down like storm waves. I was cycling back into the squall, back to 'blue sky thinking', leth-argy and towing the line. Back to the silver screen and, if I still had a job, dutifully working past midnight.

I felt guilty I didn't enjoy it. I felt guilty this seemed like a first-world problem. At home I had brooded and wrestled and said nothing. In fact, I was so skilled at keeping it all inside, I was a strong alternative to the Enigma machine. I read somewhere that women are said to speak an average of 20,000 words a day and men a measly 7,000. But I'd probably chipped that down to a thousand at my lowest ebb and around twenty over the last couple of days – and that included the 'piss off' I was mouthing at whatever was braying loudly in the next field.

I was truly stuck. Bowie, upon reaching a certain of age of maturity, and taking the briefest of glimpses back across his universe, said, 'That's the shock: All clichés are true. The years really do speed by. Life really is as short as they tell you it is.' It left me thinking things out loud. Life had gone fast. I was never really in control of it. And, yes, I was a whopping snivelling coward. The not ready to settle down cliché, the commitment-phobe. I couldn't really explain how we hadn't, or how I hadn't, at least in the way you're supposed to. Houses, mortgages, hamsters, those sorts of things. Babies maybe. I'd assumed, all internally, of course, that we were cool, we were happy, we were together. That would be enough, even if we didn't have a clear direction. Assumptions are bullshit, though. Dangerous even. We'd been to see a house we couldn't afford. The warning signs were there immediately, the hag hanging out of the window yelling not to bang the front door, the spidery cracks in the walls, the deposit we didn't have, the unaffordable commitment to mortgage repayments – and, well, the commitment again.

Lucy had looked at me with Bowie-esque decisiveness: 'We should put an offer in!'

Hideously predictable, I ran a mile: 'We can't afford it.' God, I was a one-man band arsehole. Not a good one. Some shitty banjo plucker with delusions of grandeur, sat alone in a fucking freezing cold German field. I would have tossed and turned and wrestled my anxiety, but the layers of clothes protecting me from the cold meant I couldn't move my padded body. Bowie, when talking about his space influences, had said, 'Ziggy would be something and it would relate to me ... and Major Tom, Space Oddity and Aladdin Sane were all facets of me ... I got lost at one point, I couldn't decide whether I was writing characters, or the characters were writing me.' As I gazed at the stars through the condensation on the tent gauze, I couldn't decide who was writing me either. Was it my job, our relationship, or my bastard indecisive Libra star sign that hadn't let me express any emotion? Like Bowie's space-themed characters, it was definitely written in those umming and arr-ing weighing scales in the night sky. Or was it?

What was I doing here in the middle of nowhere when I had someone waiting for me at home? Same-time sandwich man from work seemed to know: 'Weirdy, weirdy, weirdo – get a five-year plan.' As his words echoed around my wind-burnt ears and the temperature outside hovered at a Mars-like minus 73°C, I pushed away my map and thought, *Bet there's no fucking life on it.*

24. SOUND AND VISION

I needed tea, hugs and inspiration. I'd already had the tea; the steam-drenched horses next door didn't look too cuddly and the inspiration seemed behind me in Berlin where Bowie cleansed his own demons. As I stared into the deep of German winter, I thought back to the lightning bolt moment, the shower, where it all began. What caused that flash? Obviously, the mid-life crisis, but the catalyst must have been something else. The night before I'd seen Adam Buxton's Bowie BUG tribute, a collection of videos, vignettes and inspiring insights that let us wallow in his gravity. On a clip played from Francis Whately's *Five Years* documentary, Rick Wakeman talks about how Bowie had shown him the piano chords for 'Life on Mars?'.

Sitting by my damp tent, I found the clip on YouTube. Wakeman begins to play, feeling out the song's first notes, the familiar melody springing to life through the muscle memory of his fingers. We cut to the music video, Bowie in turquoise and blue-blush, singing the lyric where the heroine's friend hasn't turned up to meet her. Back to Rick, who says, 'This is a classic example of where he throws in a chord you wouldn't expect, normally after you'd get …' Wakeman plays the note as you might think. 'But the thing that makes it really clever,' he continues, 'is that he puts an e flat in the bass, which gives it a bass part you can start to move on …'

He plays Bowie's note, the song begins to turn, rising, then soaring like heaven rushing down to meet you. We cut to the song and music video, it feels like a poem. Back to Wakeman, still playing: 'Now, after that chord you'd expect it to go to …' – *he plays the chord* – 'but it doesn't …' – *he plays Bowie's instead* – and out of nowhere the song explodes into the chorus and unexpected euphoria. Even Rick Wakeman looks stunned. 'Only David would do something like that.'

I had fresh goose bumps to go with the ones winter had bestowed upon me. Bowie's genius was exposed and I had my inspiration back. I ignored the brittle air, busting onto the country roads, pedalling with purpose through the faint tang of manure. My legs remembered how to cycle again, my own muscle memory springing back to life. Getting warmer now, pedalling harder, bombing past apple orchards, through an unknown village, a long arc of gently curving road whose vanishing point flirts with a fleeing dawn. The negative thoughts melted away and sound flooded in: birdsong – goose, starling and sparrow – the wheels thrumming on the tarmac and the warmth of winter sun on my face. If I was drifting without direction before, I was back following Bowie's now.

I passed the rollicking expanse of the River Elbe, busy and restless. The air grew thicker, the K roads quickly became B roads, and cars quickly became quicker. My general zen and morning dawdle led me to believe I'd be fine. German motorists traversing the B184 tending to disagree, a disparaging beep here as Iggy's panniers caught the breeze of some Teutonic engineering, an elongated honk there as a minibus loaded with kayaks and moustachioed women forced me onto non-existent hard shoulders. The sun danced a two-step, appearing and disappearing, grey to golden and back to grey again – the traffic and my mood fluctuating with it. Sunflowers swayed to no particular rhythm; the scent of recently ploughed potato fields filled the frigid air. Conkers crunched and acorns pinged from under my wheels, but there were still no cavemen, no sailors and no girls with mousy hair.

I sought my own sunshine, burrowing away from the speeding roads deep into middle Germany. I bumped along muddy tracks, eventually stumbling across an old farmhouse café. There were carby things to dunk in soup, carby things to dunk in cheese, and carby things oozing with cream and custard. Disappointingly, the only guesthouse was full, so eyeing the vast countryside, I took a beer, several oozing pastries and my chances. As I pawed an early death into my face, lyrically I'd tied myself in knots, but perhaps a visual approach might spark something fresh. I fired up my phone.

The 'Life on Mars?' video was shot hastily by Mick Rock just nine days before the song was released in June 1973. There wasn't an idea as such, but the plain white background provided the burnt-out edges that let Bowie's sky-blue Freddie Burretti suit sing as loud as the lyrics. Alongside the distinctive bright blue eye shadow applied by our French mountain friend Pierre La Roche, it made for a timeless film. Instantly recognisable, classically Bowie.

He appears on the white screen like a mirage. First the bristling strands of firebrand red hair, then the alabaster profile of his face and the shock of La Roche eye shadow. Cut to a mid-shot where he impudently kicks a leg like a surly mule shaking off a fly. He points to the camera, asking us to focus on sailors fighting in a dancehall. In fact, he loves pointing at the camera, now telling us to check out the lawman beating up the wrong person, then pointing to the heavens to ask if there's life on Mars. We go in close, his face rapturing in orgasmic ecstasy. We cut.

Bowie dangles a turquoise leg as if waiting impatiently for the second verse. We've waited long enough. Now it's mice, in their million hordes, Ibiza, the Norfolk Broads, all played out with a mimed walk of his impossibly talented fingers. Crash zoom to mothers, dogs and clowns before he glides across screen like a fishing boat on a millpond ocean. The sailors go at it again, and by the time we know we're in the bestselling show, the camera is swirling upon high, dancing with the stars. Cut to a windmilling arm and Bowie's blue, grey, blue eye-shadowed eyes, before he feels out the piano chords with his fingers as if playing them at Haddon Hall for the very first time. In a final shot, exhausted, he holds a hand to his chest; every ounce of emotion wrung from his body, he then holds a hand to the camera as if to say, how's that?

It's worth a watch.

A sizeable tabby cat had thought similar. Winding his portly folds against my legs and in a sad, injured manner it emitted a series of soft, elongated, 'Merrs.'

Aww, that's cute.

'Merrs.'

'Yes, nice cat,' I said, delivering a skilful stroke.

'Merrs.'

'Nice stroke for you, isn't it?' I said in the odd way people talk to animals and children.

'Merrs.'

Wait a minute, did you say Marrs?

'Merrs.'

There it was again. He said, 'Marrs.' Well, 'Merrs.'

I was up for a chat if he was. Perhaps I'd pretend to be Rick Wakeman. I could play the chord unexpectedly, surprisingly, just like Bowie wanted.

I say, 'Life on,' you say ...

'Merrs'

This was great. At least for tabby's fat swaddled stomach, as every time he meowed I treated him to a shred of buttery pastry. I hereby name you Fat Bowie, I thought with a mirthful chuckle. As I put up my tent, Fat Bowie watched. His shock of ginger hair even looked like DB's in the video. I continued feeding him as I became a surreal alternate lyric in the second half of the song.

'You like that don't you, Fat Bowie. A lovely bit of pastry for you, Fat Bowie. Yesssssss, Fat Bowie.'

I'd gone absolutely fucking mental.

25. LIFELESS ON MARS

As I sat alone on the edge of an apple orchard, the comedown from yesterday's endorphin overdose in full cry, a cruel air gnawed at my flesh. I shivered again, used the last of my milk in a watery tea, then, and I wouldn't recommend this, ate muesli with cold water which had all the culinary cheer of drinking from a sawmill puddle.

I gave myself a little pep talk. 'Come on, this is OK – you're doing well,' but my monologue was cruelly interrupted. Some journeys, in order to meet their goal, encounter great loss, and my moment had arrived. In the sticker-loosening mist, the final lightning bolt on my panniers had fired away. Pushing glumly into the cold air towards Bernburg and the curve of the River Saale, my revolutions became uncharacteristically listless. I crumpled over my handlebars, a tsunami of self-sympathy washing over me, my go-faster flashes replaced by feverish flushes. Instead of being driven away by my pedalling they grew louder, an ugly symphony spreading through my body. If a man whines in a forest can anyone hear it? I did so extremely loudly, regardless. I limped to the fringes of a grotty town called Aschersleben and sat head in hands. The unconquered map of Germany looked bleak, lots of green noth-ingness ahead. 'Pretty, I'm sure, but stuffed with tales of places Bowie had visited, I don't think,' snorted the lazy devil that had appeared on my shoulder. 'Press on', 'Pull yourself together' were all words of advice I could have rallied myself with, but the lure of the bus stand across the road was whispering a little louder. 'Why not see where that bus is going?' said the devil. I nodded deliriously in agreement. The next thing I knew, a man with a seismic mullet and clip-on tie was fixing Iggy to the back of a bus bound for Düsseldorf.

'You're not cycling?' he asked.

I looked at him with an extremely sorry face. 'I've got man flu.'

He thought I was lying.

'Really bad man flu,' I added with an overly dramatic sniff.

There are many things Germans excel at – engineering, men with moustaches, women with moustaches – but sympathy isn't one of them. He merely laughed in my face as the final bit of colour drained from it. To make matters worse, the middle-aged man next to me also had the same strain of life-threatening, world-ending man-fluenza. We were placed in quarantine opposite two teenage girls. We looked at one another's leaking nostrils and aching limbs and performed a duet of pained winces and sorrowful groans.

Usually nothing enrages me more than a sniffer on public transport, the offending party and their sloppy nostrils bringing a slow build of eye rolls, progressing to annoyed tuts before an apocalyptic rage of huffs that culminate in an epic death stare. But today I just sat squelchily next to him as we roused a slow build of eye rolls, progressing to annoyed tuts, before an apocalyptic rage of huffs that culminated in 50 epic death stares and a couple of 'for fuck's sake's' from the Teutonic teens.

As the world went by in a haze of sniffles and rivers of greenish ooze, I tried to gather some thoughts. On the one hand, having a rest was magnificent; on the other, it was speeding me closer to reality: the job I couldn't hack and the kind, loving girlfriend I couldn't express myself to. Life was tricky. Life was snotty. Life was a fuggy feeling in my sinuses. 'Life on Mars?', well, we'd seen some amazing things, met some fantastic people, I'd pieced together some threads around alienation, travel, alternate worlds, dissociative writing and how he added emotion to his work – but I wasn't quite there, so that could go screw itself too. Mercifully, the cloying warmth of the heaters knocked me into a snotty coma and upon arrival in Düsseldorf, some seven moist-nosed hours later, my neighbour had vanished, possibly murdered by the girls.

26. KOSMISCHE & CRAP

Germany wasn't going great. I woke in a cheap hotel, surrounded by sachets of cheap decongestant. Was this cheating? Yes, massively. But on the positive side, there was some method among the feverish madness. Düsseldorf was on the snot-drenched Star Map.

Bowie was a man who not only inspired, but who found inspiration everywhere, especially in Germany. As well as playwrights like Bertolt Brecht, expressionist art movements and philosophers like Nietzsche, Germany's music was central to his creative oeuvre. In post-war Germany, the country was being rebuilt and bands were looking to create their own sounds. Krautrock, or *Kosmische*, as it was known locally, took its lead from world music and cutting-edge electronics like early synthesisers, tape loops and other forms of sound manipulation. And if it was zeitgeist, Bowie was there with bells and bleeps on.

He'd decided British rock was a 'toothless tiger' and wanted a new sound to inform his Berlin trilogy. He quickly formed friendships with band members from the German scene. There was Edgar Froese of Tangerine Dream whose ambient worlds and electronic spacescapes helped shape *Station to Station*, then a mix-up meant Michael Rother of Neu! didn't play guitar on 'Heroes' even though it was named after Rother's namesake song, 'Hero'. And finally, Kraftwerk.

Their get up came from Düsseldorf's visual art scene, where they partnered music against the city's industrial imagery. They were also cycling enthusiasts who would use tape recorders to sample breath, heartbeat and other bike sounds before washing them into their tracks. The respect was mutual – Kraftwerk's 'Trans Europe Express' namedrops Pop and Bowie, while Bowie travelled everywhere in his black Mercedes listening to the German band's *Autobahn* album. The musicians met frequently in Düsseldorf to discuss ideas, Bowie and Kraftwerk's Florian Schneider often chatting while eating huge pastries.

As luck would have it, Kraftwerk's legendary Kling Klang studio was only two minutes away. I pulled up outside its parchment exterior, seventies tiling and closed shutters hiding a wealth of bygone electronic music history. Dosed up and drying out on cold medicine, thoughts of FUN, FUN, FUN on an autobahn filled my mucus-crusted head. Previously the preserve of parents throwing punches at each other over missed junctions and old people going down the hard shoulder the wrong way, the autobahn did seem fun. It was also illegal on a bike. So half an hour later as I nosed Iggy towards the slipway for Bundesautobahn 57 and a feat of German engineering hammered inches past me, another thought filled my head – MAIMED, MAIMED, MAIMED on the autobahn.

The two hours and fifty kilometres along the B9 to Cologne proved equally terrifying. Not wanting to expose you to too much of my horror, the main noises were aggressive horns, clipped German swearing and me making noises like 'Woah' and 'Wurgh'. But it wasn't in vain, because before Berlin there was Düsseldorf, and before Düsseldorf there was Cologne, and the man who refused to work with David Bowie.

Thilo had added this stop to the Star Map, tipping me off that Bowie had visited Cologne to meet a man known as the midwife of Krautrock. His name was Conny Plank, the innovator and producer behind countless *Kosmische* albums, and it was down, down, down the autobahn on a pig farm where he once lived with his family. After all the stories of Bowie's success, perhaps there lay some revelations in the places he hadn't found it.

I pedalled into Cologne on a beautiful Sunday morning, feeling a little more energised. The bright sky leaned on gingerbread houses while Europe's largest gothic cathedral and ubiquitous glass buildings, which seemed to pervade every German city, decorated the skyline. One of these was the bustling Hauptbahnhof, the main station. As people buzzed and milled, the station's PA crackled into life, first in German then English.

'BEWARE! TRICKSTERS ARE DOING THEIR ROUNDS.'

I thought myself pretty streetwise having shrugged off the man flu and got this far. Those tricksters wouldn't be getting me. And it wasn't just me in a positive mood; there was an air of conviviality as families laughed and vendors dispensed newspapers and weekend cheer. That all changed when I navigated Iggy's wheels right through an archipelago of orange dog dirt. My instinct said, stand still, make a tactical retreat, but in blind panic I made a run for it and wedged the rest under my shoes.

It was the freakiest and filthiest show. This was no time for trivia, but it felt fitting to slip this in here. The last words of 'Life on Mars?' are not Bowie's existential questioning of life on other planets. If you listen carefully as the piano fades out, a phone can be heard ringing from an earlier take that hadn't been recorded over. Mick Ronson, thinking that the definitive version had just been laid down, was indignant with rage at the telephone's interruption. 'Fucking bastard, oh, for fuck's sake,' he groans. And those are the last, if unofficial words of the song. And, funnily enough, the exact words scattering pigeons and smirking German grannies as they spilled biliously from my mouth.

Wolperath sat on a hilltop 35 kilometres away, with galloping views across a patchwork of fields, pointy church spires and very small, or far away, cows. Here, among a cluster of half-timbered houses and hazy meadows swaying under a soft wind, was where Conny Plank created the *Kosmische* sound Bowie craved for his Berlin records. Plank was an unfussy man, and unfussy men from the Neunkirchen-Seelscheid region do their musical discussions around the kitchen table. It was a tough table. Although he produced records for Bowie favourites Neu! and Kraftwerk, Plank wouldn't work with just anybody. He only produced music he believed was fun, not just for the money. Enter stage right, Bono, the U2 singer and self-styled God of the Western Universe. He begged to work with him. Plank was thinking it over and had not yet given a decision when he heard Bono loudly announce at a concert, 'We are U2 and we welcome our new producer, Conny Plank!'

They never did get to record at the pig farm.

But Bowie wasn't the first to leave Wolperath disappointed. Stories vary as to whether Plank was too busy to make music with him, or that his wife wasn't keen on having a drug-user around the farm. With the future of *Heroes* hanging in the balance, Bowie instead sent Brian Eno to knock on the door. Eno was more successful, working in Plank's studio, gleaning knowledge of *Kosmische* and bringing his findings to the table at the Château d'Hérouville and Hansa Studios.

And that was that. Bowie got his *Kosmische* sound, and you can hear the strung-out glacial arrangements, motoric drumming, crisp Wolperath production and angular hooks running right through *Low* and *Heroes*. Plank tragically died at the age of 47 from cancer, and the farmhouse and studio were eventually sold off and demolished. All that remained on this day were the sounds of Sunday DIY, the rhythmic chewing of German cows and a sweep of green that wound back to Cologne.

I bowled back down the hills at speed, shortcutting through a park, juddering Iggy's wheels on potholes the size of Bono's ego. As I basked in the golden embers of the late afternoon sun, I smiled at the unfortunate events that had besmirched my shoes and Iggy's tyres and went to take a photo of the bounding green hills I'd conquered. I reached into my bar bag: sweets covered in fluff, several. Squashed banana, one. Rarely used, but very manly penknife, present. But strangely, no phone. I checked and doubled checked, but it had vanished. All my memories, photos and the Star Map gone in the time you can say, 'It might have fallen out anywhere in the last 35 kilometres.'

I looked to the skies, then got a little upset. I stood on an industrial thoroughfare, head in hands, and all of a sudden became entirely cycle weary. I wanted to jack it all in.

With the sun slipping I had about two hours of sunlight and one hour of battery life depending on whether the badgers were hammering my data roaming looking at YouTube tutorials of how to build sett extensions. I had to look for it. I'd got as far as Bono Park when I realised the hopelessness of the situation. Again, what would Bowie do? Release a timeless parable that people would sing until the end of time, or ask to use someone's phone? The latter. A kindly man agreed to let me use his, but mine rang out. Then, just as I was about to give up, along came Günther.

Günther was always the German kid in school textbooks who had a pound of sweets and you had to work out how many he had remaining after eating twelve of them. The answer, none – because Günther was a greedy guts. My Günther had my phone and a kind heart. A big kind heart that had been ringing half the numbers in it.

Seemingly at random, he'd called anyone he liked the name of: Lindy, Claire and Oida had all been tinkled several times to tell them to call me, to let me know, he'd found it. His logic was as flawed as my sentence. But I couldn't thank him enough, or, to his wife's alarm, hug him enough either.

I breathed a deep sigh of relief all the way back to the Hauptbahnhof and the scene of this morning's dirty crime. I'd picked one hell of a day to go and search for a guy who'd never worked with David Bowie. The Star Map had thrown up an interesting detour, but ultimately a red planet herring. Sure, there was some of the song's drama in the 70 kilometre round-trip, and the sights and sonic textures of Bowie's Berlin sound, but perhaps this was a warning shot from the David Bowie School of Analysing Songs. Like Plank's absence, was I simply grasping for something, like the meaning of 'Life on Mars?', that wasn't even there? I stood on the rail platform, looking to the rapidly darkening skies, and having been taught the harshest of lessons, made peace with whoever was looking out for me. Then I threw Iggy on a train before they could try anything else.

27. HEAVEN ON EARTH

When you arrive late at a destination you don't get an impression of your surroundings until the next day, the revelation that you've woken in a godforsaken ghetto or, luckily, as Münster would have it, a gentle river town draped in pretty green foliage. Surprisingly, the Star Map had even thrown up some Bowie miscellany. In 1997 he'd appeared here on a TV gameshow called *Wetten, dass ...?* (Bet that!), in which a panel of celebrities would gamble on whether members of the public could achieve unlikely stunts. Bowie's challenge was to decide whether a man could play the trumpet under water for a minute (he could!).

With Britpop at its giddiest, and an endless wave of Indie bands emerging, it would have been easy for Bowie to pat himself on the back and surf the same breakers. But with his fiftieth birthday fast approaching, he released *Earthling*. He was more interested, as always, in a counter-movement, the emerging scenes of jungle and drum and bass. Bowie riffed off their machine-gun drum loops, peppering them with a ferocious bombardment of bleeps, bass drops, samples and whatever else was left in his sonic middle-age sink to throw at it. Some journalists were irked at his old-man appropriation of the youth movement, but this was typical Bowie; he'd merely taken the energy of a music genre he was fascinated by and put it through his DB photosynthesis filter to give it its own energy, just as he had with *Kosmische* 25 years before.

He remained as creative as ever, working at pace, finishing the album in eighteen days and performing lead single 'Little Wonder' with a crop of spiky orange hair on *Wetten, dass …?* This was written using a computer programme called *The Verbasizer*, an evolution of Burroughs's cut-up technique that would spit out thought starters at random. For 'Little Wonder' the opening gambit was *Snow White and the Seven Dwarfs*. Hence bonkers lyrics where random words are placed before and after Dopey, Doc, Bashful, Grumpy and Sleepy's names to form eccentric, unusual lines. Bowie was at it again, subverting his lyrics and sending your imagination shooting off like burning comets. 'What you end up with is a real kaleidoscope of meanings and topic and nouns and verbs all sort of slamming into each other,' said Bowie. That, and a drum and bass song about the seven dwarves.

Feeling less dopey myself after a good night's rest, I blinked into the early morning light to find a man perched on the bunk opposite. 'Hallo,' he said. 'I'm Max and I am zinking you are also a cyclist.' I wasn't sure why Max was sinking but I found out he was a young student who was cycling from Münster to his home in Bielefeld. He liked the freedom it gave him. He also liked David Bowie, so we ate breakfast together, and then made ourselves brunch, lunch and an afternoon tea of cold cut rolls, yoghurts, chewy bars and anything else we could cram in our pockets.

As well as healthy appetite, Max had an articulate open mind. He liked Bowie not just for his music – 'Life on Mars?' was 'dramatic, emotional and a bit silly' – but also because, 'He brings me to other worlds.' These other worlds weren't Mars, but the German playwright Bertold Brecht, who Bowie adored and would later perform in one of his plays, *Baal*; and the philosopher Friedrich Nietzsche, who Max said made his 'thinking bigger'. With Bowie's influences acting as an art school for cyclists and offering surprise enlightenment over bowls of cornflakes, we pedalled away, parting with a handshake at the city's outskirts.

Max and *Earthling* sparked something. It was time to reboot the 'Could "Life on Mars?" be about Hermione Farthingale detective agency' and rename it, 'Could "Life on Mars?" specifically the second half of the song, be about Bowie's experiences, influences and lyrical playfulness derived from The Verbasizer, Burroughs's cut-up technique and the surrealist imagery in "Life on Mars?" detective agency'.

Well, yes, the girl in the song is seeing abstract, thought-provoking and increasingly nonsensical and wild imagery as she tumbles headlong from her disappointing reality into escape and the silver screen. What she sees – a circling disappointment of Hollywood, mass culture and society – leads her to wonder if Mars has anything better up its sleeve.

Could I apply the same principle to my escape? OK, I was still cosplaying as a teenage girl, rather than the balding, cowardly man inching closer to whatever music he faced from his employer. But life on earth wasn't so disappointing. The thought of going home to kitchen dancing, frozen food on a Tuesday and dealing with mice in the flat didn't seem so bad. This morning's roads gently lifted through apple orchards and empty cycleways, which meant I was swallowed by bursts of yellow as buttercups flooded the valley, and life was stripped to the simplicity of cycling, finding water, somewhere to sleep and the whim of slow clunking thoughts that flashed between clarity, calm, excitement and ravenous hunger.

This meant I initially sailed straight past a sign welcoming me to the Netherlands. After a thousand kilometre stretch across Germany, which I'd *mostly* cycled, I was only one country and less than a week from arriving at the end of the lyric – the Norfolk Broads. Pleased with this morning's theory, I began to relax as the Netherlands' postcard idyll revealed itself through elegant cyclists and lofty windmills, navigating Iggy along winding stretches of cycle path with a crunch of leaf and parting of acorn. Little horses appeared by the sides of the road while locals on scooters spluttered past. Amazingly, for cyclists, there are 35,000 kilometres of these cycle paths to enjoy, so later, when the clouds capsized over Scherpenzeel, I concluded it'd be best to save my legs and some *wegs* for tomorrow. I sidetracked into a campsite where young adults sauntered with carefree smiles, kids ripped around on bikes and, get this, there was a concert hall with a band sound-checking. Maybe they covered Bowie!

It was heaven. The ridiculously well-stocked mini market had an abundance of provisions for me to guzzle and drain. I took my goods to the counter where a man sat plastered with a smile so loud you suspected his mother had told him not to aim too high in life. The grinning loon spotted my cycle gear.

'You have schhycled here?' he asked, maintaining his 700-watt grin.

'Yes, I'm doing a David Bowie bike trip!'

'Oh.'

It was a disappointed 'oh'.

I tried to get the BFG smiling again: 'Do you like his music?'

'I like some of it,' he said, the grin returning as if he'd just recalled his favourite nursery rhyme.

'"Life on Mars?",' I chanced.

He just continued smiling, clearly not grasping the notion that an answer usually follows a question.

'Do you know this is a Christian campsite?' he said instead, the grin now threatening to fuse his brain.

It really was heaven.

Another person said they liked Bowie's music but wouldn't elaborate on 'Life on Mars?'. I mean, come on, I was doing the Lord's work here trying to figure out the meaning of this song by a mythical, universally worshipped figure. Perhaps I was in the right place after all.

I was invited to see the camp elder, a wise-looking man around the same height as a footstool. He examined my grizzled appearance and, with the Lord looking down, reluctantly permitted me to spend the night. As I popped up my tent, I looked around to see I was the only one camping and for some reason the site was uproariously noisy. Kids stood next to caravans screaming at thin air and mindlessly hit fences with sports equipment. Was this a centre for delinquent Christian children?

As I prepared my dinner, people came from all around to gawp at the mysterious newcomer. Who was this strange man existing on a diet of hot dogs and Snickers, occasionally swearing as he burned himself on a camp stove? Then it got dark and they went back to their toasty caravans. While Bowie was known to have flirted with Buddhism, and on *Heathen* the troubling thought that he wasn't quite an atheist, I'm not sure this would have been his scene. But inspired by his open-mindedness, I embraced it. Taking some Dutch courage, I found a beer at the bottom of my panniers and hung by the toilet block, stealthily glugging its contents. As it worked its giddy magic, and having not drunk in a while, I staggered forward, a god among mortals and bothersome children. Where was the nightlife? Ah, yes, the sound-checking band.

I wandered in, fashionably late, suspiciously intoxicated. Although the band didn't play any Bowie, they were actually pretty good, knocking out rock-pop rip-offs set to projections of swirling galaxies. As the beer wore off and tiredness wore on, a song about dinosaurs chimed out – '*God created them, so he could blow them up with meteorites, Woah, Woah!*' – or something like that. It was a real crowd pleaser judging by the mass of children hyped into a religious fervour, hopping from side to side like demented lobsters.

I shivered myself awake about 7am, the thick grey air broken only by the outside lights of caravans. A cloud of steam rose as

I brewed up, but nothing else stirred. The band possibly still jamming in a seven-berth caravan and the checkout man fast asleep with that big smile stuck fast to his face. As I warmed my hands with the hot mug of tea, a spiral of mist began to dance mysteriously before me, a dense blanket of fog shifting as dawn tried to wrestle its way through. And then, it parted like the Red Sea. I could just make out the faint outline of a figure. It moved towards me: elegant, heavenly, something tall, something from a higher plane. My God it was magnificent, shining like an angel, reaching out its arms; the miracle finally here to let me know what 'Life on Mars?' meant.

'Who said you could camp here?' mouthed Jesus, dressed suspiciously like a security guard.

'Why, the Lord, of course,' I wanted to explain, but his gruff demeanour suggested thou shall not be a cocky twerp or thou shall be punched squarely in the gob. It was time to follow the Lord's path and leave. As heavy clouds splintered with echoes of light, I observed other cyclists criss-crossing tree-lined roads, passing pretty station houses, meadows of mini-horses and twee post offices.

As I passed a sign for Maarsbergen, I had already started the self-loathing process before I'd finished the grasping question: *Is there life on Maarsbergen?* Stranded at peak pointless, luckily the afternoon ride through Gelderland compensated. Wide cycle lanes cosied up to bell-shaped houses, genteel farms and antiquated rail lines. It was inexplicably pretty. Sadly, its charm was dulled by an extravagant downpour which fell steadier and stronger than at any point on the trip. As the rain beat into my face and the wind burned cold against my skin, I realised why the bus driver in Germany had found the wheels of my bike so amusing. I'd put Iggy's mudguards on back to front, two countries ago. This revelation brought to me by the cold, wet shower my shins were now receiving. The breaching of my jacket quickly followed, while my shoes experienced their own eureka moment as freezing water poured over their sides and deep into the cotton of my socks.

The harder I pedalled, the more keenly it hunted me. Biblical, tear-shaped bullets exploded off my thighs and into my face, plummeting my body temperature to the brink of convulsions. As icy rain dripped from my hair, working its way through my eyebrows and dribbling German shower gel into my mouth, I took refuge, pushing Iggy below a giant elm tree. A miniature horse stood watching the frothing wall of white water.

'Don't know what "Life on Mars?" means, do you, mate?' I enquired.

He shook his long, sodden face.

'No, me neither.'

I made a dash for it, but the rain saw me coming; this time shaking leaves, squirrel stashes and caterpillars from trees. As torrents of water made sprinting rivulets down the cycle paths, I plundered on, the stinging cold burrowing at my skin, clawing at my bones. Fortunately, the proximity of campsites saved me again. No divine intervention this time, just an empty field scattered with dripping trees. As I peered through the locked reception door, desperate for shelter, a voice came from behind.

'Fucking wezzjja, eh?'

He'd nailed it. A man as tall as the trees said the owner was away, but to pitch up and come to his caravan for a cup of tea. Dirk and his girlfriend were with the Swedish Classic Caravan Club, and as he fed me hot drinks, I told him about the trip.

'I love journeyshhhh like that!'

'You do?'

'Yeah, it goes well in my brain. And that song, what a beauty – sailors, fucking mice!'

'Well, the sailors don't fuck the mice.'

'I know, I know. But it's batshit crazy, right? All that stuff about Mickey Mouse, cavemen and Mars!'

He was right, it *was* batshit crazy.

Could this have been what it was all about? I mean, I don't think he'd formed a fake detective agency, gone to the depths of existential analysis and cycled over 2,500 miles, but it was a valid thought. As I let that sink in, Dirk pushed a handful of shower tokens into my hand so that I would stop dripping on his caravan floor.

I pumped the coins into the shower, my skin burning as the water set to work on my weather-bruised flesh. Alone, I had time to philosophise. You know the old proverb that if you hang around a shower block long enough, enlightenment shall come? No, me neither, so luckily as rain drummed on the roof, Dirk bustled in armed with a flannel, toothbrush and some musical opinions. He let me know he didn't like all Bowie's stuff, 'China Girl was too sweet', but he *loved* the way he always tried something new, 'unlike the fucking Rolling Stones with their same fucking three chords'.

Go batshit, Dirk.

The final visitor was a bohemian mum with bouncy beach hair and her nine-year-old daughter. As I told her about 'Life on Mars?' she explained to her little girl in Dutch what I was doing. The daughter, unprompted, let out a 'Woah!' She'd obviously been played a bit of Bowie, perhaps not just the Greatest Hits. The legacy was in safe hands. The mum bid me goodnight and her parting words, accentuated with a raised fist, were a rousing salvo of mangled Dutch-English: 'The freedom, keep it in your head!'

With the approval of caravan owners, nine-year-olds and mums ringing in my ears, I began to see how Bowie inspired others, too. I waded back across the waterlogged lawn gazing at the night sky. And then, as suddenly as it had started, the rain stopped. The clouds parted like a stage curtain to reveal their own masterpiece – a black canvas dotted with pinpricks of distant light that unfolded across the sky. My god, it's full of stars.

28. THE SECRETS OF
NORTHERN HOLLAND

In northern Holland in 1974 there was a secret to be kept. A clandestine arrangement began when an RCA Records employee made a call to the Luc Ludolph Studio in Nederhorst den Berg; would they be open to receiving a surprise guest? David Bowie was making a secret visit to Holland where two producers, Luc Ludolph and his son Jan Willem, were to help record his *Diamond Dogs* album.

This record had been the result of Bowie's failure to realise his young dream of writing a Broadway musical. An aborted Ziggy Stardust play and George Orwell's wife refusing to let him adapt *1984* left him bursting with ideas and standing at a crossroads of musical directions and influences. There was the tail burn of glam rock, a flirtation with soul music, Broadway show tunes and post-apocalyptic literature. He decided to drop the lot on one album. Jan Willem was prepared, if sleepy, having stayed up listening to Bowie's entire back catalogue the night before. The next morning, a Bentley pulled onto Machineweg 12, where Ludolph describes what happened next as, 'The most beautiful time of my young life.' But he did then say, 'When he arrived we ate a sandwich,' so he might have been easily impressed.

As Bowie laid out the album's Orwellian concept – inspired by Soviet landscapes and *A Clockwork Orange* – a dystopian society where human–dog hybrids prowled the streets of Hunger City, set against a post-apocalyptic soundscape interwoven with lyrics crammed with drug references, social decay and nihilism. Or, as Bowie cautioned on album opener 'Future Legend,': telling us this was no longer Rock 'n' Roll, it was genocide.

Ludolph and son got to work. They laid down the last of his glam rock tracks, 'Rebel Rebel' built around Bowie's towering riff, and applied finishing touches to macabre gothic ballads like 'We Are The Dead' and the death-tinged disco of '1984'. The hours fell away as Bowie experimented with new sounds and guitar synthesisers, speeding away from glam rock into the looser, nihilistic strains of punk, and on 'Sweet Thing' the soul we'd later hear on *Young Americans.*

Bowie played the bulk of the instruments himself, working through until dawn. As he sang of decaying societies he'd witnessed in Russia, London and LA, set to wah-wah guitar, sax and circling synth, the album's post-apocalyptic themes mirrored his own spiralling state. Ludolph was stunned by his work ethic. The constant sandwiches his wife prepared would have helped, as did the beginning of an unhealthy communion with cocaine.

'I never saw him take drugs,' said Ludolph, 'but if he felt like a Chateaubriand steak at 11pm we'd jump into the car and drive to the Amstel Hotel.' There, Ludolph recalled how Bowie would talk about contemporary sounds … and what the future might look like.

I bet 42 years later he wouldn't have imagined it looked like a Technicolor shambles steering from the frostbitten corpses of corn fields onto the same Machineweg. Buoyed by last night's chats rather than the rainwater that blighted the roads like silver moon lakes, the morning ride was pleasantly short. I splashed past canal-lined houses and frosted fields of horses that gambolled forward to see what the fuss was about. The air was frigid but blessed with a winter sun that made the Dutch bungalows dazzle a brilliant white. This didn't feel like Bowie's Hunger City. A sign above the door read 'Bullet Sound Studios'. As I faffed around trying to lock up Iggy, a booming voice sounded: 'James! Don't worry – it's fine there.'

Jeroen was the studio's present owner, a mountain of a man with the kind of brutish handshake that gives you phalange fractures. I'd contacted him a few weeks before and he'd kindly offered to show me around. Through cigarette after cigarette, he explained how his family had taken over from the Ludolphs, pointing to sun-dappled walls where neatly framed pictures hung of the people who'd worked here. Not only Bowie, but Lenny Kravitz, Jackson Browne and Prince. We walked corridors that gleamed with the stardust of nostalgia, checking out a storage room containing master tapes and dust-dressed mixing units made redundant by the digital age. Jeroen chuckled as he pulled out old vinyl records of lesser celebrated artists who'd worked here: the ponytailed rockers Status Quo and British glamour model Samantha Fox. Crammed among the relics and outdated musical junk was his son's old bed and daughter's scooter – it remained, very much, a family studio.

'He would've come in through this door,' said Jeroen, pointing to a blue frame with a fitting diamond-shaped window. He showed me Studio 1, where Bowie got down to some serious experimenting and sandwich eating. It had the feel of someone's living room, a million miles from urban decay, as cosy wooden floorboards housed beat-up leather sofas and sprawling paisley rugs, while two chandeliers floated elegantly above a piano, and a Hammond organ sat below a tangle of microphone wires.

The tour continued apace, Jeroen telling me how today the studio's primary sound was dance music, far away from the glam rock of 'Rebel Rebel' and more in keeping with the legacy Bowie had begun to lay down with synthesisers and electronica. We stepped into the yard. 'This used to be a school playground. Bowie and his son played football here with the Ludolph family,' Jeroen explained. As fortune would have it there was a deflated ball lying in the middle of the yard. Unable to jam, I thought of Bowie kicking the ball with his son and played a neat pass to Jeroen. It rebounded off his shin, leaving a muddy splodge on his trouser leg. He shot me a look that said, 'Don't do that again, dickhead.'

Kindly, though, he invited me to walk around and 'See how it feels', and I spent a lovely half hour following Bowie's footsteps around the studio. As I poked between vocal booths, finger-tapped mics and awkwardly thwacked drum kits, I sunk into the knackered sofa and began to visualise how Bowie channelled his stage-show ideas into a sprawling hit album. The world building from his influences, how he'd move around the studio playing guitar, saxophone, Moog and mellotron; transporting me from my teenage bedroom where I read Orwell's *1984*, to Bowie's totalitarian trumpet played through a Chamberlain synthesiser on 'Big Brother' and visions of what his musical version might have been. I was lost in reverie, taking it in, quiet now, just like he wanted in 1974. I sipped my own stimulant, a cup of tea, thinking how wonderful this all was, and as I smiled a self-satisfied smile, Jeroen popped his head around the door, probably wanting to share the blissful moment.

'Anything else I can help you with, James?'

Jeroen wanted me to bugger off.

So, I did. It was time to bugger off back to one of Bowie's early loves, the style of music that shaped 'Life on Mars?'. Surely, here, some meaning could be garnered from the song's origins.

This inspiration was *chanson*. Bittersweet lyric-driven stories about love, loss and life made famous by the likes of poor old Cloclo and, before him, Jacques Brel.

Brel was the master of chanson, his songs relentlessly passionate and darkly melancholic. They grappled with themes of love, death and loneliness. These embittered verses so overwrought with emotion that when he performed his veins would bulge in agony against his temple and he'd finish wrung through with sweat. Bowie adored him, aping his songwriting and vocal style, as well as covering his songs 'La Mort' and 'Amsterdam'. Brel's version of the latter a swashbuckling tale of sailors singing, drinking and dancing with prostitutes, hinting at Bowie's own sailors scrapping on the dancefloor. Bowie's cut was recorded at Trident Studios, but a more visceral take can be found on *Bowie at the Beeb* where he delivers a rambunctious performance fraught with his muse's frantic desperation and despair. With days left, and getting a little desperate myself, it was for Brel's Amsterdam I was heading.

As it drew closer, the affluence of water grew stronger. From pottering streams with islands of lilies, grew bolshie canals that muscled their way out towards the North Sea. As a sharp bitterness hung in the air, the countryside's silence was lost to the grumble of engines and the hum of tyres on motorways. Here, I was just another cyclist, albeit not one with the informal demeanour of the local pedaller. The urban Dutch roller is an altogether different breed, blending casual everyday clothing with a spry turn of pace. I tried to keep up, my legs chuntering like pistons, but my peers bolted hastily away, deep into the city's belly and its swirl of grey canals.

I was fortunate to have a friend who lived here and was even more fortunate that she was the owner of a flat in a ravishing gable house. Having been handed the keys while she worked, I got Iggy and myself in a right lather trying to limbo him up the low-ceilinged staircase. In a city designed for cyclists, its houses strangely aren't. It was like trying to push a stubborn, plump-arsed horse into a horse box – but oilier. Iggy had gone vertical, horizontal and octagonal until the previously white roof was scuffed with incriminating tyre marks. Looking outside, the solution was obvious: chain it to the other gazillion bikes. Later, we dined and drank beer; I showered, relaxed in an armchair, had a view of the town hall and could hear, and feel, the bountiful bongs its clock emitted every hour.

Heloise spent some minutes explaining the curious nature of these narrow Dutch houses and how she'd had to move her furniture into the house by taking out the *verhuisramen* – removable windows – and using the hook that hangs from the house's gable to hoist the furniture in because the staircase was too steep and narrow. I then spent some minutes explaining how I'd tried to ram Iggy up the stairs and could she lend me a scouring cloth so I could remove the offending marks from her walls.

It was a brief return to city excess. Like Bowie, I found myself drawn to the bright lights and people in the streets below. With Heloise heading to bed, I said I'd just go for a quick walk, perhaps duck into one of the tiny brown bars where people laughed and drank beer under the haze of soft yellow light. That, and go for a joint.

I slipped into a café under a blinking neon sign where a ragtag bunch of midnight tokers sat around tables gently smoking. With a shrug, I concluded this was all Bowie-related research and approached a friendly, bearded face behind the counter.

'Hey there, what can I get for you?'

'Oh, erm, something light?'

He walked back to a plastic container containing pre-rolled joints and pulled one out.

'This should be nice,' he said breezily, handing me a spliff the size of a genetically modified carrot.

I lit up and inhaled. And without having anyone to pass to, inhaled again. I sipped at my tea, took a few more lungfuls and thought, *That'll do. Nailed Bowie's drug phase. Should really head home, lot of cycling tomorrow*. To finish, I took one final drag and headed back up the steps – and all hell broke loose. And I mean weird, wobbly hell. Although it wasn't quite so hellish and weird if you accepted the notion that your legs would only move in the lolloping steps of a recently tranquilised giraffe. That, and you happily agreed that the world would spin 600 times slower than usual and your hands were made of floppy rubber.

After a minor fascination with the white feathers and orange beaks of the swans that covered every inch of the Herengracht canal, the skies broke into torrents of icy rain. I spent what felt like a hundred years letting it hit my face, before I found myself getting confused with the saying 'nice weather for ducks', as I kept thinking 'nice weather for drugs', seemingly unable to grasp that they were entirely different words. Then, as I returned my foggy gaze to the swans, I became convinced the Cygnet committee's beaks owed me money. A strange, sleazy chanson set to maudlin strings was writing itself in my head, one built on psychoactive substances.

Nice weather for drugs/ducks
You're getting soaked through
They owe you some cash
But have lost the IOU

Happily, and strangely, I woke in a comfy bed with no evidence of how I'd got there (or whether the beaks had paid me back). No evidence, except a purple cigarette lighter, a glass of water (untouched) and being convinced I'd discovered the answer to my quest. Indeed, if you'd shaken me awake, shoved a microphone under my nose and asked me there and then what the song meant, I would have been unequivocal in my response. 'So, James, after your long, arduous journey did you find the meaning behind "Life on Mars?"?'

'Yes. Swans.'

Maybe that was Bowie's intention, find what you want in his lyrics, even while jazzed on the weakest strain of marijuana in Amsterdam. Dirk had his 'batshit crazy' meaning. Did I have my beaked and feathery equivalent? Sadly, the lingering taste of herb was the gateway drug. It was Heloise's fault, really; she'd just left it lying carelessly on the worktop and a cyclist can resist anything but temptation. That, and a Russell Hobbs kettle.

The unlimited access to an alternate herb – teabags – and a boiling receptacle had created a very British situation, so, with Heloise at work, I went to work myself, gulping down three cups of milky tea. I was more than sated as I returned to the Bowie trail, waving goodbye to beds, hygiene and psychoactive drugs. Before long the Paradiso theatre popped into view, where Bowie had played a leg on his 1997 *Earthling* tour and where Iggy at his own gig had unwisely called out some Hells Angels and taken a beating.

Its tall windows made it look like a cross between a town hall and a church. I tried its big black doors but they were locked. Fortunately, over gallons of tea, I'd had the sense to listen to a bootleg of the gig. 'Well, good evening,' Bowie said, introducing himself to the crowd. 'We're going to do two shows for you tonight … so stick around and we'll begin at the beginning.' Far away from Brel's chanson, he was doing what he'd always done, still experimenting, still giving new songs their place in the spotlight. An *Earthling*-focused first show had the atmosphere of a club night. Bowie slowly warming the crowd, jittering drum and bass beats picking up pace and deepening in juddering intensity as whoops and euphoric voices steadily rose from the crowd. He gave them a little break, 'See you in just twenty minutes' time,' before delivering a full blast of the canon, going out with the seven dwarfs' musical lunacy of 'Little Wonder'. Like the album, the gig was fresh, fun. Bowie, never afraid to keep trying new things, never afraid to walk unexpected paths – a lesson that might serve me well.

Bowie returned to the city's Amstel Hotel for a 1974 'Halloween Jack' – a *Diamond Dogs* cameo character – news conference to promote the album with Angie and Zowie; and again in 2003 for a photo shoot with second wife Iman. I made the five minute journey and approached the concierge eager to find out more: 'Excuse me, I do believe David Bowie stayed in this hotel and wondered if you had any record of it?'

The bellboy, all brass buttons and jaunty hat, was most accommodating: 'Yes, he did, actually. But there is no record of it here, the public records building will have it, though.' He kindly pointed out its location, just around the corner.

A kindly Dutch gentleman found the pictures of Bowie dressed in his 'Halloween Jack' dungarees, neck scarf and dandy eyepatch with first wife, Angie, and son, Zowie, not long after he'd finished at Ludolph Studios.

'Nice family picture,' said the Dutchman observantly, 'Not sure about the eyepatch. Maybe he had conjunctivitis?' Which, when said with a Dutch accent, makes an eye disease sound like one of the most wonderfully fantastic afflictions in the world.

As I studied the photos, he produced another envelope containing glamorous shots of Bowie and second wife, Iman, from a 1993 Tommy Hilfiger photoshoot. They stood laughing, completely at ease, atop the hotel's salubrious staircase. 'They look in love, don't you think?' said the clerk, equally lost to Bowie's aura. He was right. They looked a picture, a treat, caught in a haze of eternal romance. I was going to have to rethink the swan theory.

29. THE NORTH SEA CHORUS

Amsterdam had been short, minimal on sightseeing and jam-packed with furious herb abuse. Forever moving forward, time and Bowie's love life had left chanson behind. As I skirted the port of Amsterdam Jacques Brel sang of, now mired in a grey wall of rain, its sailors were either fighting, drinking or dancing elsewhere. Ferries drifted across its churning expanse, hooded commuters huddled like weather-beaten penguins while distant space-shaped buildings punctured the squall. Today I would set sail myself. This was the last big city. The beginning of the end. Home, or the home-land, lay on the horizon around a hundred kilometres away.

The exit from Amsterdam's ring of canals saw the heavens loosen further, rain drumming down heavier than ever before, my legs slipping on the pedals as I barrelled down empty cycle paths. By the time I'd passed Haarlem my insistence on not sorting Iggy's mudguard had left me to be hunted down by packs of destroyer clouds and given a liberal soaking.

It was a straight sprint to the North Sea. Iggy and me versus the slipping light. Three hours till dusk. As the grey sky met the ground and wind turbines cartwheeled, I pulled my hood tight to my head and shivered. The greased acorns obscuring the path and skiddy leaves beaten into the ground provided the world's smallest assault course to cycle around. I battled on, racing through parades of elms where gusts of wind shook leaves, showering me with water long after it had stopped raining.

From nowhere, a shadow rose from the cycle path. I punched the brakes, skidding to a halt in front of a pile-up. The roadblock in front appeared to have been dispensed from one of those small horse's bottoms, which seemed impossible given the size of the steaming dung monoliths that stood impervious to the pelting of rain and passing of time. I sprinted on, tearing through the administrative capital Den Haag at acorn-splitting speed, legs burning as I parted murky surface water. The slipping light and tram bells signalled the home straight, the rain obscuring my vision but not my thoughts – home soon. As my muscles tightened and lactic acid pooled around my toughened thighs, a pizza delivery boy pulled alongside and shouted something that was muffled by his dripping helmet. He pointed at my feet and laughed. I looked to see my pedal guard had exploded in a spidery tangle of black thread. Iggy was tiring. Me too. Come on, old friend.

Den Haag's shrunken Amsterdam vibes flashed by as I bulleted through junctions under the shadow of windmills and troubled sky. Finally, a traffic light held court and slowed my pace. I fell in line behind an elderly lady on a bicycle, her shopping basket loaded with colourful winter vegetables. We waited. Then waited some more. Then we had a lengthy chat about mini horses. We didn't. I made that up. Instead, I took a moment of quiet reflection, one that was broken by a volley of language that could only be described as trucker-grade filth. In fact, words that rhymed with truck, trucker and brother trucker poured with such velocity from between her false teeth they would have made her beetroot blush. 'Ja,' I offered, sharing her pain. She looked at me with a frown, jabbed a wrinkled finger at the clearly broken traffic lights and breezed onwards in a hail of profanities, her paisley headscarf flailing behind her in the northerly breeze.

A breeze.

The sea was near. The Britannia in 'Life on Mars?' still out of bounds. But for how long? It might have been easier to tell if darkness hadn't swooped in like a colony of bats. There was so much crammed on my handlebars – sweat, dead skin cells, squishy bits of banana – I hadn't any room for lights. As sea-salted marsh and weather-beaten houses blanketed the horizon, the gloom swallowed me whole. Wind hurried in from the ocean and a morose cloud converged from the south, puffy silhouettes that seemed to have been stolen from the darkest reaches of the galaxy. As paths wound and wisps of wind rallied, blinking lights began dotting the skyline like visual Morse code. 'Hoek of Holland 3km' – announced a sign. I fired on, head down, form tight, water urgently rushing to the ocean all around me. The lights returned, more intensely now, the ferry visible among towering rigs and cargo containers that reflected brightly under the glower of halogen skies. I was coming home.

I flashed my passport and worked Iggy up a corrugated ramp with a *thunk, thunk, thunk* into the ship's backside. I tethered him to a rusting barrier, patted his saddle and bid him good night. Then, as a wave of exhaustion rolled over me, I steered my stern starboard, sea legs, or something nautical, to the cabin and a message from Lucy: 'Home soon!' And with a sleepy smile I tumbled headfirst into a sunken dream. As my thoughts swam below the subconscious, I managed to cling to one: tomorrow, I would return to the island David Bowie left to bring his music to the world 46 years ago.

30. THE PIANIST'S VILLAGE

The song that began playing at 5.30am was a seriously misjudged choice of alarm call. What were they thinking belting out the whistle-infused shite 'Don't Worry Be Happy'? If someone in my cabin had bounced out of bed with a cheery, 'Rise and shine,' I would have beaten them to death there and then with a Stena Line pillow. But there wasn't, so with a Dracula swipe of the bed-sheet I stayed in bed for another hour. Last up, last off, I entered the vehicle deck as the final cars and lorries rolled into the morning murk. Unsheathing Iggy from his moorings, which had held impressively well, I took a breath, then another, and after 7 weeks and 2,962 miles, I freewheeled into David Bowie's England.

I felt excited, relieved and slightly in danger as I tailed rumbling HGVs that took on the appearance of two sausages, scrambled eggs, fried bread, bacon and a healthy dollop of brown sauce. Ten minutes later, I was consuming the same in a supermarket café. I drummed impatient buttery fingers on the table, waiting for the clock to turn seven so I could excitedly ring Lucy and announce my homecoming. Turns out I couldn't wait, and if Lucy had access to a Stena Line pillow the supermarket would have had a nasty clean-up job in aisle seven.

Meandering up along the east coast, with only 80 miles to go, I trundled through villages with curious names like Manningtree,

Cattawade and Codswallop without feeling the need to stop; their cow-plumped fields unlikely gig destinations for Bowie. But at the green-tinged hamlet of Brantham, there was a sense of unease, a shadiness that cast a dark shadow on the pleasant apple orchards and carefully curated lawns. A poster tacked to someone's garden gate confirmed as much.

WILL WHOEVER KEEPS STEALING OUR WALNUTS, PLEASE STOP IT.

Even in justifiable anger Brits are polite enough to ask for people to stop being thieving gits. Whatever next.

TWO BUDGIES STOLEN. REWARD FOR INFORMATION.

As the winter sky thickened, the plot had too. Another sign, the dark arts spreading malevolently through the veins of the Suffolk countryside. Had a travelling circus recently acquired a pair of walnut-juggling budgerigars? Bowie wouldn't believe it even if he saw it with his own distinctive eyes.

The Spiders from Mars, Bowie's band on *Hunky Dory*, played a huge role in the birth of 'Life on Mars?'. Mick Ronson was Bowie's go-to guitarist for many years. A shy Yorkshireman who went from marking out a football pitch in Hull, to living with Bowie in Haddon Hall. He had many strings to his bow. Having trained as a classical pianist, he learned the violin and was about to move on to the cello, when, instead, he picked up the guitar and became a rock and roll star. But he never lost that classic sensibility, and when Bowie asked him to play on *Hunky Dory*, Ronson agreed, on the condition he could bring drummer Mick 'Woody' Woodmansey and bassist Trevor Bolder. Introducing three working-class northern men to Bowie's theatrical world wasn't easy. He asked them to wear make-up on stage and they refused point blank. Trevor Bolder even had to run after Ronson when he bolted to the train station after Bowie asked him to wear a gold catsuit. That was, until they saw the reaction it had on women in the audience, which led to a swift change of heart, according to Woodmansey.

They went into the studio, Woody and Mick working out the drums so Ronson's guitar and classical arrangement, the first he'd ever composed, could tease itself around it. At Trident Studios, Ronson had to conduct the BBC session players, and Woody recalls in his book *Spider from Mars* how he disarmed their snootiness with some everyday rock and roll cool – by simply rolling a cigarette. The session players played, Bowie and the Spiders were wowed. Something special was happening. But the orchestra thought they could go one better, and it's their brilliant, soaring third version that sits under the final track.

There was piano, too. 'Life on Mars?' beginning with a single, and now unmistakable 'A' note. That was played by Rick Wakeman, another classically trained musician whose piano playing had equally delighted and almost been my mental undoing throughout the journey. *Diddle-ooo*. This almost never came to pass. Rumour has it that Bowie's manager at the time, Kenneth Pitt, had sent out a letter to Dudley Moore requesting his services for the album. This would have thrown a Bowie-shaped spanner in the works, as I wouldn't now be bobbing around a sun-splashed roundabout towards an exit marked Scole.

By some ungodly fate, and the ceaseless pattern of the Star Map, I'd discovered that the man who'd played those very chords lived nearby. The village was pretty in an unfussy English way. A pleasant green triangle divided two pubs, with the village store acting as peacemaker in between. I'd pop into the latter, coquettishly finger a Twix or two and ask where he lived.

Behind a stack of newspapers was a man who looked like he'd worked here all his life, and the previous one. He was tending to an elderly local in a genteel manner. I waited my turn before shuffling to the counter.

'Hello!' I said, over jovially.

'Hello,' he replied matter-of-factly.

'Bit of an odd question, sorry, but do you know if Rick Wakeman lives in this village?'

His eyes tightened with suspicion as he eyed my pockets for stolen budgies. 'He does.'

'Do you know where he lives?'

'I do. Why do you wanna know?'

He thought I'd nicked the walnuts, too.

In fact, if his eyes tightened anymore, he'd be asleep, or better still, dead. That way I could nip over the counter, check the newspaper delivery address book (a paperboy never forgets), shake his rapidly stiffening hand and have the whole thing done and dusted in minutes.

'Well, it's the funniest thing …' (it wasn't) (to him) (at all). 'I'm cycling from Ibiza to the Norfolk Broads just like David Bowie's song, "Life on Mars?"' I nodded to emphasise the magical quality of the statement, holding up my palm for the incoming high five.

'Oh yeah,' replied Mr Penny Sweets, with suspicious tones of sarcasm that left my hand hanging.

He was doubting my odyssey. It was as if people walked into his store on a daily basis and trotted out the old 'I've just cycled from Ibiza to the Norfolk Broads to find the meaning of "Life on Mars?"' whopper. The stamp dealer had me stumped. As I turned to begin a solemn walk past cans of spaghetti hoops, he tossed me an olive branch.

'You can leave something 'ere for him if you like.'

What could I leave the man who'd played piano on 'Life on Mars?'? I'd chucked my banana, lost the *Aladdin Sane* lightning bolts; I might *still* need the compass. A supermarket sausage roll provided ample thinking time. I'd track him down, give him the benefit of my sasquatch-like appearance, settle it in person. A quick look at the Star Map stopped me in my tracks. Rick was currently on a world tour with his band Yes for the next three months.

The village was small, but at the end of the private track, a bit of cyclist sleuthing bore fruit. There was a sports car bearing the initials 'RW'; the only obstacle between me and a restraining order, a tall iron gate. They say never meet your heroes, so I didn't. But they don't say never meet your heroes' cat, so I did that instead. Well, I think I did. Cats are arrogant sacks of evil at the best of times, but the black one who strolled through the iron bars had such a supercilious manner it could only be attributed to it being the mog owned by the man who played piano on 'Life on Mars?'.

She needed to be careful, pets had already gone walkies round here. I didn't much fancy climbing his fence to meet a guard dog called Ball Chomper, so in a stalkerish act took some driveway gravel as a souvenir and penned a postcard gabbing on about the trip, his solo albums I'd spotted in Moscow and that I'd seen a cat, maybe his cat!

Probably the weirdest thing he'd ever read.

I returned to face off with the store master. 'Would you mind giving this to Rick, please?' I asked, handing over the postcard.

'Arr, I'll give it to him when eee comes in next.'

His trust semi-gained, I spent a lovely few minutes convincing him about the authenticity of the trip, moaning about how small Creme Eggs were these days and discovering the quickest way to Bungay.

Norfolk was about to be breached. I pedalled forward, the blue yonder gobbled by onrushing clouds. With every rotation and heave of lungs I was riding into the eye of the storm. We collided head on, me offering an idiot-shaped surface for the sky to deposit its contents, my no mudguard policy giving my shins and backside the soaking they deserved. I didn't fancy a pit stop on a hard shoulder to fix the problem, instead bolting towards a small community called Earsham. As great globs of rain bombarded from my shoulders, exploding like gaily tossed water balloons, a cluster of oak trees lay at a bend in the road. I took shelter.

Just along the way, say two or three trees down, was a middle-aged woman in a puffy purple ski jacket who'd done likewise. My first Norfolker. I caught her eye and in expert weather-related sign language looked heavenward and rolled my eyes. She caught my drift. 'I think they're like April showers, but autumn ones,' she called with a farmer's accent so thick you could have spread it on toast. We steered through the formalities of British weather talk: the state of the weather, the weather forecast for this afternoon, the weather forecast for tonight, the weather forecast for tomorrow, the weather forecast for early next week, the long forecast and what a mild winter we were having. This spiralled into a deeper conversation about how her husband had to use the hose on the garden this summer as it had been particularly dry and the last three winters had been quite mild too, which was funny because they never used to be this mild and that that was probably down to global warming which would affect the weather even more in the future, which brought us back to the rainy anomaly of the present day in October.

We would still have been chuntering on about weather if she hadn't spotted Iggy's dripping frame and sagely interrupted protocol: 'Where you off, then?' I gave her the full works and waited for her to burst out in Bowie, but she looked indifferent, replying in a flat farmer's tone, 'Oh, right.'

We were at an impasse. It was still raining, but we'd already talked about that. I'd have to chance my arm. 'Do you like David Bowie?'

She pondered this for a second. 'Well ... I wouldn't say that. I mean, I liked one or two of his songs, and it were sad what happened, what with 'im dying and that, but they all die young, don't they?'

'Do they?'

'Yeah, take that Elvis. He got all fat and died on the toilet.' She folded her arms, satisfied with her point. But she wasn't done, and as sure as the rain kept flowing so did she. 'I tell you who never got fat.'

Gandhi?

'Cliff Richard.'

Bus driving, Christian calendar modelling, toupee-wearing, tennis crowd-bothering Cliff Richard.

'Why couldn't they 'av been more like 'im?'

Indeed.

With that denouement she looked at the brightening skies and, before we wasted the rest of the century going over the salient points of late-autumn precipitation, made an eye gesture to suggest the rain was easing so she'd be on her way.

Left to ponder why Bowie couldn't have been more like Cliff Richard, I sailed damply on, oblivious to the county I'd just cycled into. I didn't know it at the time, but technically this was it. The mice in their million hordes, the very cusp of Norfolk and not far from the Broads.

Before leaving I'd felt everything the anomic heroine had felt, the disillusionment, longing, alienation and restlessness; now, having cycled almost 3,000 miles following a lyric from the song, other than my legs and mind being completely shot, I wasn't sure how I felt at all. Like 'Life on Mars?' there was a lot to get my head around. But all that could wait, because a few days earlier I'd found something on the Star Map that might finally answer Bowie's question.

31. THE MEANING OF MARS

On an evening wrapped in brittle air, Iggy and I and set out to discover if there really was 'Life on Mars?'. But first I needed a beer and a half-hearted American-themed restaurant, which was handy as Smokey Joe's Bar and Grill was on the turnoff to Ditchingham. I ordered something meaty and cheese-laden with an auxiliary portion of double-fried chips and a nerve-steadying pint. Elvis would have been proud. Mum too.

Outside, thundery downpours had left candy floss swirls of cloud above and petrichor below, rising from the A143. With a steely determination, I fixed a head torch around my head and cycled into the black hole of the Norfolk countryside. One by one, signs of humanity were extinguished until I was faced with a wall of complete darkness. The head torch offered just a three-metre warning as to any hedgehogs, sinkholes or Cliff Richard fans loitering in the area. As I navigated invisible country lanes, the scent of damp leaves clung to trees and the only murmur was that of my shallow breathing. This was the ultimate isolation Bowie talked of. I thought of him, Lucy, family and friends, and comforted myself that I wasn't alone. And then I wasn't.

Two orbs of light glinted like sharpened diamonds half a metre from the ground – they were staring right through me. A rush of chill air dived down my neck. I pumped the brakes, my heart smashing against my ribcage as I yelped an unmanly, 'Wurgh!' The green spherules didn't move. A cloud of terrified condensation slipped from my nostrils. When it dissipated so had the demon eyes. I inched forward, freeing my legs to kick at anything occupying the grass verges. As I hurried on, a gate appeared faintly from the gloom. I could make out a cluster of luminescent onion-domes and pedalled hastily inside. As I propped Iggy against a railing, I yanked open a door, where a wall of heat rushed to meet me – but you'd expect nothing less from people who appreciate meteorites and big balls of burning gas. A wave of chatter whooshed past, flooding into the night sky. I'd made it to Seething Observatory.

I'd contacted its chairman, Andy Gardiner, to chat all things Mars and see if we could spot the red blighter. Inside, a motley crew were clustered around a telescope, while photos of swirling galaxies and bursting nebula illuminated the walls. A man with a hunter's hat and multi-purpose body warmer spotted the alien in their midst. It was Andy and he was lovely, telling me about the Norwich Astronomical Society, their current affairs and the debate of the day – whether to spend two and a half grand on a rotating telescope rig. He guided me round the site, introducing me to buildings with retracting roofs and telescopes the length of elephant trunks. His enthusiastic praise for the equipment concluded each time with a gushing summary of, 'It's fantastic.'

The passion for the night skies would have had Bowie beaming.

With regret, Andy confessed, 'It's too cloudy to look at the stars tonight.'

'What about Mars?' I pleaded.

'You would have probably seen it on your journey here.'

'Would I?'

Yes, if you hadn't been shitting yourself about badgers.

'Yes, a bright orange disc. With a telescope you can see its polar caps and surface markings. It's fantastic!'

It was, but I was desperate to know, so I asked him straight up.

'Is there life on Mars?'

'It's possible.'

The teasing sausage.

Even without immediately solving Bowie's poser, there was still an echo of Mars in the air: it was violently cold. We retired back to the club where the atmosphere brimmed with far more life than Mars' oxygen-free surface. The guest fee was kindly waived in Bowie's honour and I swapped starry small talk with the members, one of whom was a gregarious man called Paul. When I explained why I was here, his eyes lit up. Paul was a huge Bowie fan. As the others debated the merits of the telescope mount, I showed him pictures from my journey. Unlike me, Paul was alive when *Hunky Dory* was released and had followed Bowie's career all the way through to his very last album, *Blackstar*.

This was the album he'd always wanted to make. One that harked back to his first love of jazz. That first saxophone he'd saved up for, cycling the streets of Bromley, at its very heart. But it wasn't a jazz album in a traditional sense; that wouldn't be Bowie. His love of melding musical styles was helped by carefully chosen collaborators like the Donny McCaslin group and pianist Maria Schneider. The sharp wail of saxophones accompanied raw, awkward piano notes and stark, brooding lyrics that may pertain to the afterlife, or lack of. What wasn't known at the time of its conception was that Bowie was terminally ill. Paul dropped another bombshell.

'You know a Blackstar is a black hole, the end – death.'

We fell silent. I'd come here for closure about 'Life on Mars?', but this was a new revelation. Like everything that had gone before, Bowie had taken a subject and turned it into a work of art. Now he seemed to have done it with his own mortality. As always, as ever, the album was full of surprises, contradictions and mysteries: sonically, visually and lyrically. Even in failing health Bowie was involved in every aspect of the album's production, from the cover design to storyboard illustrations and ideas for music videos. One for the *Blackstar* promo was to have a familiar space-suited character, Major Tom, inside a bejewelled astronaut suit, but as a skeleton.

Bowie said, 'Major Tom still means a lot to me. It was the first time I'd been able to create a character that was very credible, for any writer I think that's a high point. He preceded all the others, so I suppose one has a special place for him. I do.' This spaceman, the ultimate metaphor for alienation, who appeared in 'Space Oddity', 'Ashes to Ashes', 'Hallo Spaceboy' and now 'Blackstar' was given a suitable ending – still isolated – but laid to rest in space.

Paul and I exchanged theories about hidden messages in the album, like the galaxy of stars that appear when the album is turned to face the sun and that inside the album's fold-out book there are six stars where every point totals 69, Bowie's age *when* Blackstar was released. But there were more: joining the constellation of stars on one page of the album booklet reveals the outline of a person – a Starman. The album's run times are written in a font named *Terminal,* found in a design suite named *Lazarus* – the title of his last single. An infinite galaxy of contradictions and possibilities about life and death. Paul saved the best for last.

'You know he's back in the stars now?' he said.

I smiled and nodded. 'I know.'

Paul, sensing I was simple, added, 'No, really. We come from stardust; we end as stardust.'

My tiny mind was blown.

Bowie worked on the album knowing he might be dying from cancer, but at the time he was also working tirelessly on something he had dreamed about since he was a teenager. 'When I was around 17 or 18, what I wanted to do more than anything else is write something for Broadway. I wanted to write a musical. I'd no idea of how you did it or how musicals were constructed but the idea of writing something that was rock-based for Broadway really intrigued me, I thought that would be a wonderful thing to do.'

A musical. Of course. There'd been opportunities to do it earlier, *1984* and *Ziggy Stardust* never worked out, but then came *Lazarus*. This off-Broadway play was based on the film character Bowie played in *The Man Who Fell to Earth* – the story of an alien who can't get home, an outsider in a place he doesn't belong. If the screenplay was typical Bowie, so was the surreal imagery: people splashing through milk, Kabuki actors invading the stage, bursting balloons, and for fans of sweaty gussets, lingerie sniffing.

Then there was the music. Bowie had most of it already tucked in his pocket – songs from *Blackstar, Low, Heroes* and a splicing of Greatest Hits material, including 'Life on Mars?'. He worked tirelessly, trying to realise both dreams simultaneously. With *Lazarus* he'd said he might not be at many rehearsals because of his cancer treatment. But they couldn't keep him away; he was forever popping in and out, smiling and writing notes with tiny details for the cast. In one instance, the character 'Girl' played by Sophia Anne Caruso was given a tip on how to project the 'a' in the lyric 'Life on Mars?'.

With delicate backing piano, melancholic saxophone and whispered drumming wrapped around a vocal that could rattle your chandeliers and smash your pint glasses, such is its lung-piping demonstration of control and bombast, she nails it. As the song drives to its epic climax, Caruso sings to the prone lead character as he lies in a rocket bound for the stars. She belts out the final refrain, lifting, then dropping, the 'a', just like Bowie told her. Newton has one final jolt of lightning crash though his body and they explode into each other's arms.

So even now, 'Life on Mars?' lives on, reinvented by the sleight of Bowie's hand. The play ends with Newton poised to leave earth and die. The accompanying song, 'Heroes', is reworked so instead of being triumphant, it's melancholy. It works. Newton has been brought back to life through his relationship with Caruso's 'Girl', rising like Lazarus to cut loose his demons, set his hopes free and accept his death. The last thing you see is Newton's expired body on stage, but his mind flying away to the stars.

The parallels with Bowie facing his own mortality are striking. While his stage work may have dictated otherwise, on earth he was still fighting; he wanted to go on. Although he wasn't thought to be well enough, on 7 December 2015 he took the bows with the cast and crew on the play's opening night, on his face a broad smile. Backstage he was inspired, he'd fulfilled his dream; he wanted to perform live again, write more music, a second play, a sequel. A month later, on 8 January 2016, *Blackstar*, his twenty-fifth and final album, was released to universal critical acclaim. It was his sixty-ninth birthday. Two days later, David Bowie died.

Today had been extraordinary, but it had all been extraordinary. I was just a plonker on a bike following a cosmos of coincidences across distant lands created from the fabric of Bowie's time on earth. The ideas, constellations and galaxies lit up his work, from the moon landings, the Major Tom inspired 'Space Oddity', a 'Starman' waiting for us in the sky, the pondering of 'Life on Mars?' and now and forever among the nebula and endless infinity, a *Blackstar*.

'Life on Mars?' was his eternal question to us. One he had no intention of answering. He even told us so on the final track of his final album, 'I can't give everything away.' From Ibiza, right to the edge of the Norfolk Broads, there had been plenty of suggestions as to its meaning: 'mysterious', 'spiritual', 'really spiritual', 'a certain ingredient', 'a magical quality', 'a girl/boy who's pissed off with life', 'a journey', 'beautiful', 'like a feeling', 'like a story', 'funny', 'special', 'poetic', 'nice', 'smartarse', 'dramatic and emotional', 'silly', 'swans' and 'batshit crazy'.

They were all true, all as he intended; it was whatever you wanted it to be. As a wave of exhaustion fell over me, right now, under the Norfolk stars, it meant many things all at once. It was being pushed towards the unknown, to a life beyond what I thought were my limits. It was accepting that not knowing everything might just be part of life, and that's OK. It was how music can take us to places that colour our grey worlds a little more brightly. It was 'we come from stardust, we end as stardust', and it's how we spend the time in between that really matters.

32. ... TO THE NORFOLK BROADS

This god-awful small affair had become rather big, and a little melancholy. The next morning, I unzipped my one-man hovel for the last time and packed at speed, eager to take my last lift off. Clothes stuffed in randomly – check. Plump panniers hooked on – check. Questionable tap water in the bidons – wouldn't have it any other way. But there was no time for looking back with sentimentality. Bowie didn't, he always looked forward. Iggy was waiting, dressed in condensation and a glistening cobweb – *a Spider from Mars*.

The co-ordinates were set: B1332. Distance: 24 miles. Destination: Wroxham. As much as I tried to sound like a set of sci-fi slanted, space-themed Bowie lyrics, it was just Iggy and me doing the same old trick: barrelling down roads, not really knowing what lay ahead.

The sun made the grassy dew wink like shimmering stars. Red berries sprang from hedges, their shiny skins toughened to repel the onset of winter, while my wheels sent grouse squawking into hedges. For all the space pomp, Norfolk was pleasingly hushed, with little to interrupt the calm except the odd newspaper billboard singing wonderful village headlines like 'Village Raven Gets New Box' and 'Snails cause A47 go-slow'. My creaking bones knew the journey was coming to a close, and like the mysteries of Mars, I didn't know what I'd find when I got there.

Ten, nine, eight, seven miles left ...

Wroxham's suburban edges revelled in the same lumpen boredom as Bowie's Bromley – orderly gardens, weekend shopping, painting the fence; all the things that drove him to bicycles, saxophones and a search for life beyond. He found it in the white island of Ibiza, the fans of Barcelona, Dalí's surrealism, Nîmes, Swiss cuckoo houses, the romance of Paris, the alien world of Soviet Russia, the new musical language of Berlin, the music he didn't make in Cologne and the chanson of Amsterdam. He found it in his friends, too.

I gazed down at Iggy, wheels still turning without complaint. I thanked him for his altruistic friendship and said sorry, again, for rolling him through a mountain of dog shit.

A van bellowed past, knocking me from my wistfulness and almost granting me my own local newspaper headline, 'Sad-looking Bowie fan taken out by fleeing walnut thieves'.

Four, three, two, one mile to go ...

Tousled hedgerows gave way to ubiquitous semi-detached houses. The sun muscled its way in front of a swamp of grey clouds. The traffic of family saloons swelled, then slowed, until they queued in orderly British fashion. Here they were, the mice gathered in their million hordes. I sailed past a man with different coloured eyes who said, 'Half a mile to go,' and then, using the freedom a bike affords, sauntered past the idling engines and breezed over a bridge into Wroxham, and – saxophone solo, please – the Norfolk Broads.

I found hundreds of tourists idling around – fussing, flopping and frolicking as far as the eye could see. Feeding the ducks. Feeding themselves. Things with cheese. Cream teas. Boat rides. Boat races. Pootling. Pottering. Pomeranians. Packets of crisps, and pints. Just how Bowie imagined – *middle-class ecstasy*.

The bristling flags of the tourist information waved in my direction. I rested Iggy carefully against the wall, gave him a fond pat and went inside. The woman with glasses behind the counter had noticed my cycling attire.

'Where've you come from, then?' she offered warmly.

'Ibiza,' I replied wearily.

I hadn't meant to sound like a gallivanting wazzock, but I was so tired I ended up sounding like one anyway. While my brain was exhausted, hers was sprightly. She joined the dots.

'You're kidding? That's brilliant. I love David Bowie. Saw him at Wembley Arena once. It was a quiet part of the show, acoustic, I think. When it came to that bit, me and my friends all yelled, "From Ibiza to the Norfolk Broads!"'

She smiled, lost in reveries, before coming back to the present and extending her arm. 'Let me shake your hand.'

By now, her younger, more bored-looking co-worker had emerged to see what the commotion was. She barely noticed.

'He had this amazing voice from right up there, a soprano, down to a low bass. Amazing!'

Some people when they complete epic odysseys demand reward – a trophy, a medal. They want to give a speech. I was marched outside to the tourist information flag and draped in every bit of Norfolk Broads paraphernalia that had ever been printed. From her colleague's rain jacket to flags, gift shop bags, pencil cases and 'What's on?' leaflets, I looked like I was auditioning for a Hunks of Norfolk calendar. She continued lauding me with barely deserved plaudits. 'I take my hat off to you.' And if that metaphorical piece of headwear had Norfolk Broads printed on it, she would have plonked that on my head, too. The sadness had lifted; this *was* worth celebrating by holding up Norfolk Broads fridge magnets.

Now what? Well, I was here, and I was a tourist, so I asked what the most typical Norfolk Broads place was to go and see. 'The place where Nelson learnt to sail.' Sounded good.

I took Iggy down mud-splattered lanes, squirrels criss-crossing in front as I ducked under pear tree branches and let clouds of midges smash into my grinning teeth. I reached a stream that chuckled heartily under a wooden walkway and pedalled on until a swathe of bluey grey stretched out in a rippling panorama – the Norfolk Broads in all their glory. I watched tiny sailboats bob and reeds dance as wind whispered through water grass and the cold hooked onto my skin. Alone, I was tired, alienated and homesick, and so, like Rick Wakeman's last caress of the Trident piano, I called it the final note.

The euphoria was hastily replaced by hunger. It demanded sloppy tourist fodder, and pints. I dined in a fish and chip shop. The touristy mice ensured that two waitresses, girls in their fledgling teenage years, were rushed off their feet. As they were overrun, one accidentally left the patio doors open, allowing a pleasing breeze to spirit inside, where on it floated a tutting voice: 'Well, I don't think she's very good.'

I looked round to see a curmudgeonly crone forking chips into his miserable thin-lipped mouth. His pallid face was mapped with a petty gnarled complexion, as if his other half had been frying eggs on it for forty years. The wife, who might have been his brother, was sitting opposite, grumbling in agreement and equally desensitised to the sunshine of life.

To be fair to the misery peddlers, the girls were useless. Just shocking. Stone cold appalling. Instantly fireable. Some of the worst weekend workers I'd ever seen. They dropped cutlery with a bothersome clang, peas rolled from plates like lobster pots at sea, tea was sloshed onto pieces of cod, and chips tumbled with alarming regularity to the floor. Neither should really have been working a busy weekend lunch shift without a senior staff member to supervise them.

But those first jobs are essential. If only so you can find your inspiration, chase your dreams and wrestle the ones you love to the ground. Everyone has to do it. I did my paper round; Bowie, inspired by Little Richard, took a butcher's bike and rode it from

Bromley to Berlin and on through an infinite cosmos. I wanted to believe there were others who might be daydreaming of life on other planets, of finding a way out, to leave a trail of stardust that would last for millennia, and although I suspected the young waitresses might spend it on crap from Claire's Accessories, I left them a generous tip hoping they'd go and buy a saxophone and change the fabric of the music universe all over again.

The scent of spilled vinegar knocked me from my daydream. I gathered my belongings and got ready to leave. But just before I did, I turned to *The Twits*, still forking chips between their sullen lips, and called them a pair of miserable lifeless prats.

It was time to go home. I lifted Iggy gently onto the train to London and we wove from station to station, daydreaming through a network of darkening rail lines and grassy fields that passed like country poems. Over 3,000 miles, the places we'd seen were merely a blink in his space-time continuum, but we'd been through a lot: from the bandstand it was written, we'd seen sea, mountains and revolutionary walls – from Ibiza to the Norfolk Broads. Escaping into his influences, inspiration and artistic expression, a blazing trail of stardust to get lost in however you pleased, I'd got really lost. Behind the cosmos, I'd blurred the songlines of fiction and reality while riding an ever-shifting tide of meanings. Yet with the traces of the Star Map – a serendipitous snapshot of Bowie's life and music – I'd found a way through. Through my own bombast of frustrations, wrong turns and petty dramas; through my own surreal journey of people and places – just like the girl hooked to the silver screen. Wherever she is now, I hope she did too.

Yet as my reality inhabited her world, and I shambolically tried to untangle the song, something changed. All the while I was isolated and alienated, the sky was slowly beginning to clear. Stars were gently rising, winking subtly, guiding me to what mattered.

To knowing that when the darkest moments come, not every corner of a blackened sky needs your attention; to let those things fall, until there's only one thing left to see.

As I wheeled Iggy off the train, I looked south – around the buses, fast food restaurants, neon signs and a family wearing matching yellow fleeces – jeez, get out the way – all the way to Brixton. I gave a grateful nod and turned Iggy's wheel north. Racing home with toughened thighs and dodgy tan lines, we punched through autumn's chilly trim, darkened blues settling on rooftops as the city's hum crackled and burned. Together, we made one final turn, before I expertly hopped off for the last time. Hoisting Iggy up the steps to my flat door, under the ochre of streetlight, my head began to swim. Excitement rushed in, pushing away all the moments I had been confused and alone. Although, truthfully, I was never alone. There had always been someone up there who'd occupied my thoughts. Not just the writer of a song who started this god-awful small affair, but some-one who made me smile when my legs grimaced, who told me to go forwards when I would have turned back. I thumbed the doorbell and waited, stealing a last look at the stars – endless and infinite. Then the door swung open, light rushing past, everything falling away, and all I saw was a smiling face.

And then I knew. It was just like he always said.

This was a love song. And maybe that was enough.

EPILOGUE

One December morning I'd taken the tube to Oxford Circus, a stone's throw from the old Trident Studios, where that first note echoed from the Steinway piano to record players, headphones and countless showers. But as I stood on the escalator my heart vaulted and began clattering against my chest. I caught sight of a man wearing a heavy Manila coat, a tatty leather satchel tucked under his arm, fair hair tumbling from a Panama hat.

My head swirled with galaxies and supernovas. I could play it cool, but being an unabashed idiot, I didn't. So, I waited for Rick Wakeman, the man who'd played piano on 'Life on Mars?', slipping into the peloton of pedestrians behind him. As I quickened my stride, I drew level, filled with panicked thoughts of what I'd say.

'Excuse me, are you Rick Wakeman?' I spluttered.

'Yes, I am,' Rick Wakeman replied, confirming he was Rick Wakeman.

'This is a weird coincidence, but I was the man who cycled from Ibiza to the Norfolk Broads.'

Rick politely and patiently replied, 'Oh, wow. How was that? Hard work, I bet.'

I told him I'd left a postcard at his village store. He said he was off to the BBC to play a medley of *Hunky Dory* songs. In a breezy daydream of easy-going conversation, we exchanged tales of David

Robert Jones: his perfectionism, his dedication, his artful genius and his legacy of inspiration. Then, with all said and done, I shook his hand, the one that played those chords, and wished him a Happy Christmas. Or I would have, if someone up there riding around on a butcher's bike hadn't cursed me, and as I bid him goodbye with a handshake instead said, 'I've met your cat.'

It had been eight months since David Robert Jones left us all on planet earth. Life had gone on. But slowly. It hadn't been the same for his fans. People had taken comfort sharing thoughts like, 'The world is over four billion years old and yet you somehow managed to exist at the same time as David Bowie.' We were lucky. We carried on cycling, we listened to his music more than ever, the Beckenham bandstand where he'd written the song was fundraising to have it refurbished. Dad still thought he was weird, Mum had stopped yelling no/get a hotel if you're cold, and his Greatest Hits, my portal into his dimension, was sat between some other lucky CDs in their house. Bowie really *is* kind of everywhere, scattered across our galaxy: in the radio, on the turntables, among the rebels, the queens, the quiet ones, the kooks – and the stars. And although you can't always see it, they always shine a little brighter when his music plays.

As for me, I found the patience to put something together without launching it across a room; I lost my beer swaddle and felt that seeing the places he'd been somehow brought me closer to his music. But most importantly, I learnt to stop saying yes to things that didn't really matter. To not always follow expected paths, but to ride my own occasionally – even if people thought I was weird. Life on earth no longer had me cornered. For the first time I could kind of see where I was going. Like Bowie, I'd found my own road. I had to travel down it to see what lay ahead, may that be happiness, heartache or whatever. But that's the point, I guess. We never really know unless we stop just letting stuff happen and choose our own paths instead. So, I left the job that made me unhappy and started expressing myself to the people who made me happiest most of all. Who knows, maybe that's what David Bowie would have done too.

ACKNOWLEDGEMENTS

Who knew that cycling a David Bowie lyric would be the easy part. After 'Life on Mars?' faded out, bringing this story to the pages you've just read was a god-awful monumental affair. For this, I owe a huge debt of gratitude to a band of confidants, cheerleaders, family and friends; one that hugs, handshakes, thank yous and a thousand beers will never do justice to.

To Mum and Dad, thank you for setting me on the right path, letting me find my own way and never doubting me (at least to my face). Mum, you can stop worrying – and texting every four hours – I'm safe and warm. Dad, you can tell completely random strangers you used to play for Leeds United by using this very page in this very book. To my sister, Claire, thanks for letting me pilfer your CDs. Keep caring for animals in need, they're lucky to have you.

Thank you to Kate, for your unwavering support, forensic eye and general ambivalence to my idiotry as we freewheel down our own road. I can't think of anyone more brilliant, intelligent, angry – about all the right things – and passionate – about all the good things – I'd rather have cycling, walking, or arguing about the washing up by my side. Sea kisses.

Before the book, there was a scrappy handwritten diary, shabbily organised thoughts and endless drafts labelled FITTNB1 to

FITTNB1million. A giant thank you to my early readers, sounding boards, therapists and chief encouragers, Adam Simcox and Nicky Lianos. Their brilliant, brutal, book-enhancing notes and constant support were the spur I needed to keep going and make this a better story.

An LP of superstars made the book a reality. To my agent Nick Walters, at David Luxton Associates; thank you for taking a chance on me. You are exactly the industrious, skilful, progressive dynamo our screaming rollercoaster of a football club Tottenham Hotspur could do with in midfield. Thank you also to the rest of the team at DLA; Sam Rak and Rebecca Winfield.

To my publisher, the brilliant, good-humoured and welcoming team at Icon Books. Special thanks to my musically minded editor Connor Stait for telling me when to stop recounting toilet breaks, what sandwiches I had eaten, and for knowing so many obscure bands I lie awake at night worrying about all the music I'll never listen to. To Elle-Jay Christodoulou and Amelia Kemmer for their creative expertise, skill and enthusiasm in getting this book into people's hands and out into the universe. To Steve Burdett for recounting his weekend breaks in weather-beaten detail, for teaching me grammar and punctuation, and when not to refer to people's arms as sausage meat.

Words, lyrics and music are nothing without an album cover and sleeve notes. Thank you to the talented Mark 'kid-ethic' Swan for the wonderful cover design and the equally blessed Kate Fahey for the elegant and complete finisher-esque 'Star Map'. To the wonderfully kind people who offered words of endorsement you see on the cover, thank you for generously giving up your time to read an enthusiastic stranger's work, and for supporting a debut author.

On the journey I was indebted to the support, friendship and encouragement of Lucy, Lee Ashton, Chris Holt, Laurie McCall and Heloise Hooton. Thank you also to the people I met serendipitously along the way. Both for making the journey beautifully unpredictable and for sharing your meanings, music and passion for the Starman. A special thanks to the key players who saw through my dodgy BBC accreditation, but opened their doors to a dishevelled cyclist all the same; Thilo Schmeid, Jean Taxis, Jeroen van Kooten, Andy Gardiner, Paul from the observatory and Jonathan from Argentina, whose surname l still don't know.

Thanks to creative siblings: Ciara O'Meara, Michael Nagy, Toby Derham, Théo Dufaÿ, Gareth Rice, Felix Heyes, Mark Lewis, Felipe Pires Dias, Neil Gurr and Nat Cantor – it's never not a pleasure to meet around a creative table knowing we'd rather be anywhere but. To the Yeovil lot, especially SJB, sorry for calling you all virgins. To the London Beer Bums, thanks for always suggesting 'one more?' To McGrath, looking forward to your impression of the cover. To the Liverpool lot, 'Who invented the skip?' And to Diggy Stardust – Molly Isaacs – for your care, encouragement and love. Thank you for letting me be part of your story; this one would never have existed without you (bear wave).

To the patient musical academics I subjected to obscure enquiries as I sought to untangle Bowie's lyrics, thank you – Dr Leah Kardos, Professor Alexandra Lamont, Professor Lauren Stewart and Dr Caspar Addyman. For anyone seeking more Starman, the following never fail to entertain, educate and amuse; the inexhaustibly comprehensive *The Complete David Bowie* by Nicholas Pegg, Chris O'Leary's extraordinary Pushing Ahead of the Dame website, Marc Riley and Rob Hughes' entertaining *The A–Z of David Bowie* podcast, Arsalan Mohammad's David Bowie AlbumtoAlbum podcast, Francis Whately's documentaries, and the many others who've written so passionately and eloquently about him.

To you, the reader: a Bowie fan, Kook, cyclist, wanderer, or someone ready to get lost in music; it means the world that you picked up this book and gave it a go – thank you. To Iggy the bike, whose wheels are still turning without complaint – although currently under siege from a summer fizzing with spider webs – let's hit the road again soon. And finally, to David Robert Jones – the Starman waiting in the sky. Like you, I just wanted to be a writer who created characters and stories. Thank you for being the main one in mine. You made my childhood dream come true.